Life and Other Times

Leslie Grantham

TIMEWELL PRESS

First published in Great Britain by
Timewell Press Limited
10 Porchester Terrace, London W2 3TL

Published by Timewell Press Limited 2006

A catalogue record for this title is available from the
British Library.

ISBN-10: 1-85725-216-0 (cased)
ISBN-13: 978-1-85725-216-3 (cased)
ISBN-10: 1-85725-217-9 (tpb)
ISBN-13: 978-1-85725-217-0 (tpb)

Typeset by TW Typesetting, Plymouth, Devon
Printed and bound in Great Britain by William Clowes Ltd,
Beccles, Suffolk

All photographs courtesy of the author with exception as
follows:
© Mirrorpix.com 9(b); © Paul Elliott 10(t), (b); courtesy of
BBC. © BBC 11(t); photography by Stephen F. Morley
© Stephen F. Morley 11(b), 12(t), (b), 15(b); reproduced
courtesy of ITV PLC (Granada Int'l)/LFI 12(b);
© Mike Vaughan 13(t); © Radox 13(b); © Geoffrey Reeve
14(t); © Qdos Entertainment plc 15(t)

Dedicated to the love of my life
my wife Jane
and
Spike, Jake and Danny

CONTENTS

BEFORE YOU START

My life has not been an easy one, although a lot of my troubles have been of my own making. I have tried to tell my story how it was, how it is. If I could turn back the clock I most definitely would. Along the way I have hurt a great many people, all of whom are innocent. In one act, I destroyed several families, and of that I am ashamed. It is the thing I find the most difficult to live with. I have never denied that I took a man from his family, and I have thought long and hard for the last forty years about the events of that night. To say that it will be with me until I die is an understatement. The guilt and remorse will never go away – it is always in the present for me, while I can't change the past. It happened. I don't seek forgiveness. What I did was unforgivable.

But others have had to live with the consequences of my mistake, their only crime being married to me or being my children. I could have devoted a huge chunk of this book to relating what was going on in my head, as I lay in my cell, waiting for the door to open. I could have spent hours relating the sheer desperation of coping with the dreadful crime I had committed – but that would only depress the reader. I would like to be remembered as a man who was given a second chance in life, seized it and brought some pleasure through the characters he has been fortunate enough to play. I have tried to make the book as entertaining and as real for the reader as it was for me.

1

IN THE BEGINNING

Quite some year was 1947. The Thames burst its banks and flooded poor old Windsor; *A Miracle on 34th Street* broke box office records all round the world; the United Nations agreed on the partition of Palestine into Jewish and Arab states; and the UK suffered one of the coldest winters on record. So extremely cold was it in Camberwell, south-east London, that people were limited to buying coal by the bagful – sugar bags, that is. They had to burn anything they could lay their hands on in order to keep warm. This crude lesson in home economics no doubt accounts for there being no family heirlooms to hand down to future Granthams. Because yes, there was one more earth-shattering event that took place that year. The debut appearance of one Leslie Michael Grantham.

I was born in the early hours of the morning of 30 April 1947, at 14 Flodden Road, Camberwell, the second son of Walter William Grantham and Adelaide Victoria Grantham, née Flinders. In reality I was the third child of my mother. Her first child, Matthew, had been struck down by a chest infection. She had named the child after Captain Matthew Flinders, from whom she claimed to be a direct descendant. I was told that I was a difficult birth.

My Dad had been one of the first to volunteer, having been a member of the local branch of the Territorial Army, whose barracks just happened to be at the bottom of our road. He had joined the Royal Fusiliers and had risen to the rank of colour sergeant. He was one of the thousands of nameless heroes at Dunkirk, where he spent almost thirty-six hours in the water and on the beaches, waiting to be taken off to safety by the flotilla of small boats that had sailed from England. On returning home, he was posted to Shorncliffe Barracks in Essex, where he became an instructor training recruits. One of his duties was to instruct new recruits in the art of throwing hand grenades. Before and during the war grenades were primed in factories and despatched to the services with the detonators already inserted. Although my Dad instructed recruits day-in day-out, one such session was to end in tragedy.

In the sandbagged area, Dad was guiding his recruits through the standard grenade procedure – pulling out the pin, using the non-throwing arm as a guide to the point where it was to land, like a bowler sending a ball to a waiting batsman then launching the grenade from behind his lower back. But on this one dreadful occasion, all hell broke loose. He had taken a grenade from its box as usual, and was going through the various movements when the grenade just exploded; the pin was still intact. Two recruits lost their lives and quite how my Dad survived the blast, I shall never know.

He woke up a day later in a military hospital, having lost his right arm below the elbow. While my Dad's accident didn't in itself cause the munitions factories to change their system of pre-priming the grenades before despatch, it was a contributory factor to their changing the practice. But we were living in modern times, and heard stories of new frontiers in medicine and the wonders that surgery could achieve these days. If that were the case, then it must have been part of the Official Secrets Act. The radical new breakthrough they tried on my Dad went as follows: a bread knife was placed in his left hand. A (rather stale) unsliced loaf was placed in front of him. He was then directed to slice the loaf, using his left hand. Ah, the miracles of modern medicine! With the after-care consisting of teaching himself to write with his left hand, Dad was eventually given a medical discharge from the army.

Before the war, he had been working for a printing company in Camberwell, also in the despatch department. But when the company offered Dad his old job back, he saw it as charity and turned them down. My Dad was a proud man, from London working-class stock. His own father had been a mechanic in the flying corps, and a tanner and part-time painter and decorator; his mother was a Tory councillor in Lambeth. As a child, Dad earned his pocket money by cleaning out the ovens at the local bakery and being a bookies' runner. He had never been shy of hard work, and having one hand wasn't going to stop him now. He tried – as hundreds of others had before, during and after the war – to get work through the local Unemployment Office – or the 'Labour', as it was known. He didn't do himself any favours, there. When told that the only job he could do, or might be fit for, was as a postman, he became enraged and, after nearly destroying the office, chased the clerk halfway down Camberwell New Road. Once he had calmed down he was even more determined to do it his way (fitting, really, as he was born the same day and year as Frank Sinatra).

Dad eventually got a job at Boots the Chemists, where he met my mother, who was working as a nurse. She had a young child who – she said – was the result of a brief wartime liaison between her and a Danish sea captain, who tragically had gone down with his ship. My mother was often to be found at arm's length from the truth, however. Her personal history would range from being a direct descendant of Captain Matthew Flinders (who sailed with Captain Cook and named Australia) to claiming kinship to Sir John Franklyn, who perished trying to find the Northwest Passage. She also alleged that her Dad had been an officer in the First World War, after which he stood for Parliament (and failed) and lived in a grand house in Ripon, North Yorkshire. Of course, I believed her; what child wouldn't? But as I got older and began to meet my relatives, we were half amused, half disappointed to discover that my mother wasn't the only one with an over-active imagination. Her own mother (my grandmother) had been doling out these tall stories throughout her childhood. All the supporting evidence – photographs, pamphlets and other references to Captain Flinders and Sir John Franklyn –

had been acquired over the years from a variety of jumble sales and junk shops!

After a whirlwind courtship, my parents married. Before long, my older brother John arrived. Dad continued to work at Boots, while my mother stayed at home to look after the baby. In London, just as all over the country, there was a baby boom in the immediate post-war years, and two years after John's birth, I was born too. Along with the baby boom, there was a housing boom to house all these new arrivals. Whole new satellite towns and overspill estates were constructed on the outskirts of London and, after some deliberation, Dad decided to move his young family to a brand-new council house. So we upped and moved to St Paul's Cray in Kent.

The house we moved to was in Clarendon Road, halfway up a steep hill. The front and back gardens were mud and the fences that would later separate the houses had not been erected. At the back was the railway line that ran up to London and down to the south coast. My early memories include being stuck one Christmas morning on the hill, unable to move because the wind was so strong. My Dad was secretary of the sports and social club at Boots, and part of his brief was to organize the firm's sports day, the annual dinner and dance and the children's Christmas party. Because of the hours that he worked we hardly saw him in those days. He worked Monday to Saturday, leaving the house at six in the morning and returning home at half-past seven in the evening. On Saturdays he came back early, just after lunch. My sister Angela was the latest addition to the growing family, and we moved the short distance to a bigger house in Ringshall Road. Before long the Grantham family line-up was supplemented by the arrival our baby brother, Philip.

Apart from the smell of Philip's wet nappies and the grinding boiler, the main thing I remember about Ringshall Road was the news that Everest had been conquered and Queen Elizabeth's Coronation in 1953, and the wonderful street party that followed. We didn't have a television, so we all crammed into Mrs Brown's house across the street, to watch it on hers before heading out to the street party. Her family also had one of the few cars in the street, in addition to a motorbike and sidecar. At the time we thought of the

Browns as millionaires, though they lived in a council house, same as the rest of us. I was all of six years old, yet I remember the day with almost cine-reel clarity. I went to the street party dressed as a pirate, while my sister Angela went as a fairy. The party seemed to go on for ever and, with it being such a significant day, and such a balmy summer's eve, too, us kids were allowed to play out after dark. It was magical.

After the Coronation we bought a television, as I am sure most people in the country did. Although it had only a nine-inch screen, we had a magnifier fixed to the front to make it bigger.

My Dad's nightly ritual would be to rise from his chair at about ten to nine, detach the hand of his false arm, which was permanently covered by a brown leather glove, lay it on the arm of the armchair, wind up the clock and go up to bed. Most nights of the week my Dad had a large cooked meal ready for him when he came home from work, but Friday night was slightly different. As the housekeeping money had run out, his usual fare would be herring roes on toast. And when he rose from his chair at ten to nine he would do his arm-detaching-clock-winding-go-to-bed routine, but on this night he would put the housekeeping behind the clock.

The housekeeping would cover food and gas and electricity for the week. Wednesday morning, my mother would draw my Dad's war pension from the post office. This money was to cover the rent for our council house and was used to pay what we owed to the tallyman. We seemed forever to live on tick. There was a constant line of tallymen calling at our door – collectors demanding the latest instalment on hire-purchase furniture, television, insurance, assurance. But we always seemed to be hiding from one or the other. As the money began to run out, the rows seemed to be never ending. My Dad swore blind that he had left enough to cover everything, my mother was adamant he hadn't. Somehow my Dad would produce money to pay the debt. One day I came home from school to find my mother tucking into a plate of cream cakes. I guess that's where the money went.

Boots, however, was good to us. They kept us in toiletries, medicines and Lucozade. Anything that Boots sold Dad could buy at cost price and bring home for the family. The firm kept us warm, too. Boots lorries would turn up with packing cases of wood to put on the fire; sometimes farm eggs and meat, which his drivers picked up on their journeys, would also appear. So we never starved.

When I started school I was ambidextrous, though I tended to favour my left hand to write with. I attended a Church of England school, and the teacher used to hit me with a ruler on the left hand every time I wrote with it. (I'm sure she believed only the Devil's progeny wrote left-handed. I later learned that *sinister* comes from the Latin for left!) So I feigned illness and said I didn't want to go to school. When asked why, I showed my bruised hand to my mother. Once my Dad got in from work my mother told him what I had said. My Dad took time off work to come into school with me to try to sort it out. The teacher denied hitting me, and said I was making it up. Reluctantly, I pulled my closed fist out of my pocket and, with pain, straightened out my fingers. Observing my black and blue fingers, she became a little flustered but insisted I must have fallen over in the playground. It was clear she was lying and my Dad decided there and then that we had to find another school for me. Fortunately, a new school nearby was nearing completion, so the next term I was to go there. I still had to turn up at my existing school until the end of term, though. I hated going in, and dreaded having to go into that classroom every day to be taught by this woman who had whacked me and then lied about it. She started to make comments about my writing. By now I was afraid to use my left hand: I would have to write things over and over again.

My new school was great: large and airy, unlike my previous establishment. When we studied Captain Cook I became a minor celebrity when I said I was related to Matthew Flinders – I quite liked the feeling. On the way to the school we would pass a quaint little shop called the Crow's Nest, which was run by Mr and Mrs Crowe. It backed on to an orchard, which obviously was a temptation to all of us. We would climb into the orchard and knock apples and plums down. Whenever we had to buy something from the Crow's Nest, we were told by my mother to see if there were any apples lying on the ground and to pick them up and bring them home. So dutifully we did, though this had to stop when I fell out of a tree and landed on an old iron bed frame grazing my back badly. Although in obvious pain, my mother's only comment was, 'Where's the fruit?'

As our family increased, we once again moved, this time to St Mary Cray over the other side of the railway station, to a larger house with a fairly large garden. My Dad loved the garden, although it must have looked odd seeing a one-armed man using a fork and shovel to dig the vegetable patch. But dig it he did. There was a very well-established rock garden at the front of the house. At the bottom end of the back garden there was a shed, as well as a row of gooseberry bushes.

It was about this time that our Saturday afternoons would take us out of the house. Both John and I would go off to the Boots sports ground in New Eltham to watch the company teams play either cricket or football. In this environment, away from the tiffs and tribulations with Mum, Dad was transformed. He was a different bloke here, and the staff seemed to love him. It was Wally this, Wally that. It was a family affair, everyone would be there. I remember the secretaries in the summer sitting in deckchairs watching the cricket. When I was about eleven I started playing for them myself. I was told I could bowl a bit – something that would bring great pleasure and a welcome relief from the pressures of work for myself, my wife and my own kids in years to come. When I was about thirteen I started to take my mates along to the sports club. Every weekend there was something going on.

I remember a time when Boots drivers had to be balloted about going on strike, something to do with orders from the transport union. Dad was obviously deeply worried. Very much a don't-rock-the-boat person, he was a great believer in the establishment. At Christmas we had to keep quiet while the Queen's speech was on and the same when the Remembrance Day service was on television. So I know he was at odds with his workmates over the strike.

Once in the early 1960s war was declared in our house, when Eric Lubbock led the Liberals in Orpington, and my mother took great pride in sticking a Liberal poster in the front room window. Dad was furious. He wasn't going to have that rubbish in his window. Of course I am sure that my mother only did it to wind him up.

The day of the strike meeting duly arrived. After a long-winded speech from the shop steward, my Dad stood up and said, 'I don't know about you blokes, but I can't afford to go on strike. I *will* cross the picket line. I've got four kids to provide for.' Others seemed to be of the same opinion and the strike never took place. No one seemed to hold it against my Dad. In fact my memories of the Boots drivers are of a happy bunch who enjoyed their work and were well disposed towards Dad.

Dad was proud to have served his country and enjoyed his time at Boots, just as years later he would be thrilled about his achievements as a local Tory councillor after he retired. Nevertheless, he was reluctant to speak about his war experiences, though I am sure he had many. He didn't even keep his medals, though I'd have loved to have seen them. His only regret about Boots was that he never rose above manager of the department he worked in, whether it was despatch, transport or assistant warehouse manager. He wasn't university-educated as that was Boots' criterion for senior management.

Dad would come in at the same time every night. Once when he was late, so late that even my mother was worried, we didn't know what to do. (We had no phone so there was no way of knowing where he was.) Suddenly the television flashed an announcement that there had been a huge train crash at Lewisham. We feared the worst, but eventually my Dad turned up in a police car. No, he hadn't been arrested, though he did look dreadful. No, he hadn't been in the crash. He had been on a station waiting for a train, when the announcement was made. Seemingly he had commandeered the station master's phone and, co-ordinating with the police and emergency services, had managed to despatch drugs and other emergency equipment to the hospitals that were to be used for the injured (whether he did this by himself or through his bosses at the warehouse I am not sure). Boots paid for us to have a phone installed after that, although Dad said it was to be used only for incoming calls. So there we were with a phone, but we still had to trot off to the end of the road to use the phone box. We were under pain of death not to tell people we had a phone, so we wouldn't have the awkwardness of having to turn them down when they asked to use it. In retrospect, it's just possible that the wires leading from our house to the telegraph pole might have tipped our neighbours the wink, though.

Holiday times were wonderful, and laid the foundations for my love of a good, family holiday to this day. There was nothing more exciting than setting off for the break, either by train or, if we were lucky, one of Dad's driver mates would give us a lift. Our usual destinations were those tropical outposts of the English coastline. Leysdown. Eastchurch. Jaywick. Camber Sands, of course, and Dymchurch – although once we did travel further afield to the uncharted northern climes of Blackpool. Sadly, my only memory of that trip is an agonizing, slow-motion playback of our newly-purchased beach ball blowing away in the first gust of wind as we stepped off the tram. There was always a competition to see who could catch first sight (or smell) of the sea. Somehow, in our childish imaginations, we assumed that no sooner had we turned the corner of our street we'd be able to smell the sea. In reality, the only thing we could smell was the pong of us kids. It was the same on the train. No sooner had the train left the station than we'd be craning our necks out of the window, convinced that we'd seen the sea.

But there was no denying that when we did eventually arrive, it was like being in Wonderland. It didn't matter if it was sunny or raining or shrouded in fog – we were at the seaside. The smell of candyfloss, the noise of the amusement arcades and the sights and sounds of holidaymakers enjoying themselves made us kids think we were in heaven. More often than not we'd stay in caravans or chalets, and with there being six of us, it was always a matter of getting up as soon as we could in the mornings and getting down to the beach or the amusement arcades away from the cramped living quarters and the smell of wet towels.

While the others were watching Punch and Judy or trying to grab the sweets with the crane, and the adults were playing bingo, I would tend to wander off by myself. I was captivated by the various shows going on, usually on a bandstand or in some public space, or down on the beach on an impromptu stage. These shows would typically include the usual knobbly knees competitions or fancy dress, but there'd always be local talent contests, too. One particular day, I spotted a sign for a Junior Talent Contest later that week. I decided there and then that I would enter it, although I had not the faintest idea what I was going to do.

The nearer the day came to take part, the less confident I felt. Eventually, I told my Dad that I wanted to take part in the contest, but I didn't have a routine. His face burst into the biggest grin and he just said: 'Make 'em laugh!' It sounded easy enough in theory, so I swotted up on the joke pages in a comic and perfected possibly the least amusing jokes ever to regale a British seaside talent extravaganza. When it came to my time on stage, I took a deep breath and started to go through the motions. No one laughed. I tried another gag. All I could hear was my father, mother and brother, over-compensating for my lack of chuckles with their big, booming guffaws. It's an odd thing when you're up on stage, but you actually can't take in much detail in the audience. People always say: 'Did you see me, waving?' and you say that, yes, of *course* you saw them – but you're too busy concentrating on giving your best up there. I do recall that day, though, people turning round to see who was making all the noise over the unfunny jokes. As I swallowed my pride and went to take my bow, I tripped on the microphone cable and performed what could be construed as a perfect pratfall.

Now *that* brought a huge roar of laughter, and got me through to the next heat. Sadly for the audience the jokes were no better in the next round and that was as far as I got . . . but it gave me my first taste of showing off, and my first fix of laughter and applause. It made me want more.

Encouraging my interest in being an entertainer, Dad gave me a Christmas present to behold – an amazing set of stage makeup in a beautiful, varnished wooden box. He probably never even dreamed I would end up on stage in any capacity, but that gift was one of the big factors in stimulating my love of dressing up and playing out parts. I spent hour upon hour 'being' Coco the Clown or Mr Pastry or Al Jolson. These solitary performances brought much more satisfaction than the next time I was to appear in front of an audience, playing a shepherd in the school Nativity play. All we had to do was spy the bright star in the sky over Bethlehem and point at it in awe and wonder. Sadly, while the rest of the cast performed impeccably, Leslie Grantham was looking in the wrong direction!

Much later on in life this penchant for entertaining would get me through my prison sentence. Even when I was a boy soldier, I managed to bring the house down: lingering in front of the hardest, strictest, most humourless drill sergeant in the barracks, I looked into his eyes and sang Freddie and the Dreamers' 'You were Made for Me'. Even he saw the funny side – for a minute.

When I was about thirteen or so I decided to go camping. A lot of my mates were doing this at the time – it was the latest thing. After getting hold of a really basic tent, I set off to Canvey Island via the Woolwich Ferry. I hiked around until I found a campsite and managed to get the tent up, with a little help from fellow campers. They may well have thought it was a tad unusual for a young boy to be pitching up on his own, but if they did, they kept it to themselves. I was as happy as a pig in muck out there. Mind you, I wasn't allowed to do any cooking. Some kindly neighbour would intervene just before I incinerated my sausages, either preparing my own food for me or inviting me to share theirs. I remember two sisters a lot older than me, checking to see I was all right. These two would always include me in whatever they were doing. I was having the time of my life, but just as I was starting to get used to my independence, my short burst of freedom was shattered. Out of the corner of my eye, I spied a fearsome sight.

Bustling through the camp gate was my mother, with my sister and my younger brother in tow. Without pausing for introductions or niceties she commented on how thin and dirty I looked. Although I'd only been away a few days and had been treated like a king, she was adamant I must be half starved, and that was that. She proceeded to dismantle my tent, pack up my duffel bag and, immune to my protests, took me off to the campsite café where we all had lunch. Even the other camp dwellers who came over to say cheerio assured her I'd been fine. She told them 'Mummy knows best'. We trooped back to the train station and returned home, my great outdoor adventure cut short in its prime.

Sometimes we didn't have a week or a fortnight away, just day trips out to one of the seaside resorts on the south coast. Our destination would, more often than not, be decided by the weather. For reasons I have never quite worked out, these day trips always seemed much more exciting than a full family holiday. We'd spend more time in the sea, less time in the arcades while Dad and my mother sat in a deckchair with a tea tray. We always had fish and chips for lunch, and always finished up with a plate of cockles and winkles before boarding the train back home. And if, as often happened, the weather took a sudden turn for the worse, at least we knew we'd be going home to our own beds rather than some cramped caravan or chalet. No matter what the weather, Dad always stayed covered up because of his arm. He couldn't join in with all the fun in the sea, but holiday times were – and still are – some of the best times I have ever known.

My mother was pregnant. Dad, though, was in extreme pain with his teeth, and boils started to appear on his neck at an alarming rate. I can see my mother now applying magnesium sulphate to his neck, and little bits of metal would be drawn out. Dad had a great set of teeth, even for a smoker. Dentists could find nothing wrong with either him or his teeth, but you could see him becoming more and more irritable with the pain the longer it went on. Eventually he decided to have all his teeth out. The dentists were right, in that there was nothing wrong with his teeth; it was his gums. But, as Dad said, they couldn't take his gums out and leave his teeth. When the grenade had exploded, shrapnel had entered his body and over the years had travelled through his system and ended up in his neck: hence the boils and the deteriorating gums. The amount of shrapnel that came out with his teeth was phenomenal. Later, he would have to have half his stomach removed because of this shrapnel.

Our little brother, Simon Keith, was born without kidneys and obviously in considerable pain. Still, my mother was allowed to bring him home. Eventually he went back to hospital. Now, years later, having had a child of my own with a disability, I realize how hard it must have been for my parents. Although I was preoccupied with my new baby brother, I was taking my eleven-plus; I did what I had to do and sat the exams. The day after my exams I was called to the headmaster's office. Mr Bird, whose only contact with me hitherto had been regarding disciplinary matters, now seemed kind and caring. He asked me to sit down and told me that Simon had passed away ten days before; on speaking with my parents he had decided that it would be best if the news were kept from me until after the exams. I felt devastated.

2

SCHOOL AND SCANDAL

As I slowly moved up the education ladder, it became increasingly obvious that I would be pre-judged by the shenanigans of my elder brother. John had had a patchy school career: he had played truant and refused to carry on at Dartford Technical School, at which point my parents had him transferred to St Mary Cray Secondary Modern, affectionately known as Herne's Rise. John was intelligent and very popular, but sometimes popularity has its down side. He seemed to mix in strange company, and because he liked to smoke – we all did; it was all part of the glamour of being a teenager. My mother didn't try to stop us, knowing we'd only go and smoke on some street corner, and preferring to keep an eye on us herself. In fact, she went as far as buying the cigarettes for us – our front room would be full of six or seven boys smoking.

When it was my turn to go to Herne's Rise, the teachers, having remembered my brother, earmarked me as a Grantham. I was told, in no uncertain terms, that I was being closely watched. (My sister, Angela, received a similar reception a few years later.) From my first day at my new school it was a rocky ride, and I hated it, not because I couldn't cope with the lessons, but rather because I couldn't stand the constant needling and snide comments made about John.

I felt like a goldfish in a bowl, and like a goldfish I tended to spend my time looking out of the window. The more I looked out of those windows on to open green fields, the more I wanted to be out of the bloody classroom! And out of it I got: I started to play truant. At first I played truant at my mates' houses. School was becoming unbearable for me, too, and I was getting caned more and more, mostly for cheek and truancy. On numerous occasions I was caned in front of the school; so often, that as soon as the deputy headmaster, 'Daddy' Day, began to call names out, I made my way up to the stage to receive my six of the best, though there was nothing best about those six. 'Daddy' Day caned your backside, whereas the headmaster, Mr Fawcett, caned your hand; Day did it in front of the whole school, Fawcett in his office. Once I went up and Day was surprised to see me, as I wasn't on his list. Another time he put so much pent-up fury into the act of whacking me that he snapped his braces. When he retired I presented him with a new pair in front of the whole school.

Truancy had taken over; I started fruit-picking and got myself a job with a greengrocer on his horse and cart round. I remember feeling so brave as we drove the horse and cart past the school gates, knowing I should be back inside there. I also got a Saturday job, down at the local bread factory. We would grab the WH Smiths van as it dropped the papers at the local newsagents, and hitch a lift to the Bridge House pub, where we would jump off and then walk the short distance to the bread factory. We would all wait outside until the drivers came out, whereupon they would pick their boy helpers and drive off. In the beginning, we used to shout out, 'Want a boy, mister?' in the hope that we would be picked. (Imagine how that'd sound today. They'd have a social worker round before you'd got to the end of the road!) Eventually, after a few weeks, I ended up working regularly with a driver who was a fantastic character, as kind-hearted and generous a man as you could wish to meet.

One Christmas all the lads were loading up the vans for the next day's rounds, when the factory caught fire. It was the day before Christmas Eve, so we were there late and ended up driving vans, lorries and barrows of bread, chocolate yule logs, cakes and Christmas puddings out of harm's way. I think we saved a load of people's Christmas that year.

As if school wasn't bad enough, my relationship with my mother was becoming difficult. One day, her brother arrived with his family from Manchester, and because I had been cleaning out the van, I looked like something out of Richmal Crompton's *Just William*. As I walked in the house to say hello to my uncle, my mother caught sight of my appearance and went ballistic. My poor aunt, who was sticking up for me, enraged my mother further, and a full-scale row ensued. By teatime, I had been sent up to my room, and my aunt, uncle and cousins had got into their car and driven back up north. Sadly, this was not to be a one-off.

My mother's changeability must have run in her family. My maternal Nan was difficult to please, too. She only came down once a year from her home in Hertfordshire to visit us. But what should have been a great, joyful day usually ended up being a terrible letdown. No matter how hard we tried not to irritate her, we would inevitably be sent out of the house for bad behaviour, usually something unforgivable like forgetting to cut the cake. Even looking back it on it now, I find it hard to understand her coldness towards us. Both my Mum and her own mother carried an air of disappointment about them, as though they were destined for better things. It's been my experience that women like that find children an inconvenience. It's almost as if the mere existence of kids challenges their vanity, reminds them that they're no longer in the first flush of youth themselves. Whatever it was that irked them, we never felt the closeness that we grew to know and value in other of our relatives.

My mother took a job for a few months as a nurse in a nursing home. She was over the moon when John Glen – some big star or other, according to her – used to drop by the home to see his mother, who was a resident there. Of course, she became incredibly superior and dined out on this tale for months. But no matter how much money was coming in, more and more was going out. Fortunately, John and I didn't have to rely on our parents for money as we had always worked to bring in our own spends.

'The Huggetts' had been a very popular radio show, which had been turned into a few films with Jack Warner. So when the Huggett family had moved into the Seven Stiles pub, it was only right that

Jack Warner of 'Dixon of Dock Green' fame should be asked to open it. The turnout for the ceremony was phenomenal. John managed to get his picture taken with Jack Warner, which appeared in the local paper. I say his picture but it was actually a rather splendid image of the back of his head that made it into shot, as my brother turned to watch Jack waving to the crowd. John went on to get himself a job as a barman in the Seven Stiles, and Harry Huggett, who had the best car in the neighbourhood, took all of us tearaways under his wing. He was in his element, driving us around here, there and everywhere. He and Ada, his wife, had no kids, so they treated John and me like their own. If Harry was off to see another publican, he would take us with him, and we would sit outside drinking lemonade while he talked business. I got a job as a pot man and then when it was busy, served in the bar, to supplement the money from the bread round. Harry Huggett had the local residents in the palm of his hand; we loved him and Ada. And the Seven Stiles became the centre of our universe.

I had become friendly with several people on the estate, one of whom was also called John. He worked for Burroughs Wellcome. I had a key to his house, and would make my way there most days. John's Dad was dead, but his mother, Eileen, who worked on the buses, treated me like a son. Eventually, when it came time for me to leave school, John managed to get me a job at Burroughs as a junior laboratory technician, making tetanus injections and sheep inoculations.

John invited me to his sister's wedding, where I met most of Eileen's family. As we waited for the bride and groom's pictures to be taken, the police suddenly burst into the churchyard and marched over to Eileen's brother. When they grabbed him, something flew through the air and landed at my feet. I looked down and saw a handgun. I quickly stamped on it, and because the ground was wet it eased into the earth. As the police dragged her brother away, Eileen looked everywhere for the object she had seen looping through the air. When she came to me, I tried to sound as calm as I could: 'It's here.'

I lifted my shoe to show her. No gun. I lifted my foot right up and, this time, we could just see the outline of the gun in the mud.

She grabbed my arm, and we left for the reception. I don't think Eileen and her family ever went back for that gun.

My last year at school was a doddle, although I fell foul of the establishment on many occasions, especially when elected house captain. This did not go down at all well. I had beaten the head boy easily: he got three votes, and I got the rest. The housemaster tried to force a re-vote, but the electorate had made their decision. It was Grantham for PM – well, house captain, at least, for now. My career in politics lasted about twenty-four-and-a-half hours. The following night, on leaving school, I had cleared the school perimeter, made sure the coast was clear and even then left it all of fifteen minutes before lighting up a cigarette. As I took my second puff, the gleeful housemaster leapt out from a bush, smirking from ear to ear. Triumphant, he told me I would be seeing the headmaster the next morning. So it was six of the best, and I was stripped of the house captaincy.

Shortly after we had finished our end-of-term exams, I was set all the dirty jobs, like clearing out the boiler room and stacking up the fuel in neat piles. It was clear to all the staff that I wouldn't be staying on to higher education, so they gave me all the jobs they thought I would hate. When I finished my tasks, I was given others: cleaning out the clay bins in the pottery room, for instance, which was not as much fun as clearing out the boiler room. Nevertheless, hanging around the pottery room did have an added bonus that the school could not have foreseen.

The art teacher, who was helping me clear out the storeroom, came to see how I was getting on. Apart from clearing up, she showed me how to keep the clay moist. To do this she had to bend down into the huge bin and agitate the clay. As she did so, I couldn't help but peer down her top. And, hallelujah, she wore no bra: what a result for a young man! Obviously I raced to the pottery room each day now, eager to plunge my hands in up to the elbows. Whenever she came in, she checked the kiln and moved stuff out. She also used to knock up a few little pots, and in so doing, had to keep supplying herself with more clay. I was transfixed. Apart from my mother and a few *National Geographic* magazine pictures of bare-breasted African women, I had not seen anything like this before. Shortly after bidding my farewells to the school, I was buying some cigarettes when I happened upon a *Health and Efficiency* magazine; I swear that was the pottery teacher on the front cover, leaping in the air, extolling the virtues of naturism.

My schooldays ended when I was fifteen, and I started at Burroughs Wellcome, where I worked in the autoclave room. I was given a guided tour and went into a laboratory, and was shocked to see the people there grabbing the mice by their tails and swinging them around, before crashing their heads on the table. They then slung them in a huge paper bag, which was taken away and burnt.

Part of my lowly job was to clean out the stables and get to know the horses. These were either rescued or old brewery horses that had been sent to end their days here. Little did they know! We had animals of all shapes and sizes; one day a monkey, which was being experimented on, escaped, only to be located and shot. On another occasion, I was approached by a senior technician, who gave me a scalpel, a long rubber tube and a huge glass bottle with a rubber bung in it. He told me to cut the horse's throat, stick the rubber tube in it, and drain off the blood. The blood had to come straight from the main artery and, once collected, needed to be taken to a lab; the horse would then be cut up, and its flesh minced, cooked and used in the manufacture of tetanus injections. I had had enough; I handed in my resignation there and then.

Because I didn't want to admit to being a failure, I didn't tell my parents. I applied for a few other jobs, but nothing came of these inquiries. Fortunately, I still had the pub job, so I did more nights to keep the money coming in. By now, I had progressed from the baker's round to a Saturday job in menswear on the high street. Walking the streets, looking for work, and having to stay out of the house, was not the most invigorating pastime. The problem was that, when it was raining, there were only so many cups of tea you could drink.

I often think back to that rainy (and fateful) day, all those years ago, when I ducked under an awning to escape the huge downpour. It was to be the moment that changed my life – for better and for worse. If I hadn't joined the army, I would never have killed a man. But if *that* hadn't happened, who knows? I may never have pursued my love of acting. I can't alter any of it. Things have happened in the way they have, and my taking shelter from that downpour was, I now think, my next step on the journey that would ultimately take me to Albert Square and beyond. As I stood there shivering, I heard a voice behind me say, 'Don't stand there – come on in.' I turned and followed the voice inside, and only then did I realize I was entering an army recruitment office. I decided to bide my time, waiting for the rain to stop, by going through the enrolment procedure; I never in a million years intended to take the final plunge. As I finished answering the questions, and wrote down my preference for which regiment I would like to join, the rain stopped. I stuck the paperwork in my pocket and headed for home, assuring the recruiting officer that I would get my parents to sign my papers as soon as possible.

The papers lay in my pocket for weeks. One Friday morning, Dad, having come down to get ready for work, found there was no gas and the meter empty; he couldn't shave or boil a kettle to make a cup of tea. Looking through my pockets, I found him a shilling piece and, of course, out fell the enlistment papers. An ex-volunteer himself, he was obviously thrilled for me and didn't hesitate to sign them. I was now lumbered. But, after a while, the idea of joining up grew on me: it would get me away from my mother and this increasingly dreary life at home. And the pay, although nothing marvellous, would be a step in the right direction, too. So I duly returned the papers. In the meantime, I got a job in a menswear outfitters in Bromley, and waited to hear when I was to be called up.

At that time I was the runt of the litter, no taller than five foot six or seven, with a size-six-and-a-half shoe. John was already six foot, and Philip and Angela were as tall as me, although two and four years younger respectively. After a few weeks of working in the menswear shop, I had the good fortune to strike up a friendship with a girl on the train. We met on the platform in the morning and caught the same train home every night. On a particularly snowy evening, we somehow ended up in the woods near where I lived, and another of life's debuts was successfully negotiated by young Grantham. A close enounter of the brief kind, however, right down to the railwayside setting.

Eventually I was summoned to report to the Junior Leaders' Regiment in Oswestry, Shropshire, where I would go into the boys' service. After a farewell party, I bade goodbye to my friends and set off for a prolonged stretch in uniform. Little did I know that the uniform was not to be the one I thought it would be, and the stretch would be significantly longer than I'd signed for.

On our arrival at Gobowen station, line after line of army trucks awaited us. The train I had been sitting in for over three hours was probably three-quarters full of new recruits, along with a smattering of more experienced soldiers. Various uniforms greeted us, worn by training instructors who'd come from every regiment in the British army. The journey to the barracks was short and we were allocated our quarters. We weren't given uniforms, so spent the first evening in our own clothes, which, I believe, was meant to mark us out as rookies to the old hands.

Once we had been 'fitted' out with uniforms, a process which basically revolved solely around how tall and fat we were (how anything fitted I will never know, but fit, in a fashion, it did), barracks life started for real. It was unrelenting: drill, polish, spit, drill, march, drill, march; dawn inspections, morning inspections, evening inspections. Sometimes we were woken at two in the morning and told to parade on the main square in our pyjamas. If we weren't fast enough this just went on night after night until we were. We abseiled, boated, climbed Snowdon, and we polished, cleaned and spat.

By the time six weeks had passed we could march, halt, present arms, about turn, right wheel, left wheel, and could strip a rifle or machine gun blindfold. It was on Snowdon, while carrying the radio, my kit and the general-purpose machine gun, that I got a radio message saying Kennedy had been assassinated. However dangerous it might have been on that part of Snowdon, carrying enough equipment for three men, Kennedy's death put it all into perspective.

Obviously, being new recruits, we were open to all forms of intimidation. We were always on tenterhooks lest the instructors found fault with us; and we hated it when some of the older soldiers came in and wrecked the barracks. They always seemed to travel in packs and pick on a lone soldier. After six weeks, however, we were allowed to go into town, but dressed in uniform – so what little chance you had of meeting a local girl was made even less likely dressed to the nines like Action Man. Sometimes a dance was held in the barracks, but the majority of girls who attended were already spoken for by soldiers from an older group; these guys had first call.

At one dance, I got on very well with a girl from town and walked her to the gate. As I was now allowed out in my civvies, I arranged to meet her at a dance in town the following Saturday. Lights out was at ten o'clock and, unless you had a late pass, you had to be in bed by then. Lights had not been out for long when I was visited by three squaddies, who wanted to know what I thought I was up to. Apparently the girl I had chatted up and kissed goodnight belonged to this corporal. Quickly deciding that discretion was the better part of valour, I claimed that I'd had only one dance with her, and maybe someone was winding him up. He was full of all the usual bluster, but after threatening to kick my head in and telling me to watch myself, that was that.

Saturday evening arrived, and I made my way into town. When I got to the dancehall I told the girl that it might not be the very best idea if we were seen out together. She asked me whyever not, so I repeated what her boyfriend had said. She burst out laughing at the preposterous notion he was her boyfriend; he'd been trying to get her to go out with him for weeks and she just wasn't interested. In light of this startling new information, I elected to take up where we had left off. Later that evening, I felt daggers aimed at my back; I turned around and saw my three squaddies standing in a group, looking particularly intimidating as they gesticulated at me and made throat-cutting gestures. Wholly unimpressed, the girl stormed over to them and gave her 'boyfriend' an earful in front of his mates, listing in detail the reasons she could never contemplate a date with him, even if he were the last man on earth; at which point this supposedly 'macho' type turned on his heels and slunk off. As hilarious and as richly deserved as his public humiliation was, I had a nasty feeling it would be me who'd be feeling the backlash. I realized that getting involved with other soldiers' girls – even if they were not going out with them – would make my life unbearable, and I decided never to venture into town again. The only time I broke my own embargo was when the whole of the Junior Leaders' Regiment had to march into town (in full dress) to see *The Longest Day*.

When my leave came, I travelled in uniform down to London, where my family met me at the station. My mother, Dad and Angela all walked straight past me, not recognizing the man I had become. Having been the runt of the litter for so long, I had now shot up to nearly six foot and was wearing a size-nine boot. That first leave shot by. Much more confident in myself now, I asked out a lovely girl, who worked at the local baker's. We were pretty inseparable over that fortnight and, before I headed back to camp, became lovers. But to say I was still innocent in the ways of womankind would be to understate the case significantly.

To escape the monotony and tedium of weekend barrack life – unless we were on weekend guard duty, we just hung around, twiddling our thumbs – I visited my uncle, who lived in Manchester. This was a godsend for me, and made some of the more unpleasant aspects of army life easier to bear. All my mates were now mods and I wanted to be the same. It was the summer of 1964 and we'd head off to the coast each weekend, where there was more fun to be had. I was there the day the famous photo of the battle of Brighton beach was taken; and I'm sorry to have to say that the fighting between the mods and rockers was all staged for the newspapers. How little times change! We were only kids and were more than happy to repeat the same action sequence for them, over and over. I clearly remember stopping our flight across the beach to help a young mother carry her pushchair down the steps. Over the years, though, mates have bragged about the 'Battle of Brighton'. Read something often enough and you start to believe it must be true.

After our passing-out parade, I was posted to St George's Barracks in Sutton Coldfield, the regimental training depot. On arrival, I was put into a barrack block full of new recruits, and made to complete training all over again. For the first few weekends, we couldn't go into town dressed in civvies, though none of the locals wanted to know anyway. Most weekends were now spent at home anyhow.

After a few weeks, given that I was too young to join my regiment, the Royal Fusiliers (City of London Regiment) in Germany, I was designated to help with the training. As well as training the new recruits, I still had to mount the guard. Every now and again, a young lady would approach the sentry at the main gate – myself included – and try to engage us in conversation. As this was against the rules, I ignored her. One morning the barracks descended into a blind panic: the armoury had been broken into, and weapons and ammunition had gone missing. Seemingly, the young lady had found a gullible squaddy to fall for her charms, and while they were busily engaged, some IRA sympathizer emptied the armoury.

I can't say that my time at Oswestry or Sutton Coldfield had made me into a better person; I was still very much the cocky (now not so little) kid I had been at school. Only now I knew how to obey orders and how to jump when told to jump. As well as discipline, the only other thing I was taught was how to keep things clean. Uniforms, boots, equipment, weaponry – whatever it was, I knew how to clean it.

The time had now come to play with the big boys, and I was sent to Germany to join my regiment. It was the first time I had ever been on a plane. On arrival at Belfast Barracks in Osnabrück, it was as if I was suffering from *déjà vu*. I was back in training company with all those squaddies who had completed six weeks' basic training. I may have been a new recruit, but I had been in the army for nearly two years.

3

DON'T MENTION THE WAR

Army life, as portrayed on screen, has certain elements of truth to it, whether it be the brutality or the camaraderie. But, in reality, it's the sheer monotony, coupled with physical and mental abuse, that sticks in my mind. From the moment the bugle was sounded to the moment the dormitory lights were switched off, we were under a microscope, constantly at someone else's beck and call. And because of the mind-numbing regimentation, soldiers tended to group together to beat the system. (Strange, really, as the modern British army is a volunteer force.)

But beating the system entailed many things: whether it was getting someone else to polish your boots, to press your uniform, to clean your equipment, to keep your locker tidy, or to do your guard duty, it was all about getting some poor squaddy to perform whatever wretched tasks you'd been allocated – so much so that if you could have made someone do your marching for you, you probably would have done so. Some soldiers made a good living out of cleaning and shining boots. NCOs didn't pay; they used their rank to intimidate and ensure they received favourable treatment. And then, of course, there were the mini-mobs of bullies, who would just railroad the unfortunate new recruits into doing their bidding. Life in the First

25

Battalion of the Royal Fusiliers was very easy for the bullies, whereas it was very difficult for the new recruits who felt unhappy and homesick, slowly realizing that the army was far from being the heroic institution they had imagined. After a period of time the toughest of them became hardened to it and, before long, they were bullying the next intake of novices themselves. A vicious circle of abuse and intimidation we had to endure.

Forty years ago, before the advent of the package holiday, the world was a smaller place. When I was a teenager no one I knew travelled abroad for holidays. One boy at school had a French cousin to stay for a week. At first we stood off and treated him as a curiosity, as if he were from another planet. (As the crow flies, he lived closer to Kent than my cousins in Manchester!) So to be not only abroad, but also miles from friends and family, was a shock to many a new recruit. Even those who had been in the army a while suffered from homesickness. Sadly, a lot of new recruits never made it back from their first leave home, and several deserted while in Germany. It wasn't hard to understand why.

Barrack life for us new recruits was all drudgery and routine. In the morning, the duty NCO made his wake-up rounds by riding his bike through the dormitory, or bashing a dustbin lid. If you weren't up by the time he had completed his second round, you were tipped out of bed. If that didn't work, you were charged with disobeying an order. Obviously, not all duty NCOs used these methods; some just turned the lights on and told us to get out of bed. (That's what I did when I was an NCO.) But whichever method was used, you were expected to be dressed and have all lockers neat and tidy (their contents had to be folded to the required length) for inspection. If anything was out of order, there would be a further inspection that night, either for the whole section or the platoon. Clearly, this put a lot of pressure on all concerned; more so if it messed up any social activity that might have been planned. Any misdemeanour led to loss of pay or privileges, often both; the usual punishments, or jankers, included confinement to camp, extra guard duty, painting the parade ground stones white, or cleaning pots and pans. And if any of these weren't punishment enough, there was also the constant threat of bullying and intimidation from the older soldiers.

God forbid anyone was heard crying himself to sleep; this would be just the sort of chink in the armour that these bastards preyed upon. It soon became apparent to me that anything could be taken as a sign of weakness: choice of reading material, music, football team, or even a photograph of a girlfriend or loved one. No one reported anything, such was these bullies' power; if anyone was foolish enough to do so, a bed end would be taken to them while they slept.

It was pretty obvious that some soldiers, however hard they tried, just couldn't hack it, mentally or financially. Wages were low, and with everything on tick – from cheap beer to radios – in the NAAFI, it was all too easy to spend more than you earned. There was absolutely no supervision as to how much you spent, so long as you could pay it off. The problem, for many of us, was that we couldn't. Theft was rife, and so was loan-sharking. Money borrowed had either to be paid back at extortionate rates or worked off – so pity the poor squaddy who couldn't come up with the cash to pay his creditors.

Being in Germany didn't help. It was obvious that, because of the British soldiers' attitude, we weren't welcome in too many places in Osnabrück. It was only twenty years since the war had ended, and as we were an occupying force, there was not much love lost between the locals and us. (Looking back on it, we were just like English football fans abroad, with a brash and vocal minority given to picking fights with little or no provocation.) Equally, though, during all the time I was in Germany I never met a single German who would admit to having fought the British; they had all fought the Russians. Osnabrück had been a major recruiting area for the Nazis and the Hitler Youth; they had painted a barracks with red crosses while leaving the hospitals exposed, so when the Allies bombed the region, they of course hit the hospital, and not the barracks. The story consequently circulated that the British had bombed a hospital, but nothing was ever said about how the barracks had been painted with red crosses in the first place. These stories helped keep up the barriers between us.

In fact, the British were hated. Part of the reason was that the city was the main base for the British Army of the Rhine, but another major contributory factor was that the men couldn't handle the strong German beer. Quiet, retiring men would suddenly take on a demonic, violent turn as steins of strong lager transformed them. Bars and restaurants were off-limits, though this did not unduly inconvenience quite a few of the soldiers. The brothels may have been *verboten*, but we did have great fun playing knock-down ginger. Most evenings, however, would be spent in the big NAAFI over the road from the barracks, or in the corporals' mess. It was pointless watching television, as most programmes were in German, and although facilities were provided to do so, few of us saw the point in learning the language. As long as we could order a cup of tea and chicken and chips, we were bilingual enough.

Being under eighteen, and being on boy soldier's wages, I had to augment my meagre wages by babysitting. This allowed me to earn a few marks and save money for the NAAFI. I had about four or five regulars, and life was all right. And I'd started writing to the sister of a mate in my platoon, so I received mail regularly. Dad, of course, being ever so proud of me, sent the local paper and a few bob every now and again. Nevertheless, I was beginning to spend more and more, not on alcohol, but going out in town and buying clothes. I still thought of myself as a mod and wanted to look smart; I also needed to keep up with my peers, and not look out of place.

My first leave at home, however, was a disaster. No sooner had I walked through the door than my mother, without even a 'Hello, son, nice to see you', said, 'Where's your housekeeping?' As I was home only for a week, I bit my tongue, and thrust a pile of notes at her. This was most of my leave money now gone. Dad, however, was especially pleased to see me, as were Angela, Philip and John, while the Huggetts made a huge fuss of me as always. I tried to spend as little time in the house as I could get away with. I got through the week by going off to see mates and relatives, and I was increasingly spending time hanging around mod clubs in the West End. We saw some fantastic bands before they'd really broken big: the Temptations, the Four Tops; there was even a visit from 'The Beatles' that our local promoter claimed was a personal favour, payback for putting them on as the Quarrymen. It sold out straight away of course, but those who attended couldn't be absolutely certain that the Beatles who went through the greatest hits that night were actually John, Paul, Ringo and George. More likely Tom, Dick, Harry and Fred from the social club in mop-top wigs!

By this time, I had been selected for the NCOs' cadre and, although not promoted the first time round, I passed on my second attempt. One of the few truly rewarding days came when Dad visited for a few days with a coach-load of war veterans. This was arranged with the Royal Fusilier Association, and we entertained them with demonstrations of tactics, drill and weaponry. I think he really enjoyed himself, and it's always nice to make your old man proud of you. I know he went away as the main man among his friends after that visit – for the time being, at least.

My first duty, in charge of a section, was to go to Norway and take part in a NATO exercise. The weather was atrocious; it rained non-stop, so much so that the roads collapsed under the weight of the armoured personnel carriers and tanks. Given my section was in the last vehicle, the first battle lasted only forty minutes. Suddenly we came under artillery fire – all blanks, of course – which bogged our side down. Because of the grim conditions, we had stopped on hearing the gunfire, left our vehicle and climbed the hill behind the enemy position. My first battle in charge and we had managed to capture the enemy! Unfortunately, the army marshals disallowed our clever manoeuvre and ordered all of us to start the battle again. Spoilsports!

On another exercise, we went up to Denmark to take part in manoeuvres with the Danish army. The majority of our time, however, was spent visiting the Tivoli Gardens and Carlsberg brewery, where the men were shown brewing techniques. At the time, Carlsberg had a beer called Elephant, which certainly knocked all the German beers we were drinking for six. I have never seen so many drunken soldiers together at one time. I'm certain the Danish officers introduced us to the lethal brew on purpose; the next day we were soundly defeated, though many of the men would have been too hung-over to notice.

At this time, we were testing new equipment, like the Carl Gustaf rocket launcher and an amphibious armoured personnel carrier. As a section leader, I had the unenviable task of learning how to drive it as well as command it. During an exercise on Ackmer, which was our usual training area, we drove around on trial, the army's equivalent of a driving test. The problem was that the whole area was littered with huge bomb craters. So there I was, standing up in the hatch, while the driver was steering the vehicle blind. Suddenly, we hit a large mound, rose up and, as the vehicle crashed down, the cable connection to my headset was ripped from its socket. Although I could see a crater full of water in front of me, I couldn't communicate with the driver on my headset, and as I shouted out instructions we suddenly pitched down into a huge crater. The vehicle was a write-off, for which I was fined twenty pounds, to be taken from my pay in weekly instalments.

Believe it or not, I was now really enjoying the army. I wasn't being bullied or harassed; I was fortunate in that the training company's quartermaster, who had served with Dad, was looking out for me. Maybe it was also my cheeky-chappy or Jack-the-lad attitude that made me immune to the bullies. Usually, I could talk my way out of anything by cracking a joke or two. And because I spent my free time babysitting, helping out with the wives' shooting club and attending quite a few parties in the married quarters, I didn't much hang about with many of the regular soldiers.

This halcyon period turned out to be short-lived. It was becoming apparent that those of us promoted on the last cadre – those, like myself, who were very young – were inadvertently causing a lot of resentment among the older men, especially those who had failed. As time went on, it became increasingly obvious that things were being done to undermine us young NCOs. (Had we not been as clued-up as we were, there could have been tragic repercussions.) Maps were lost, radios didn't function, vehicles weren't greased or filled up properly. One commander of an armoured personnel carrier was nearly decapitated when the cover of the coolant compartment blew off and missed his head by two inches. Eventually, however, the troublemakers got their way, by resorting to violence.

Of course, as young men, we were obsessed by meeting girls, which was difficult given the no-go areas and the obvious language barrier. So it was a surprise when a mate and fellow NCO arrived at my door on a Sunday morning, and asked me to mount guard on the shower room door to stop anyone going in. My first thought was that it was another 'brooming', where they covered a soldier in scouring powder and then scrubbed him with a large brass broom. When I said I wanted no part of it he told me not to worry, as it was nothing like that. I got dressed and followed him to the shower area; I checked inside and saw it was empty. He ran off and a few minutes later arrived back with an attractive young lady, whom he said he had met driving back from England. While we waited outside, she went into the shower and reappeared after what seemed an eternity, wearing his shirt and carrying a bundle of wet clothes. He hurried her away, making sure that no one saw her with him, as it was against the army regulations to have civilians (especially female ones) in the barracks. How he got her in was anyone's guess; most likely he had hidden her in his car as he passed through the main gate. He was a hero with the lads, until he picked up a very nasty dose of VD.

The long, lonely weekends were beginning to take their toll on many of us, and drinking games and drunkenness seemed to be the order of the day. Many a morning, at inspection time, you would find people still drunk from the night before. Mattresses were so piss-soaked, after weeks of their occupiers flopping into bed and peeing themselves, that they sagged until they touched the floor. Whenever you have a large body of men together, trouble is only just round the corner; mostly this trouble was caused by alcohol, more alcohol and boredom: the destruction of many a good (and not so good) man.

After one nasty experience I stopped drinking altogether. During one particular drinking game, where you downed as many different concoctions as possible, blissfully unaware of their content, I began to hallucinate. Paranoid, and convinced an army was coming to 'get' me, I tried to throw myself out of my top-floor window. As I stood on that window ledge all I saw were tanks coming towards me. Fortunately, the catch on the window frame snagged on my belt and saved me from falling on to the tarmac below. Several people saw me hanging there, rushed up to my room, and dragged me back in. God knows what was in those drinks, but apart from having my stomach pumped, I wasn't about to find out. All I know is that it can't have been totally alcohol-fuelled. Like I say, boredom has proved the downfall of many a good man.

Given that alcohol was cheap in the NAAFI (similar to prices in a workingman's club), a lot of money and time was spent drinking. Quite a few soldiers ran up bills that would have to be paid at the end of the week, or on payday. This inevitably became a Catch-22 situation for many of us: no sooner had we received our wages, than bills would have to be paid, and the cycle would start all over again. The NAAFI also allowed soldiers to enter hire-purchase agreements for radios, cameras and clothes, which had to be approved by the company commander. But, as with everything else, if you happened to miss one payment, you were constantly playing catch up from that point on, robbing Peter to pay Paul.

The NAAFI was also a great source of income for a select few: shoplifting was rife. When the authorities cracked down on this, soldiers were allowed in only in pairs (not dissimilar to those signs you see in newsagents, 'SCHOOLCHILDREN – ONLY TWO AT A TIME'). After having been broken into at night once too often, huge security locks were fitted to keep the thieves out. Nevertheless, the gang managed to replicate that scene in *Rififi*, where a small hole is cut into the ceiling of a shop, and an umbrella is dropped through it so as to load up the loot. The spoils would be sold cheaply within the regiment. As far as I am aware, no one was ever convicted of these offences, although two drunken soldiers, who broke into the garrison NAAFI and defecated and urinated on the clothes, were subsequently dismissed from the army.

Another source of income for many a hard-up soldier came via the practice of 'rolling' Germans. If you've ever seen Sergio Leone's gangster classic *Once Upon a Time in America* you'll get the picture. It was a fairly crude affair that entailed going out at night, waiting for a suitably inebriated German to stagger by, and robbing him – which of course was fairly easy. In the mid-1960s, far fewer Germans spoke English, so, with your head down and collar turned up, it was very difficult for them to distinguish one British soldier from another. The tragic thing was how easy it was for so many to be drawn into that way of life. They felt that, as foreigners in a strange land, they were somehow anonymous – and it was easy pickings.

By now, I was so getting desperate for money, I could not sleep at night. I owed several weeks' pay without having the means to cover the debt. I had stupidly, and irresponsibly, started borrowing from my fellow soldiers; I wasn't just robbing Peter to pay Paul, there was also Matthew, Mark, Luke and John to consider. There was nothing Christian, however, about some of the people I was borrowing money from.

I was becoming scared by now, starting to dread what might happen to me if I couldn't pay. I managed to keep up a façade of bravado, but I'd seen what happened to some of the other kids in debt. But as an NCO, I thought there was only so much that my creditors could do to me. On one particular evening, which still makes me shudder to think of it even now, an event took place that sent my life into a downward spiral and led to the death of an innocent German. But this was nothing to do with creditors. I just happened to be in the wrong place at the wrong time.

After a visit to the mess, I went back to my room and pressed my uniform, cleaned my belt, gaiters and polished my boots for the next day. I also had to make sure I had a tidy locker and room: I could hardly give a member of my section a roasting for an untidy locker and a slovenly dormitory if my own weren't spick and span. And we were subject to lightning inspections, besides. Just because I was a section leader with an NCO's stripe didn't make me exempt from the random checks and possible repercussions of a less than perfect locker. So I got down to it. Once I had tidied my room I had to plan the next day's agenda, which would typically involve trying to digest mind-numbing manuals on the very latest weapons or tactics.

No sooner had I settled down, than the end-of-evening noise drifted up the stairs. This would usually be followed by people banging on doors, pretending to be the duty sergeant and harassing new recruits with 'Stand by your beds'. Some poor bloke who had just arrived would stand there dreading the inspection, while someone else would throw him a pair of dirty boots and order him to clean them. Other pranks included apple-pie beds, removing bedsprings and hiding mattresses in the showers.

So I really didn't pay much attention to the noise down the hall, as I expected it to die down as quickly as it had reared up. Unusually, it continued. Those responsible for the racket were knocking on the door of another section commander called Steadman, a mixed-race guy with quite a strict approach to discipline. I knew that he wasn't expected back until much later. The knocking stopped, and the hallway fell silent. Suddenly my door flew open and three members of my section stood in the doorway. They asked politely if they could come in. Of course, I replied. They asked where Steadman was, and when I told them he had a late pass they started to slag him off, calling him every name under the sun. It would seem that these lads had had a run-in with him earlier that day and he had reprimanded them, probably on someone else's orders. It was obvious they had been drinking; the longer the tirade went on the more manic and unstable they became. The three were called MacDermott, Renton and Commanchio, and they were missing a fourth member of their gang; he had gone to bed early, though he probably had full knowledge of what they were about to do. Years later I read that he had gone home on leave after being told his new bride was having an affair. He had either smuggled a rifle through customs or managed to get hold of one somehow; and when his wife's lover turned up, he had shot him. He could have saved himself a long prison sentence by staying with his mates that night.

They were becoming more and more aggressive, and I should have asked them to leave. Instead, I gave them a cigarette each, thinking that changing the subject might help defuse the situation. It didn't. They spotted my pressed uniform on the door of my locker and yanked it to the floor. They then emptied the contents of the locker I had so industriously tidied. Their attention now turned to me. Who the fuck did I think I was . . . telling them what to do? The problem was that we had all been mates before I was promoted, and I was several years younger than them. They had all failed the NCO cadre. Standing in front me, itching for trouble, that mix of resentment and strong German beer made for an ugly combination.

If Steadman *had* been in his room, there was no doubt he would have been beaten up. Bullying was rife in the regiment at the time, though no one would tell on whoever was doing it. Most of the attacks took place at night; the victim would either be hit with a bed bar or urinated on. On this occasion, one of my attackers had plugged in the steam iron while I had been trying to placate them. I thought I had managed to convince them that they should forget all about it, and that I would have a word with the other section commander in the morning, ask him to soften his attitude a bit. I still clearly remember my last words to them: 'Night, lads, see you in the morning. Do us a favour and turn the light out for me as you go.'

They made as if to leave, but suddenly I felt this excruciating pain shoot through my face and eye. I had been so busy watching my back to make sure I wouldn't be bed-ended, that I failed to see the iron coming towards my face.

All I could hear was sizzling and a voice screaming, agonized.

It took a few moments before I realized all the noise was coming from me, and the howling was my own.

My mouth was clamped shut with a hand.

'You fucking say anything to anyone and it won't just be your fucking face that's burnt,' said one of the three.

I must have passed out, because I don't remember them leaving. I woke up hours later, my face in agony and unable to open one eye. There was a smell of burnt meat in the room. I made my way to the washroom and saw that the whole side of my face was bloody and peeling; my eye resembled a large false one stuck in too small a socket. I tried to touch my face but it was too sore. Luckily the iron had either been on low heat or the steam had protected me, though I had two rows of steam holes on my cheek. Panicked, I tried to bathe my face. I staggered, in my underpants, to the guardroom, where the guard commander took one look at my face and asked who had done it. It was obvious to him that it wasn't an accident.

I was taken to the medical officer straight away, and then driven to the BAOR eye hospital. After extensive tests, I was told that the eye wasn't damaged, though the steam and its effects had made it seem abnormally large. I had to wear a surgical pad over the eye for weeks, and I was excused duties.

My attackers were arrested and charged with grievous bodily harm. After an initial holding charge of assaulting an NCO, they were remanded for courts martial. Strangely enough, the assaults on sleeping soldiers seemed to decrease after that. Whether this was due to their incarceration or because the incident had sent other bullies and assailants under cover, I never did find out.

The problem now was that I was no longer the victim, but the villain. I began to receive threats about giving evidence; my room was trashed repeatedly while I was out; my radio, camera and any other valuables were stolen. And I was given the silent treatment by many of their mates. It was soon impossible for me to go out into town. I became increasingly paranoid, and felt that I was being followed. I turned inward and lost what little confidence I'd had previously.

Still, I was going on leave soon, back to England, so at least I would have some respite from this nightmare. I had been offered medical leave, but because I didn't want anyone to see my face I had declined it. Nevertheless, I wasn't a complete outcast: I still had all my babysitting contacts, and Bunny Dearsley, Vic Parrish and plenty of others stood by me. But I felt I always needed to look over my shoulder. Back in England I could forget my worries for a while, and on my return it wouldn't be long before the trial of my three assailants. I hoped it would all go away so I could get on with my army career. Oh, how little I knew . . .

4

CALM BEFORE THE STORM

I may have been back home on leave, but things were really no better there than in Germany. Looking back on it, I must have been close to a nervous breakdown. I should have seen the signs but, in the mid-1960s, people were less willing to acknowledge these things. I felt hesitant about leaving the house, though being in close proximity to my mother was the last place I wanted to be. After a few days, I didn't even want to venture out at all. Part of me wanted my leave to end, and yet part of me was terrified of going back to Germany to face my attackers' mates. I knew there would be repercussions; I dreaded to think what was going to happen on my return. I counted the days to the end of my leave.

When the time came for me to catch the boat train, I left it as late as I could. I thought that by leaving everything to the last moment, I might have the decision taken out of my hands, and yet I was frightened of missing the train, of not making it back to barracks and the subsequent nightmare that might ensue. As I said goodbye to my family, little did I know that I would never see some of them again; others I would see only after a fourteen- or fifteen-year hiatus.

On the boat, I bumped into another soldier from our regiment; he was a friend to all but close to none. He went on the front foot straight away, letting me know exactly what he thought of me: 'Didn't think you'd show your face again.'

'What?' I was taken aback.

'Didn't think you'd have the bottle to show up. You can't fucking do what you did, and expect to be walking about the place.' He wasn't smiling.

'Hang on a mo',' I said. 'I'm the *victim* in all this. I'm the one who got fucking burnt with the iron!'

He seemed not to hear. 'You shouldn't have interfered. It's none of your fucking business, anyway . . . it's got fuck all to do with you.'

I couldn't believe what he was now saying.

'How you gonna cope with all the aggravation you're about to bring down on your head?'

'Don't worry, I can handle myself,' I said, not even remotely believing it.

This conversation reinforced all my fears. I was dreading – literally sick to my stomach with fear – the shit I was walking into.

At my trial, he related a slightly different and more lurid version of this conversation. Nevertheless, years later, when I was appearing in pantomime in Belfast, he sent a note to my dressing room. It was all the usual kiss-my-arse stuff: how we had been mates in the army and what good times we had. (He may have done, but I certainly didn't.) He told me to ring a number, and after three rings I should hang up and he would ring me back. I couldn't believe what I was reading. In the end, I tore the note up and threw it into the bin. Why should I be friendly with him? And, given this three-ring business, what must he have been thinking? I had no desire to see him, let alone talk to him. The way he was carrying on in his note, you would have thought he was Northern Ireland's answer to James Bond! Yet, on the same trip, I was humbled to be invited to the barracks of my former regiment, the Royal Fusiliers. I was paraded around the sergeants' mess like royalty in front of genuine heroes, men who had fought in the Falklands and the Gulf War, and here was me, the man who had disgraced the regiment, being celebrated as one of its alumni. I was honoured to be their guest but made sure they knew that, truly, I was not worthy.

When I arrived back at the barracks, I found that the door to my room had been kicked in and the room itself had been trashed beyond recognition. The bottom suddenly dropped out of my world; I could feel it in my guts. This was going to be the beginning of the end. After I tidied up my room, I made my way to the mess to get some food. I was suddenly approached, one after the other, by the three married servicemen I babysat for. Each of them had the same thing on his mind: what did I mean by telling other people I had slept with his wife? I didn't know where to turn or what to do. I tried to look them in the eye: 'Er, when exactly am I supposed to have made these claims? I've just got back from leave . . .'

They backed off a little, but they were unconvinced. Clearly, while I had been away, the rumour mill had gone into overdrive.

Over twenty years later, I was in a newsagents in Wimbledon when I was approached by a middle-aged man. He made a fuss of me, and after he reminded me who he was, I remembered him. He had been the first one to berate me about what I was supposed to have said about his wife, and now he was all over me. How people can change! Apart from babysitting, I had been helping out with the wives' shooting club; but since this was run by the RSM and his wife, nothing could possibly have happened. The whole thing was just another way for the bullies to get at me.

By now, I had had everything I owned taken from me. My room was being constantly trashed, and my personal belongings were either stolen or broken. My radio, camera, and what little money I had disappeared. The problem was that I was still paying for the things I had bought on tick. I was desperate: I owed roughly £27 right, left and centre, with absolutely no means now of paying it, and my prospects diminishing by the day. Although I had felt threatened before, I was even more terrified now MacDermott, Renton and Commanchio had been arrested. I became paranoid, feeling that something terrible would happen either to me or to my family at home. I had been warned that my family weren't safe, and that someone back home might get hurt. They never let up with the intimidation, even though they were under arrest. On one occasion, one of their henchmen tracked me down and told me that my mother would be carved up. In other circumstances, I would have dismissed it as nonsense, but isolated in Germany as I was, I panicked.

Intimidation of this nature tends to work only on the fragile-minded, by magnifying certain aspects of life out of all proportion. This happened to me; I became nervous and paranoid. Everything that was said, however innocent, sounded sinister. Soldiers who had hitherto been my mates seemed to become bit players in McDermott and Co.'s little game. With my mind in such a fragile state, the burden became increasingly difficult to bear. I didn't feel as though I could turn to anyone, as going to my superiors would undoubtedly have made my situation even worse.

In retrospect, I should have given up. Why didn't I check myself into the army hospital? Or have myself discharged and sent home? Why had I made things go from bad to worse by pathetically trying to cope on my own in such a hostile environment? Why hadn't I asked my family for financial help in the first place? These are questions I have asked myself many times. Had I been sensible and looked after myself, I might never have thought of going out on that night, or on any other night. Looking back, I realize that when I was home on leave, I was running the gauntlet of my mother's moods. I also felt completely out of place in my own home. We were not a rich family: my father worked very hard and was continually having to work extra hours to live within his means, while my mother's total disregard for money only made the situation worse. My brother, John, was an apprentice and would never have had the money to lend me, so there was no way I could have borrowed it from him. I suppose if I had asked Dad, he might have helped, but then here I was, a big boy in the army. I didn't want to disappoint him, so soon after making him so proud in front of his pals. And besides, I was a soldier now. Shouldn't I have been able to look after myself?

Since the attack with the iron, the outlook seemed bleak. I was (and still am) someone who kept (and keeps) his emotions bottled up inside. I felt at the time that I was in a desperate situation, which had spiralled completely out of control.

What happened next was to impact on the lives of many people.

The repercussions of the tragic events of 3 December 1966 have long continued to haunt all those concerned; some of whom weren't even born at the time. This is something I have never previously spoken of in public. Even my own wife was ignorant as to the true course of events that unfolded on that dreadful night. Jane was pregnant with our first child when the press brought the devastating truth to our own front door.

That night I went out with the intention of stealing money, to pay back all I owed – not with the intention of taking an innocent man's life. But that is what transpired, and I fully accept my own guilt in the matter. The fact that I had no intention of harming anyone, and didn't ultimately steal anything, in no way absolves me from my own responsibility, nor does it relieve me from my ongoing torment. I was a boy in a man's world with nowhere to turn, and the panic decisions I made have had lasting repercussions.

It was a cowardly plan, and in the event it all went horribly wrong.

I met a very drunk businessman in the town centre, who asked me for directions, and I walked with him for a while. Having enjoyed his company, I found I couldn't go through with my plan, and left him at his lodgings. I then caught a taxi back to the barracks. After being taken on what seemed to be a roundabout route, I asked the driver to pull over so he could let me out – and that's when I decided to go through with it. I wasn't prepared for what happened next.

I pulled the gun out and asked him for his money.

The courageous man grabbed the gun and tried to wrestle it from me.

It went off.

In my panic I just ran for it.

I intended to use the gun only as a threat. I didn't know it was a loaded gun. I was mortified when, in the ensuing struggle, it went off fatally wounding the driver. It never occurred to me that he wouldn't just hand over his night's takings. What did I think I was playing at? The whole thing was such a pathetically flawed scheme, and the consequences were truly horrific. I thought I could go out and commit a robbery without anyone getting hurt.

By the time I had got back to the barracks I had taken a man's life, deprived a decent family of a husband and a father, and destroyed my own family back at home – even the one that didn't exist yet. Be in no doubt that they have suffered as much as anyone over this.

Frightened as I had never been in my life before, I climbed over the barrack fence and made my way to the armourer's room. Shaking, I grabbed hold of the store man and asked him if he knew the gun was loaded. He said he didn't. Realizing that he had signed out the gun and would be implicated, which would at the very least mean the end of his army career, he offered to clean the gun and said he would say it had never left the armoury, should anyone enquire. I will never forget his parting words: 'It will all blow over soon.'

I wanted to turn myself in, but because of my stupidity and belief that it would all blow over soon, I grasped that thought and convinced myself that the driver would be all right. I decided foolishly to try and blot out the events and carry on as if nothing had happened.

When I got to my room, I looked at myself in the mirror. I realized there was blood on my suit and I saw that I had spots of blood across my face. I froze. I couldn't believe what had happened. What I had done.

I despise myself, and will always be ashamed. No matter how much I try to shift the blame, and look for excuses, there are none. I cannot alter history and I can't make everything right again – would that I could.

After the shooting, it became increasingly difficult for me to carry on as normal. I was continually being harassed by MacDermott, Renton and Commanchio's cronies, as well as having to live with the burden of the terrible thing I had done. The death of the taxi driver was far more disturbing than the attentions of the bullies, yet, at the same time, the bullying was becoming too much for me to take. I was in a fragile state of mind anyhow, so I now felt close to breaking point. I spent most of my time looking over my shoulder, worrying myself sick about the next trick that might be played: trashed room, missing mess kit, soiled civilian clothing.

I was also dreading the tap on the shoulder, although in some sense I was in denial, having convinced myself that the incident would go away. It just goes to show what my state of mind was: I was ready to believe in anything that might get me out of the deep hole I was in. Even if I had not been arrested, this mental turmoil would have never gone away. (And it never has.) Every time I approached the armourer and told him I had decided to turn myself in, he kept telling me that it wasn't a good idea, and that, so far, no one knew about it. All I needed to do was keep quiet.

I tried to do as he said, after all he was a good mate, but it was extremely difficult and when I was finally arrested, as I deserved to be, my relief was palpable.

I was told I was wanted in the orderly room, by a rather nervous messenger, and made my way there. I saw that the parade ground was ringed by soldiers all carrying pick axe handles. I was taken to the guardroom and then moved to an RMP (Royal Military Police) barracks a few miles away, where my interrogation started.

I don't remember much about this interrogation, except that those questioning me were very kind. I did, however, try to deny all knowledge of what had taken place, which was not surprising, callow youth that I was. I was in complete and utter denial, trying to put off the inevitable.

Eventually, I broke down and confessed to the shooting. In that moment, there was relief: it was all over, or so I thought. But the guilt and remorse, not to mention the sheer anguish, I would later experience were far worse than anything I had ever contemplated in my life.

5

TRIAL AND ERROR

I was charged and, as word got out where I was being held, I had to be moved to various British barracks around the Rhine. Tensions were running high after the shooting: the State Attorney's office had put out a reward for the killer's arrest, so too had a local publican. At one point, I was nearly run over, at the RMP barracks, by a German civilian who drove for the army. There was also talk that the German authorities would take over and try me, and also a rumour that they were going to ask for capital punishment to be restored. Thankfully and mercifully for me they didn't.

In each of these guardrooms, I was listed on the detention board as someone else; I was ordered never to tell anyone what I was being held for. A simple enough request, you would have thought. Except that no one bothered to remember the army rules and regulations. Even though I was a prisoner awaiting a major trial, I was being held in army guardrooms. I was, therefore, subject to the same rules and regulations as those serving seven or twenty-eight days for minor breaches of discipline. Each evening, the orderly officer on duty had to check on the men in the cells. On one occasion, my cell door flew open, and a young officer stood in the doorway.

'Name . . . number . . . rank?'

'Can't tell you, sir,' I said.

'Why not?'

When I eventually had no choice but to tell him, the look on his face was one of sheer horror. He did a quick about turn, slammed the door shut and disappeared down the hallway.

The cells I was banged up in were austere: wooden benches – with raised headrests for pillows – fixed to the wall; no mattresses. I exercised alone and was not allowed to come into contact with other prisoners. I was forbidden newspapers, and my day entailed, apart from the brief exercise period, sitting in my cell reading books or sleeping. There were no tasks to perform, so I just stayed banged up. If I wanted a cigarette I had to ring a bell, and one would be given to me; I was not allowed to keep cigarettes or matches in the cell. Sometimes an officer from my regiment would come to see if I was being treated all right, and would bring me any letters from home.

I remember one evening when I was in agony with stomach pains, yet no one would call a doctor. In the end, I was given some tablets, which did nothing for the pain. I later found out these were placebos.

During this period in custody, I was constantly having meetings with doctors and psychiatrists. On one occasion, when I was being held in Münster, I was asked to look at a book, which was made up of page after page of ink or paint drops, pressed together to make shapes. As I looked over each page, I told the psychiatrist what I saw. I then came to a blank page.

'There's nothing on this page,' I said.

'What do you mean?' said the psychiatrist.

'I can't see anything.'

'Don't be so ridiculous. Surely, you can see the cottage by the lake and the birds flying? Can't you see the big black bird, hovering in the grey skies above?'

I looked again, turned the page and leafed back, but all I could see was a blank piece of paper. He tutted, snatched the book from my hands and left the room. As he passed a young woman seated behind a desk, I could hear him say, 'He's mad, you know . . . completely mad.'

Well, I must have been: I couldn't see the cottage, lake or birds. Had I lost the plot completely? Or was he just playing a game?

After being moved around the Rhine for a few months, I finally arrived at a barracks back in Osnabrück, where I stayed until my trial. I was now allowed the freedom of the guardroom, and wasn't banged up in my cell unless it was absolutely necessary. The military police would check up on me and leave a bottle of beer on the window ledge outside the cell.

By this time, my platoon commander, Second Lieutenant Hugh Oliver-Bellasis, had arranged for a firm of solicitors, Kingsley Napley, to represent me, and one of their number, Dennis Goodwin, would come and see me every so often. But first there was the preliminary hearing at Belfast Barracks, which would decide whether there was a case to answer. The Germans may have wanted to claim jurisdiction for the trial, but the case was automatically handed over to the British authorities. All crimes at that time, perpetrated by foreign soldiers on German soil, were tried by the occupying army in question. The hearing very quickly found that because I had admitted the killing, there was a case to answer. I would now have to stand trial at a court martial in Bielefeld.

While awaiting trial, I had to give evidence at the courts martial of McDermott, Renton and Commanchio. I now had nothing to lose. In court, I recounted how I had been bullied and subjected to the horrendous assault with the hot iron. Once I had given evidence, I was taken back to my cell. I later heard that the courts martial had lasted no time at all, and the accused were either sentenced to imprisonment or given a dishonourable discharge from the army. Although I felt relieved that this chapter was over, I had too many other things on my mind.

Eventually, I was transferred to a guardroom in Bielefeld in order to await my trial. My parents were flown over; I was so glad to see my Dad, less so my mother. But what could I say to them? What was there to say? I remember Dad saying, 'I can't condone what you've done, son, but I'm with you all the way.' Poor man. What Dad felt I sadly never did find out; even after I came out of prison he kept his counsel on the subject.

After a brief exchange with my parents, they went off to have dinner with the trial judge, and I settled down to sleep, trying to prepare myself for the days ahead. I hoped my mother would behave herself, as most mealtimes tended to end in tears. But I knew that by the end of the trial there would be even more than usual.

I was up early the next morning. After a short visit from my parents, during which my mother kept telling me how nice the judge was and how they had dined in the officers' mess, I was picked up from my cell and escorted to the courts martial building (where I had given evidence against MacDermott and Co.) by the same NCO who had told me I was wanted in the orderly room all those months ago. As we made our way to the court, the photographers were out in force.

I waited nervously in a small anteroom, where I was visited by my QC, Michael Eastham, and solicitor, Dennis Goodwin, and a defending officer. Soon after they left, I was marched into the court. I remember standing there in the dock; in front of me was the Judge Advocate General, S. H. Bean, and several army officers sitting on the top table. I was in shock; I couldn't take it all in.

To tell the truth, I remember very little about my trial. Once the prosecution started to make its case, I gave in mentally. I had already admitted my guilt, so there was nothing left to fight for. I suppose it's different if you're innocent: you fight for survival and try to refute all the prosecution's arguments. But I was carrying so much guilt; I didn't really take in what was being said. I remember it felt like being constantly struck over the head by a rubber truncheon; after the first blow, you don't remember the others. In the end, I didn't care what would happen to me.

I felt ashamed yet, at the same time, completely cut off from the proceedings. It was as if the trial was happening to someone else and not to me. But when the taxi driver's wife came into court, the enormity of what I'd done struck home. I felt sick: I couldn't look at her; I couldn't bear to be in the same room as her. As I stood there, ashamed of what I had done, I could feel her eyes bore in to me.

The rest of the trial passed in a blur. I was confused, scared and unable to cope under the sheer weight of the evidence and witnesses keen to testify against me. A dozen soldiers – some of whom I had hardly ever given the time of day to – were called in, relating, with great aplomb, conversations I was supposed to have had with them. The store man had changed his statement three times. I had always, after my initial denial, admitted my crime. My only real defence was that I hadn't known the gun was loaded.

When it came to my defence, near the end of the five-day trial, it didn't matter what I said; I had done the deed, for which I now needed to pay the price. Eventually I gave evidence myself.

I remember the Judge Advocate explaining to the court that, had I gone out with the intention to rob *and* shoot a man, I should be found guilty of murder. On the other hand, had I gone out with the intention to rob but *not* shoot a man – whether I had known the gun was loaded or not – I could be found guilty of manslaughter. On the evidence, and what I knew to have happened, my lawyers thought that a verdict of manslaughter would be returned. So too did Dad and my mother; they were, they said, quietly confident.

Towards the end of the trial, there was a very emotional moment when my father took the witness stand and gave evidence about my character. Good old Dad, he did the best he could for me, saying that I had changed during my time in Osnabrück. But I guess by that time it was all too late.

At the end, we all awaited the verdict. I stood there in my uniform, without my beret and belt, waiting for the sentence to be handed down. In truth, I knew there could be only one outcome: 'life'. I was shocked; I couldn't take it in. And then the silence – that's what I remember – the magnified silence that comes after that word – life.

After a tearful farewell to my parents – where the solicitor whispered the words, 'Eleven and a half' – I was taken back to Osnabrück. I was locked up in the guardroom, where I awaited the appeal procedure, which was automatic in the army. Although I had been sentenced to life imprisonment, disgraced in the army and reduced to the ranks, I still had my stripe as I was waiting for the appeal court's decision.

Life in the guardroom was the same as before, but now it was just a question of counting the days until I moved on. I was still in uniform and still subject to army discipline. My solicitor visited more frequently, and I was allowed a mattress and pillows, as well as cigarettes and matches in my cell. I still had no tasks to perform, but to alleviate the boredom I volunteered to clean the back area of the guardroom, and when there was a big parade I cleaned the red carpet. A few other prisoners were in the guardroom cells at that time, but apart from the odd nod or hello, I had nothing to do with them.

My appeal was turned down, and I then awaited the date of my transfer to England. When it came, I was to be flown from Gutersloh Airport. As I had to be transferred to a guardroom near the airport to await my transport, I was taken to a tank regiment's barracks and put in the guardroom there. By now I had been stripped of my army uniform and was wearing civvies. It was a Sunday afternoon when I arrived there; I sat reading in my cell, when the door crashed open and there stood this provost corporal, slightly the worse for wear. He had obviously been having a liquid lunch in the corporals' mess. The board outside, listing the names of the prisoners, still contained no reference either to my name or my crime.

'Stand up when I talk to you, and address me as Corp . . .'

'You know I don't have to, but if it makes you happy I will,' I replied.

In response, he became animated and threatened to show me who was the boss; this was *his* guardroom and he could make life easy or hard on me. He spotted my cigarettes and matches, and threw a fit.

'Look, I've been given permission,' I said.

'You're a fucking liar,' he shouted, throwing his hat on the floor. 'NUMBER! RANK! REGIMENT!'

'I'm a civilian; I don't have a number and I can't tell you the charge.'

At this, he became even angrier, slamming the door behind him so that we were locked in together.

'If you don't fucking tell me now, I'll make life very difficult for you,' he snarled.

I didn't tell him that life was pretty difficult for me already; neither did I want to give him a heart attack. I just told him what my crime was and what my sentence had been. Well, if I thought the orderly officer had reacted as if he had been shot, this guy acted as if he had been blown up by a mine. He stopped ranting, looked at me as if I were mad, did a 360-degree turn and tried to disappear through the closed door. He then realized that he was stuck in the cell and began frantically banging on the door and ringing the bell. Eventually someone let him out and off he went. Twenty minutes later, he appeared with a cup of tea and a camera; he asked to take a picture. He seemed completely oblivious of his behaviour of half an hour before.

The next morning, I was handed over to two military policemen and taken to the airport. I was put on a military aircraft, a troop plane with a few seats bolted to the floor. We landed at an airfield near Oxford, where I was rushed through the aerodrome. I was handcuffed to two policemen, so when I asked to go to the toilet, I could see the look of disbelief on their faces. They couldn't unlock me, so they had to stand there while I peed. Our transport arrived and we made our way to the prison where I was to spend the next eleven years. First stop: Wormwood Scrubs.

6

BARS AND STRIPES

On arrival at Wormwood Scrubs prison, I was taken to reception, where I was processed and inducted before being allocated a cell. Obviously, being under twenty-one, I was classified as a young prisoner or 'YP'. Induction consisted of changing out of civilian clothing, having all your personal items, such as watches and rings, taken off you and then having a bath. This consisted of six inches of water in what was a standard tub, which had brown, yellow and green stains – from limescale, or I so hoped. I assume the bath was rarely cleaned, having seen a large number of prisoners, day in, day out. The soap was a smallish bar, though slightly bigger than the ones you get in cheaper hotels. It was called 'White Windsor'; apparently it was the same soap the Royal Family used, or at any rate those who scrubbed the floors for the House of Windsor. Here I was, in one of Her Majesty's Prisons, using her soap. Shame there was nothing royal about it, apart from it being a royal mess. Once I was out of the bath, they stuck a piece of paper under my nose and asked me to sign for my personal property. I looked at the list and signed. If I hadn't been so interested in looking at all those faces around me, and wondering what they were in for, I might have noticed that neither my ring nor my watch made it on to that list. But I guess I had other things on my mind.

The prison uniform arrived: grey trousers, a blue and white striped shirt and a navy-blue army-style blouson, together with severely discoloured grey socks and a piece of blue material that was supposed to be a tie. I was also given a pair of blue workman's bib and brace, and a pair of shoes that seemed to be made out of compressed cardboard, which had obviously been worn by several hundred prisoners before me. I was also given a pillowcase containing a razor (but no blade), a toothbrush, tooth powder and a bar of 'White Windsor'.

My name was then called by a prisoner officer with a white hospital-style jacket on; he signalled me to follow him. After negotiating several metal gates we entered the grounds of the prison itself. I could see a church and well-kept gardens, around which several prisoners with different-coloured armbands were walking. These, I later discovered, were 'trusties'. A 'red band' was allowed to walk around on his own, whereas a 'blue band' could escort other prisoners. And then there were those who had yellow stripes on their jackets and trousers, or 'patches' as they were known. These guys were an escape risk and had to be escorted everywhere; they had a book that had to be signed every time they were collected and delivered.

After a short walk, we arrived at the other building, which although it had gates and bars was the prison hospital. Here I was interviewed by the medical officer; my shoelaces and pillowcase and tie were taken from me, and I was put into an observation cell. For the uninitiated, an observation cell is a normal cell, but instead of having a narrow spyhole, it has a larger, window-style opening through which the prison officers can observe you at all times. The cell was practically bare: it contained a bed and mattress, no chair, no table, not even a piss pot. If I wanted to go to the lavatory I had to ring the bell; a guard would then escort and watch me while I performed the usual bodily functions. It was obviously a suicide watch.

This seemed quite alien to me, months after being sentenced and having been in a military guardroom, with a radio and my washing and shaving kit, plus a set of cutlery as well as various other forms of equipment at hand. I definitely wasn't suicidal at that time, although later in my sentence I became so.

I had arrived in the hospital shortly before mealtime, and I was hungry. I think I was under the impression that prison food would be somewhat akin to army food – mass-produced but by no means inedible. How wrong I was. Suddenly the door of the cell opened and an appalling smell wafted in. For a fleeting moment I thought it was the drains – but when I was handed a plastic plate that had at one time been white, but was now a very discoloured yellow and deeply striated with scratchmarks, I realized that the smell was emanating from the cud that was stuck to the plate. This was what they proposed I should consume with gusto. I couldn't even have consumed it with mustard, lashings of it, to obliterate the stench. (Years later I was reminded of my first encounter with prison cuisine while watching *The Dirty Dozen*, in which one of the characters says something like, 'I've have never eaten food like this before, though I've have stepped in something similar.') With what they were fancifully describing as 'goulash', came a slice of not very fresh bread and a pat of butter. I've known meat to be tough before, but not bread, for God's sake! Foolishly, I chose to ignore the goulash and just ate the bread and butter instead. I say foolishly because for the rest of the night I was absolutely starving. Still, there was always breakfast. They couldn't mess up breakfast. Could they?

The night passed uneventfully enough, although I didn't sleep much, given the hunger pains and the continual noise of the observation hatch being opened and shut every half an hour during the night. Eventually morning arrived, the door opened and I was escorted to the toilet. Probably due to a combination of lack of food and being watched, I failed to perform any bodily functions. I was then handed a razor and a bar of soap, but no shampoo, as that was not standard prison issue. And as I shaved and then washed I was watched. As soon as I had finished my shave the razor was taken from me. I was then handed a piece of fabric that was a cross between a tea towel and a post office mail sack in texture, tough enough not to tear in strips and hang myself with, yet not absorbent enough to use to dry myself. Then back to the cell, where breakfast was waiting. I say breakfast, because in the crudest possible sense these would be the meagre morsels with which I'd break my fast. But what a miserly business it was! Two slices of bread, a scraping of butter that was tasteless before it was fashionable for butter to be tasteless – and a runny concoction they insisted was jam. This was the menu for my very first breakfast inside. A prison officer watched me throughout as I chomped my cardboard – as though the variety and excitement of the grub might provoke a rush of blood to the head – and as soon as I had finished, he whisked away my plate and plastic cutlery before I did anything foolish. The ritual was by no means over. He handed me a mug whose exterior was only marginally less discoloured than the liquid it held; it was the same colour and consistency as mud, a shade or two warmer (i.e. lukewarm) and presumably meant to be tea. I drank it slowly, but then I had little choice. It took two minutes to slide out of the mug. No sooner had I drained it (and chewed it) than the receptacle was snatched back and the door slammed shut.

Lunchtime came and as I was about to collect my plate of food I was handed my pillowcase, shoelaces and tie. I was now told I was going to A wing, where I had been allocated a cell. I guess as I hadn't tried to top myself the night before I was no longer a security risk, saving a lot of paper work for the duty officer. The walk from the hospital wing to A wing wasn't a long one: you had to pass through an arch and into this long, tall Victorian building. All I could see was landing after landing, and a mass of fence-like wire that ran the length of the first level separating the ground floor from the landings. They said it was to stop prisoners throwing things from above on to people below. In truth, it was there to catch anyone who decided to throw himself from the landings. Thank God no one tried that while I was there. The wire was so buckled and in need of replacing that it wouldn't have saved a six-month-old baby, let alone a grown man or boy.

After a while the wing didn't seem so big and so high; in fact, there were only four landings and a third of the wing was bricked off and known as 'A Adults', as it housed prisoners who were sex offenders or had other psychological problems, as well as those waiting for, or recuperating from, operations. Most of these were performed in the prison hospital, although some prisoners did go down the road to Hammersmith Hospital for the more serious ones. One chap I saw being escorted from the adult wing to the hospital wing had a nose that looked like a penis and nostrils that looked like a pair of testicles. He was affectionately known as 'Prick Face'. He was here to have plastic surgery to make his nose normal, as it was felt that his looks had contributed to his turning to a life of crime.

I was told to collect my bedding, which comprised two sheets, a pillow and a blanket and one of those towel-like things from the stores, plus a plastic mug and a piss pot. From there I went to my cell, which had a bed and mattress in it in addition to a small square table and a corner unit on which was a metal washbowl and a metal water jug. The cell itself was thirteen feet by seven, with small square windows that had bars on the outside. The walls themselves were white and covered in graffiti, which listed nearly everyone who had been there since the walls had last been painted. The floor was made of black bitumen, and had indentations in it from the metal bed legs. Apart from the graffiti on the walls, there were blood and food stains, and near the washstand were traces of excrement and urine.

I hadn't heard the door close behind me, and as I turned around to question the officer who had unlocked my cell I realized I was locked in. I stood on the chair to look out of the window, but all I could see was the rooftop of another building. I put my pot under the washstand and draped the towel over the wooden bar that ran along the front of it. I unpacked my pillowcase and laid out my razor, soap, shaving cream and toothbrush with the green tooth powder on the shelf under the washstand and started to make my bed. No sooner had I finished making the bed than the cell door opened and a prisoner officer was standing there. He handed me a book of prison rules and regulations and then told me to go and see the Chief. I made my way downstairs and found the Chief's office. I knocked and was told to go in. The Chief told me what I could and couldn't do and also said I would be working in the toyshop. Because the wing was overcrowded, he told me I wouldn't be able to have recreation in the evening until people had left the wing either through transfer or discharge, and as there was a waiting list that might be a while. I was number forty-three on this list, but in the meantime the stores had some books I could borrow to read in my cell. Recreation, I would later learn, involved watching television or playing table tennis.

Since A wing was used as an allocation unit, the majority of the inmates were borstal boys who would subsequently either go the short distance from A wing to B wing (the borstal wing), or would be sent to various borstals round the country to serve their sentences. They were mainly housed three to a cell and spent the day either banged up or being assessed. There were also a small number of young offenders in the wing, with sentences ranging from three months to six years, and of course me, with a life sentence. Some of the young offenders would be here only for assessment, and then would be transferred to prisons such as Aylesbury, or else be released. Once they reached twenty-one, some would go to C wing, a short-term wing. Those with longer sentences would go to the long-term wing or another prison when they became adults.

So it was back to the cell via the store, where I picked up several paperbacks. James Hadley Chase seemed very popular, as did Mickey Spillane and cowboy books. As I headed up the stairs to my cell I suddenly realized I had no idea where it was, and half-panicked. I heard my name being called; I looked up and there on the top landing was the prison officer who had earlier sent me to the Chief's office. Right, so there I was on the top landing; that was one part of the puzzle solved. But where was my cell? To my relief he told me to go to the wing office and pick up my cell card, on which was my prison number, cell number and category and length of sentence. My religion and dietary needs were also listed. My number was 1047, which was later changed to 261006 on my becoming a man.

Once back safely in the right cell, I felt at a loss: the wing was empty, apart from the inmates in the stores. The borstal boys worked in the wire shop, where they stripped cable and extracted the various metal wires and piled them up in skips, which would then be collected by an outside firm and recycled. The YPs worked in the toyshop, where they made the wire frames for Bendy Toys and also painted them.

Suddenly the silence was shattered by the sound of the inmates returning. From silence to bedlam in one foul swoop. As these prisoners passed my cell, several looked in to say hello and ask what I was in for. Those who read my cell card, which was pinned on a little wooden board outside, commented, in unambiguous terms, on my sentence. Apparently having a lifer in the boys' wing, although not altogether new, was something of a novelty for all concerned. No sooner had the boys arrived back than the cells would slam shut, not like in some American film on a centrally operated hydraulic scheme, but by the landing officers individually closing each door. Once shut, they would then go round again, this time putting on the bolts, which was their way of counting heads. Any empty cells or cells with prisoners absent, either on visits or assessment, would be left open. Once each landing tally was shouted out, and if all numbers matched, the cry would go out: 'Unlock!'

Once unlocked I was told to go to the canteen. Wow! I thought. How civilized: a canteen. But this wasn't to eat in, it was where the prisoners spent their hard-earned money. Now, as I hadn't worked, and seeing as I had only just arrived, I was entitled to an advance against my two shillings and eleven pence a week. So I bought a sachet of shampoo, a quarter-ounce of Old Holborn, cigarette papers and matches. I was also given a reception letter and envelope so I could write home. Cheekily I asked for another, and got it. That was my first evening in my cell taken care of: I could fill in the time till lights out writing home. As I made my way back to my cell I was passed by stream after stream of inmates pouring down the stairs, all holding mugs. Must be teatime, though having no means of telling the time made it all seem so strange. As I arrived back at my cell, I was suddenly caught up in a mad dash, as the prisoners on the landing made their way down to collect their food. I was just about to deposit my stuff from the canteen when a low voice said, 'If I was you, mate, I'd hide it, as it's liable to disappear.' For just a moment I wondered what he meant, and then of course I realized where I was. Why did I think that being in prison would stop someone stealing my stuff? The other inmate leant across and slammed my door shut, and I now followed him down to get my tea. Although more substantial than the hospital fare, it was just as inedible. Later I was to realize that all the good stuff was commandeered by the 'red bands' and 'blue bands' or sold to the gangsters in the long-term wing. Once the food was eaten in the cell the trays were collected, and we were allowed to fill up our jugs with water, carry out any ablutions and watch television or play ping-pong. In my case I was banged up till bedtime, with the cells being opened to empty pots and collect water. Luckily I had used the toilet facilities so didn't need to go again, and having seen and smelt the slop-out line I made a vow that I would never use the pot. Thankfully, apart from two occasions, I never did. How those prisoners who were three to a cell and banged up twenty-three hours a day coped I can only guess.

My first evening banged up, apart from the supper call, where a bun and a mug of tepid tea were thrust in, was spent uneventfully: early to bed with lights out at eight o'clock.

7

SETTLING IN

My sleep that first night was pretty much non-existent, what with the door banging, people screaming out of windows, and what seemed to be the continuous sound of someone checking through the spy hole. I guess I must have slept for a few hours, but as music blared out over the Tannoy system, I sat up wondering what the hell was going on. Suddenly bolts were slammed back, and voices shouted out numbers. I leapt out of bed, grabbed my clothes, got dressed and made my way to the wash area, carrying my jug to fill up with water with which to wash and shave. As I passed the other open cells, the stench was overpowering; bodies spilled out of cells carrying pots that were overflowing with urine and faeces. On returning to my cell, I found a razorblade on my bed. I washed, shaved and prepared to get ready to go down to get my breakfast. The razorblade was collected, and put in a board next to my cell number. After breakfast our cells were unlocked again, and I made my way to the toyshop.

The toyshop consisted of bench after bench, where inmates trimmed and painted various rubber toys. These were mostly Disney characters – Mickey and Minnie Mouse, Bugs Bunny and Pluto. All were sold under the name of Bendy Toys. For those who have never bought one, they were most frequently seen adorning the front of dust carts as they made their way around estates picking up household rubbish. The toyshop was manned by two permanent prison officers who wore brown overalls, but another prison officer, usually a new member of staff, would patrol the shop, checking on discipline. Sometimes an older, more experienced officer would be allocated. There was never any trouble; most of the people in there were doing only six months or so, although there was a sprinkling of one or two longer-sentence prisoners.

A lorry would pick up the completed toys once a week, and the first time a pick-up was due, a rather bolshie-looking prison officer came into the shop, told me and another inmate to grab the barrow and load up the boxes of finished toys. This I did, and when the barrows were finally loaded, he told me to follow him. I tried to tell him that I wasn't allowed to, as I had to be signed for, and had a book that had to be filled in everywhere I went. He screamed, 'Do as you're told!' and made me pull the barrow. He didn't even inform the two officers who ran the shop where we were going. As the other inmate and I pulled the barrow through gate after gate, I realized that we were heading for the front entrance to the prison. The inner gate opened up and we passed through it, and as we did so, the outer front gate was opened and I saw the van that we were supposed to be loading the boxes into, parked up ahead. Suddenly there was mayhem: I was yanked back, the doors were closed, I was frogmarched back to my cell and the door slammed loudly behind me. I stood there stunned. I wasn't kept guessing for long, though: I was to be charged with attempting to escape.

I was hauled in front of the Governor. In spite of my protestations, the officer who'd ordered me to help him pull the barrow gave his evidence. He said nothing, of course, about how I had told him I wasn't allowed to leave the toyshop. My turn came. I gave my evidence, trying to explain the situation. I was told to wait outside, and as I left the Governor's office, the officers in charge of the toyshop went in. I waited outside and the officer who had given his evidence waited outside with me. He was then called back in. After a few minutes he came out with a face like thunder, glared at me and left the prison wing, slamming the gates after him. I waited for what seemed like ages, and then the two officers in charge of the toyshop came out. They too left the wing, but this time without slamming the gates. I was summoned back inside the Governor's office. He looked up at me from the book in front of him on his desk, and said, 'Case dismissed. There will be no mention of this on your record. However, please be mindful of your future conduct.' Bloody hell . . . I hadn't even done anything wrong.

I returned to the toyshop, where no one could believe I hadn't been banged up for trying to escape. The officer had obviously been bollocked, and whenever our paths crossed in the future he made a point of making things difficult for me, whether it was on visits, or if he was in charge of recreation. Visits were particularly harrowing when he was involved, as he made a big deal of searching me, dragging the whole process out as long as he could and only granting me what little time remained afterwards.

After a few months I was determined that I had had enough of prison, and decided that I would try and escape. My plan was this: I would be hidden in a box of toys, carrying in my hand a razorblade with which, once the lorry had travelled some distance, I would cut the string around the box, hurling myself from the lorry via its Perspex roof. The two blokes in the store would load me on to the van. I got into the store and was just about to get into the box when, with uncanny intuition, the officer in charge came in and said: 'Grantham! No pick-up this week. Van's broken down.'

It wasn't like this in *The Great Escape*. The bolshie prison officer did get his come-uppance, however, when an argument took place in the toyshop between two of the inmates. As he rushed to break it up, making the biggest meal of it that he could, he suddenly went arse over tit and ended up covered in paint, like something out of a farce. He never returned to the toyshop while I was there.

Shortly after my failed attempt at breaking out, I was moved from the toyshop and put in charge of the stores and the hotplate in the wing. This basically entailed handing out the blankets and taking them back in when people arrived or left, collecting the food and stores, and, of course, serving the food and keeping the hotplate area clean. Food was always short in the boys' wing: we barely seemed to have enough to go round, and on my first Saturday in charge, we ran out. So we asked for more from the main kitchen, but that too ran out, and there were still loads of inmates who hadn't eaten, as they were still on visits. The officer in charge of the wing phoned up and was told that we had had our allocation. I pointed out to him that we had given out only one piece of corned beef and one piece of cheese and an orange to each inmate. Milk had been ladled out to the right amount, and of course bread was rationed to two pieces each and a knob of butter. He had been watching, so he knew what I said was true. In addition, each boy had taken his food to his cell and had then been banged up, so no one could have come up twice. And the boys serving hadn't been fed yet.

The officer in charge went to the Chief and told him that he and I were going over to the kitchen to sort it out. There was just a 'blue band' there and no officer. The 'blue band' was getting the supper ready, buns and tea. He made a big fuss about how someone must be stealing food; he had loaded it up and counted it himself. And anyway he had none left, so we would have to go without. He then made the fatal mistake of saying, 'Well, they're only kids anyway.'

'No, they're not all kids,' I said. 'And it wouldn't matter even if they were. They're entitled to food. I'm a kid and I want my grub.'

'How long are you in for?' he asked dismissively.

'Life . . .'

His attitude suddenly changed. Food appeared from nowhere. And from that day on, we didn't go short; there was always some little extra put in the barrow, and extra tea, milk, sugar and coffee just for me. Obviously he was on the make: and in order to supply the gangsters in the long-term wing, who paid him for extra food, he stole it from the boys' rations.

In the stores we had our own television, which was separate from the one that all the other boys watched. On Saturday nights I would sneak it into my cell, put a blanket up at the window, plug the TV into the light switch and watch 'Match of the Day'. This went on for several months. No one seemed to notice and as I was first to be unlocked in the morning, I would sneak it back into the stores while the officer was doing his round. One Sunday morning the chief officer opened me up, and as the kettles started boiling, said: 'Yes please. I'd love a cuppa.'

As he turned to walk away he stopped, turned round and said: 'Oh . . . get that television back in the stores before anyone else notices, will you?'

'Fucking hell, Chief – anyone would think I was in prison!' I replied.

He laughed and said, 'Two sugars, 1047 . . .'

Being in the stores also meant you stayed out of your cell later than the others because you had to wait for a new batch of prisoners, and also get the supper from the kitchen. Depending who was on, you could stay up until the night patrol came on duty.

During the day you handed out stuff and dealt with the meals. Because the wing housed lots of borstal boys, some working and some not, there were lots of visitors, including vicars, social workers and the like. There was one particular social worker, a rather attractive woman in her mid-thirties, who went to see the boys, and walked quite freely around the wing. She had an office in the wing, and I would take her cups of tea there. Years later when I was working in Piero de Monzi, and she visiting a local hospital, she recognized me and we had a coffee together. Tiny things like that, having a coffee and being taken at face value, really help that process of stepping back into society and starting to believe you can actually leave all the rubbish behind.

One night, just as I was going to bed, my door was flung open, and I was told to get dressed and open up the stores. Some other establishment of Her Majesty's was on fire and they were sending all their young offenders to us. The inmates of the boys' wing were transferred to the borstal wing, and we had to get extra blankets and beds from the main stores, and prepare to receive them. They arrived at four in the morning, and life in the wing took on a different shape for a month or so, while they were allocated. Next door to the boys' wing were the adults, sex offenders and those with psychological problems. In theory these prisoners would never come into contact with the young offenders but, as with so many things in prison, it was difficult to enforce. One day I found a note describing in quite graphic detail what one particular prisoner wanted to do to me sexually. I was shocked, as I had not encountered anything like this before, so I decided the best plan was attack. I confronted him and told him that I would rip his fucking head off. He didn't seem overtly homosexual, and of course it dawned on me, he didn't want someone who was obviously queer: he wanted a straight boy, so he wouldn't seem queer himself. This became much more obvious when I was later transferred to the long-term wing. Some of these married guys, all of whom had a wife and kids outside, had straight-looking boyfriends so it wasn't obvious they were having sex. A few admitted they were queer only in prison, though I never bought that. I myself didn't have any homosexual leanings. I think they were really homosexual and just could not admit it.

My father used to send books in to me as well as the odd girly magazine, and West Ham used to send me their match programmes. I was called up to see the Governor one day, and told I had received a magazine that was obscene. It just so happened to be the first edition of *Penthouse* to show pubic hair.

I looked at the Governor and said, 'With respect, sir, my bollocks dropped when I was sixteen. I've been in the army, I've killed a man, I'm doing a life sentence, and I've had sex . . . I don't think a little bit of pubic hair is going to corrupt me.'

He looked at me and said blusteringly, 'Well, you can have it for the night, but it must be returned to the office in the morning.'

Looking him straight in the eye, I said, 'No thanks, sir . . . I don't want it.'

And then I left. Unsubstantiated rumours swept the wings of a shady-looking Governor hastening out of the gates with a concealed package under his jacket, sweating profusely. I think the staff were even more hard up than the inmates when it came to thrills.

A few months later I was summoned to the hospital wing, where I was told that I was to be sent to the Atkinson Morley hospital in Wimbledon for a scan. Apparently, the army had sent my medical documents to the prison belatedly, and the doctor there, on reading them, had seen the report about the iron attack.

An appointment was made and I was subsequently taken to have the scan. Years later I was to move to a house just around the corner, and as I passed it every day, I remembered that first feeling of being outside walls and wire. Obviously something was wrong in the scan as I was then sent for a check-up to Hammersmith Hospital, where a specialist did some tests, and decided that I had to come in to undergo further investigation. Hammersmith Hospital was next door to the prison, so the journey wasn't a long one. I was put in a ward with other patients, although I had a prison officer guard day and night.

After a few more days of tests and observations I was taken to a room where I was given an anaesthetic, and a tube was inserted that took a picture of my brain. After two days I was sent back to the prison. What was found or not found I never knew. That was what prison was like in those days: you never did get a straight answer.

Shortly thereafter I was told to pack my stuff up. I was being transferred to Wandsworth Prison, where I would be assessed and interviewed for reallocation. I arrived and was put into a wing with adult prisoners (there were no boys in Wandsworth). I was called up in front of the wing governor, and I asked him why I was there.

'Long-term allocation,' he replied.

'But I'm only nineteen,' I said, though the fact was that I was closer to twenty.

'That's the way it goes,' was his curt reply.

I was now allocated to one of the prison shops to earn my pay. I was in the mailbag shop, which was like a tailor's shop in appearance, as most of the time the machines there were used for altering prison clothing, rather than sewing up the mailbags. My job was to take a stencil with GPO on it and print it on the blue bags. Some of the other inmates were stitching the old canvas bags. I seemed to fit in with them, although I did have a run-in with a particularly tough prison officer, who went out of his way to make things difficult. One lunchtime I was in the toilet area filling up my jug.

'Grantham, what are you up to?' he asked.

'Sir,' I smiled, lifting my jug to him. 'I'm just filling my jug.'

'Are you taking the piss?'

'No, sir. I thought I'd just stick to the water.'

He started walking towards me. Another prisoner, very much on the edges of the gangster fraternity, told him to leave me alone. And surprisingly enough he did.

During my interview and assessment sessions, I kept thinking that maybe I was mad, because nothing they asked me ever seemed that relevant to me or my case. On one occasion, when I answered 'No' to a particular question, they looked at me strangely and made notes.

Life in the mailbag shop was pretty tedious, so pranks were plentiful. These consisted mainly of sewing up people's jacket sleeves so that as they went to have a visit, and went to put their jackets on or sometimes trousers, they would find they couldn't get their arms and legs in. Obviously this banal and childish prank caused some light relief. I didn't have many visits, so they couldn't do my clothes, but they decided that I needed to be paid back in some way. We all trooped into work, and after a short while, they started to complain about the food, which wasn't that bad really. So after a few hours it was decided we would have a food strike, which entailed getting our food, and on returning to our cells, throwing it over the railing on to the floor below. We collected our food and went to our cells. On three the word went out, and I threw mine over. The others laughed and then went into their cells with their food. I looked down and saw the officer who had been picking on me look up. Before he could say anything, I shouted out, 'Accident . . . I . . . I slipped . . .' He bought it, and after clearing it up, I returned to my cell, without food. Meantime, I wasn't getting mail forwarded from Wormwood Scrubs. I was, however, getting some mail addressed to another Grantham, which I dutifully handed back.

When my assessment period was up, I was informed by the governor of the assessment panel that I was to be transferred to Albany Prison on the Isle of Wight, probably the toughest maximum-security prison in the UK. Within the next few days, my father came to see me and when I told him where I was being transferred to, he couldn't believe it and went mad. Orders came though that I was to be moved the next day. After breakfast, we were told to pack our stuff up and be ready to move. Suddenly the door opened and I was asked to go to the Governor's office.

'What are you doing in Wandsworth prison?' he said.

I told him: 'Long-term allocation.'

'But you're only nineteen,' he said.

'That's the way it goes, sir,' I said.

He looked at the file in front of him, looked at me and told me to return to my cell, which I did. After a while the door opened, an officer told me to grab my stuff and I was escorted, with the others who were being transferred, to reception. There we changed into civvies and sat waiting to be called. The names started to be called out and bodies rose and made their way to the prison bus. Name after name was called out; still I remained sitting there. Before long, I was the only one left unsummoned. I sat there for what seemed ages, and then I was given lunch. No one said anything, and all sorts of thoughts ran through my head. Maybe they'd all been carted off elsewhere; maybe it was only me going to Albany. After lunch, a prison officer arrived whom I recognized from the boys' wing at the Scrubs.

We went to a prison van and, still puzzled, I asked what was going on. He shrugged and said he didn't know, all he knew was he had been told to come and take me back. We arrived back at Wormwood Scrubs. I changed back into my uniform after the obligatory bath and was taken to the boys' wing. The Chief looked at me and said: 'And there was me thinking I'd managed to get rid of you.'

He then told me to get back into the stores.

I couldn't begin to work out what was happening, but little by little a picture started to emerge. Apparently my father had phoned our local MP, who was a junior minister at the Home Office, and had told him what I had said about Albany Prison. The MP had phoned an executive in the prison service who was quite adamant in telling the MP that, not only was Leslie Grantham not being allocated to Albany, he was not, and never had been, at Wandsworth Prison, either. According to their records, which were infallible, young Grantham was where he'd been all along – safely tucked up in Wormwood Scrubs. All that implied was that my father was lying, and the MP knew him well enough to know that he wouldn't. The long and short of it was that this other Grantham (no relation) was down for Wandsworth, but in the confusion I was sent there. No wonder they looked at me stupidly when I answered their questions. No wonder I thought I was going mad. No wonder the prison service was, and still is, in a complete state.

On returning to the boys' wing it was obvious that the difference between Wandsworth Prison, which housed adult prisoners, and A wing at Wormwood Scrubs was pretty profound. No adult prisoner would put up with the crap that the boys endured. Cell conditions, toilet facilities and the food were all completely different. We had no shower facilities, and the only washing facilities were a jug of water and a bowl. No hot water; the only place to get it was the pantry, where the food trays were washed after meals. We were allowed a bath once a week, and then we would change our clothes. No wonder the place stank. The hotplate, where food was served, was near the toilet area on the ground floor.

Most prisons were built around a central hub, from which each wing branched off, but the Scrubs was built so each wing was independent and stood alone. Of course the prison was Victorian, outdated and not built to house the number of inmates it held. The infrastructure had to give, and give it did, periodically. Waste from the toilets above the hotplate would spill out and overflow on to it, and usually this happened at mealtimes. Obviously all the waste from the inmates built up and the system couldn't cope. We had become used to the pigeons that nested in the roof crapping everywhere, but the food was crap enough without having real stuff added to it.

The works department decided to put plastic corrugated material on the wire to prevent the hotplate being hit, but as inmates left with their food, they would still get hit. Eventually, it was decided that the wing would be updated. No more inmates were admitted and work began. The black bitumen floors, which over the years of non-stop boot polishing had become black glass, were tiled, the toilets were ripped out.

Obviously a project like this would take years on the outside, using teams of skilled workman. But the prison system couldn't cope with this, so it was a quick bodge job, and although the end product looked a lot better, it was only really papering over the cracks. The sagging wire was replaced and a nice airy-fairy canopy put over the hotplate. The pigeons, during the refurbishment, had even more scope and when the old wire was ripped out they would dive-bomb the inmates preparing each finished cell. So the Chief Officer instructed us to catch them and put them out of the building. We had quite a success rate, but as we had cornered one and were about to put it in a box with the others, we heard a voice asking us what we thought we were doing. We tried to explain, but logic is not, I believe, something that was taught at officers' training college. The man in question saw the large box at our feet starting to move. Programmed to disbelieve and investigate everything and anything the inmates told him, he proceeded to open the lid. Just like Tom from *Tom and Jerry* peering down the barrel of a blunderbuss, he craned to look inside and, as he did so, six or seven pigeons flew back out to their perches, depositing their thanks on his hat as they did so. By now I think even he realized maybe less haste might have been called for.

When the water tanks in the roof were removed, they were found to contain more dead pigeons than water. That's why the tea always tasted so lousy. The loft floors were knee-deep in pigeon shit, and borstal boys were used to get rid of it. Nowadays this couldn't be done; protective clothing would have to be provided. But, hey, what the hell? These were only kids between the ages of sixteen and eighteen. Thank God there were no chimneys to sweep.

The only good thing to come out of this, apart from the smart-looking wings and cells, was that while we were clearing it all out – and covered head to toe in dust and filth – we were allowed an extra bath and a change of clothing. But as the prison bathhouse was struggling to accommodate nearly everyone, and only the long-term prisoners in D wing had showers, the extra bath was a hit-and-miss affair.

Eventually the wing was finished and filled with prisoners. There was no mass inrush, because as each landing or part-landing was finished, inmates would occupy the finished cells. But before too long the newly painted or sprayed walls would become covered in graffiti and chipped. Although the toilets didn't contaminate the food any more, they soon became tacky and smelt as bad as before. And with three inmates to a cell sharing a pot and banged up from anything from twelve to fifteen hours a day, with only one bath and one change of clothing a week, such deterioration was always likely to happen. Because I was in the stores and we had two huge sinks in the pantry in which to wash the meal trays, I worked out a scheme to at least make myself more presentable for visits. So the night before I had a visit I would fill up the two sinks with hot water and have a good scrub and wash my hair. And yes, I did scrub the sinks out afterwards, so my dirt didn't affect the trays.

In 1968 I came of age. I was twenty-one, an adult, and about to celebrate this milestone with a move to the long-term wing. Apart from the birthday cards from friends and family, my only presents were new, designer clothes – prison design, that is. I had had a brief 'fitting' of them before, when I had been sent for long-term assessment to Wandsworth, so this wasn't going to be a surprise, and they weren't going to be new, although it would be a new beginning for me.

8

SCRUBS

It was now time to leave the boys' wing of Wormwood Scrubs and travel the short distance across the prison exercise yards to D wing, the long-term wing. Normally I would be in the stores making tea for the prison officers and doing various chores just to appear busy. Having been told at breakfast that I was to be transferred to the long-term wing, though, I was locked up in my cell until after everyone had gone to work.

Once all the other boys had left for work, I was unlocked and told to take my bedding, apart from one pillowcase, and my pot and eating utensils, to the stores and hand them in. My razorblade was collected from me as was the norm, and I did as I was requested. The pillowcase was to be used to carry my uniform to reception, where it would be handed in and exchanged for an adult one. Before I could leave A wing I had to have a medical, which consisted of answering a few questions: 'Do you feel all right?' 'Do you have any problems?' The doctor then signed a piece of paper, and handed it to the medical officer, and I was then told to wait by the wing security gate, where I would be escorted to the prison reception. A prison officer appeared with a line of half a dozen other young prisoners. I joined on the end and off we ambled to reception.

There, the other boys were herded into a waiting area after being processed and then locked in cubicles to await collection by a prison van to be taken to various destinations. Sometimes they would be waiting till 6 p.m. After being processed, which amounted to having my white, YP-stamped cell card replaced with a blue one, I had to strip and have a bath, again just the right amount of regulation water: barely covering the buttocks and just enough to cover the genitals. As soon as the bath orderly popped his head over the cubicle door (apparently to check if I was all right, but really to have a look at the family jewels), I told him to fuck off or I would rip his fucking head off. He scurried off, no doubt to look at someone else's privates.

Once washed I left the bath cubicle area with a towel wrapped around my waist and headed to the store area to pick up my adult prison uniform, blue and white striped shirt, grey trousers and grey army-style blouson. Apart from the colour, the uniform was exactly the same as the boys' uniform. I guess because I was a lifer and I had been in the Scrubs for a while, the uniform actually fitted, although the con handing out the uniform did comment on me 'fucking off' the nonce in the bath area. So I guess it was a combination of everything. Some of the guys who were getting their uniforms ended up looking dreadful in ill-fitting trousers and jackets.

Once dressed, I collected a pillowcase with sheets, extra socks and eating utensils and a mug, and sat by the gate, which looked directly into D wing. It seemed so huge compared to A wing, which was divided into two parts: A Boys and A Adults. And whereas the boys were mostly in for petty crimes, this was the real thing. Yes, I know I had been in Wandsworth Prison for that short period of time, and I had held my own reasonably well. But this was going to be completely different.

Eventually an officer told me to follow him, which I did. He unlocked the gate of reception and I headed straight ahead. The gate closed and he unlocked the gate of D wing and I entered it. I heard the gate lock behind me and the regulation 'one on', and I was led to the box where the wing officer sat. After handing in my card I was assigned a cell and told to report to the landing officer. Which I did, and after dumping my bed linen in the cell I was told to report to the medical officer. I tried to explain that I had been examined only that morning in the boys' wing. But this fell on deaf ears, so I made my way back down to the ground floor and looked for the medical officer's room. Easy enough one would have thought . . . But no . . . there were two doors marked 'Medical Officer', and along the wall between them was a row of the usual aluminium and plywood chairs. Sitting at each end was a prisoner, one at one door, one at the other, with empty chairs in between. The medical rooms were basically two cells knocked into one. After a short deliberation I decided to sit next to the inmate at the far end. He was wearing shirt and trousers and wore glasses and seemed very sheepish. No sooner had my backside touched the plywood than I heard a voice from the other end say, 'Don't sit there.' My heart sank. 'Sit here,' the voice continued. So I upped and moved next to him. I started to apologize, said that I was new here and all the usual, face-saving, crawling, not wanting to upset the applecart, but he was deaf to all that. He just told me he'd got a dose. Meaning VD. My reaction to this was one of panic. What the hell had I let myself in for?

Although homosexuality was part and parcel of the boys' wing, it really had never bothered me that much. This, however, was a whole new ballgame. Sexually transmitted diseases. Was I safe, I wondered? My thoughts were interrupted by the appearance of a prisoner mopping the floor some twenty feet to my left. He was about five foot six and was wearing just bib and brace overalls. He had the hairiest back I had ever seen; hair covered his upper body. He also had a monkey-style gait.

The prisoner next to me said, seemingly without moving his lips, 'See that dirty bastard there?' He indicated the hairy one. 'He gave it to him.'

Before I could reply, the prisoner next to me suddenly upped and went into the medical room. I had been so intent on my own thoughts that I hadn't heard him being called. I also didn't see him leave, and was barely aware of my own name being called until I realized that the shape in front of me was not a prisoner but a medical officer. I followed him to his room and answered the same questions as I had put to me in the medical room in the boys' wing. Then I was told to go back to my landing. Well, thankfully, I hadn't contracted any diseases travelling from the boys' wing to the long-term wing, although if I had no one would have known.

Lunch came and I was assigned to a table. In the long-term wing you had a choice of eating arrangements. You could eat out, on association, which consisted of rows and rows of tables at one end of D wing ground floor. Each table had a locker to keep knives and forks in, and obviously any extra food you had bought from the canteen with your pay. At the far end of the wing was a television, and also a dartboard and snooker table. Some cells had also been converted into showers, so the sooner you finished your eating, the sooner you could watch television or play snooker, darts, or cards.

Whereas the boys' wing was badly maintained, possibly because of the sheer turnover of bodies in and out of the place, D wing was immaculate, or seemed so. Table one was always the 'hierarchy' table, for train robbers, Kray gang members and other well-known characters in the criminal fraternity. They always seemed to have better-fitting clothing and edible food. I, however, was allocated to table four.

After a while, you could apply to eat in the recreation hall, or 'rec', which was where once a week they showed the film. It also had a stage, where plays were put on, and where various outside organiz-ations would also put on shows for the prisoners. David Frost came in with Julie Felix. At other times we had Jet Harris, Long John Baldry, Chris Farlowe and Rod Stewart, well before he was famous. Also various magicians, snake charmers and female impersonators, and of course the lovely Larry Adler and Kathy Kirby. She sang very nervously, but she was wearing a beautiful blue shimmering evening dress, with a low-cut front. As she took her bow, the inmates erupted; you could (even from the back) see most of her breasts. The inmates stamped, yelled, whistled, screamed for more. And the more applause she got, the more she bowed, obviously thinking she had given a great show. Well, she had, but the inmates were not applauding her singing. She got a better reception than Johnny Cash in Fulsom Prison.

You could choose to eat in your cell, which meant you were banged up. Obviously all this had to be approved, and it was always some concern to the authorities if an inmate chose to be banged up instead of associating with other inmates. Some had reasons that were innocent enough: they were studying, or doing handicrafts. Others had more therapeutic reasons.

As I made my way to table four, I passed the inmate who had given me the medical history of the two prisoners earlier. He told me to sit on his table, which happened to be table two. I explained that I had been told to go on table four. Suddenly he called a screw over and said, 'I want him on this table.' The officer ummed and aahed for what seemed an eternity, pointing out that it would mess up the paperwork, all the time my food going cold – not that it mattered: crap food is no better off being hot than cold. Eventually it was agreed that I should go to table two. I nodded to all seven prisoners on the table.

As I started to eat my food from the metal tray I got a proper glimpse of the inmate who seemed to be taking me under his wing. He was about mid-thirties, dark-haired, looked slightly Italian, and was called Tony. There I stopped, the fork of food halfway to my lips. He was wearing the most atrocious wig I had ever seen, not that I had seen many. It was obviously made of nylon and had a side parting that you could drive a bus down. It really was a monstrous thing. No one, I found out later, had ever seen him without a wig on, and no one mentioned it unless he did, in case he went ballistic. He told everyone that he was badly scarred on the head by being beaten up with truncheons when he was arrested. And he was suing the Home Office and police for compensation for the injuries he'd received. I heard one story that he had done it himself by falling through a skylight when he was robbing a place; the fall had taken his hair and scalp off. But as everyone spoke in telephone numbers when talking about how much they stole, or anything else, it was always hard to fathom out the truth. Subsequently, I found out that he had two wigs, one for work and one for best. By this I mean for visits. They were Home Office issue. When I found this out, I prayed I would never go bald. Trouble was, his visit wig was just as bad. It had a midnight-blue sheen to it. Although he was a known hard case, if trouble flared in a work space near him he would scurry, holding his wig on, to the loo or office in the shop he worked in, in case it came detached and fell on the floor, humiliating him. Maybe the other blokes might have played football with it. I had many a chuckle to myself as I thought of him being on Governor's orders for a breach of discipline: whereas the majority might get loss of wages, or bread and water or loss of privileges, he might get loss of wig. Now there's a thought. But no, sad to say that never happened.

I decided to stay at the table and watch the tablemates play cards. Obviously they wanted to know what I was in for, and they told me what they were in for. Robbery, violence, manslaughter, fraud and murder. A mixed bunch. As I was watching them play cards, I was summoned to the gate, where the orderly officer told me I was to be working in the mattress shop. Normally the Assistant Governor would see you when you arrived in a wing, but apparently he was on a course, and would see me when he got back. At the end of lunch, as after breakfast, each work party would be summoned to the main wing gate and you would stream off, under supervision, to your places of work. The long-termers worked mainly on the works department, bricklaying, painting and plumbing, refurbishing the prison. The laundry was entirely manned by long-term prisoners, as was the mattress shop and the library. There were also a number of other jobs that involved some short-term prisoners and long-term prisoners working together, such as the bookbinding shop and the tailor's shop. Plus jobs for a select few in the library, officers' mess, visiting room, education block, gardens and kitchens and reception and hospital.

As I entered the mattress shop all I could see was piles of old horsehair mattresses and new mattress covers. I was assigned to the piles of old mattresses, which I had to unpick and pull the hair out of, putting it in one long wooden barrow. Believe me, this horsehair got everywhere. (Thank God there were showers in D wing.) The mattress covers went in another barrow and once these barrows were filled, they would be transported off to the laundry, where they would be washed and then returned. Some other prisoners would then refill them with a mixture of new and washed horsehair, sew them up, and then they would be redistributed. Any torn and damaged mattresses would be sent, after being laundered, to the tailor's shop to be repaired. When the mattresses were replaced a few years later, they gave us foam-rubber ones. What a stupid idea that was! Most ended up having holes cut in them and female shapes drawn on them by the inmates. The mattress shop was then turned into a gym – from one treadmill to another. Before that time, most prisoners worked out in the showers, which served as many things: for washing, obviously, as a gym and as a meeting place for homosexuals, and a still room for making hooch, illicit home-made booze.

After tea, we all went off to the recreation hall to see a play performed by the prison drama group. This play was called *Norman*, a comedy about two men in love with the same woman. As we filed into the rec, I saw row upon row of chairs, and a stage raised at one end with rather nice theatrical curtains. As I took my seat, the lights dimmed and the curtains opened. We were in some drawing room; they all have drawing rooms, or so it seemed. I had a front room in *my* house. Anyway, there was a woman on stage pacing about, when through a door came the man who that morning I had briefly sat beside, the one who had VD.

The woman said something to the effect of, 'I'm sorry, I can't' to which he said, 'Why, oh why, won't you marry me?' Well before she could answer him, a huge roar went up from the audience: about five hundred prisoners shouted out, 'Because you've got a dose, you dirty bastard!' From that moment on, it was absolute chaos. Then to cap it all who should appear through another door onstage but the grey monkey dressed in biker's leathers. Well, if you can remember the 'Bilko' television series with Phil Silvers, you will remember Doberman, the poor put-upon serviceman, who was the butt of all Bilko's schemes. The grey monkey was Doberman with long arms and masses of body hair. As he uttered his lines, no doubt with a sense of dread as to what was to be verbally hurled at him from the audience, it came out so monotonous and lifeless that I heard myself saying, possibly out of sheer bravado, 'I could do better than that.' To which a voice from behind me said in the campest, most theatrical voice, 'Well, why don't you then?' I turned around to see this sixty-year-old with long bouffant silver hair, long nails and a shawl thrown around his shoulders. He looked like a poor man's Quentin Crisp. When I said I would, he told me to put my money where my mouth was and join the drama group.

The next day I applied for the drama group, and then off I went to work in the mattress shop. I was up to my knees and elbows in horsehair, when I heard my name being called. I looked up and there was a prisoner officer with a basket on his arm, similar to those carried by bakers' roundsmen. He was wearing a brown overall, his name was Pascall, and he was in charge of the library. In the basket were piles of books and magazines. It was a new delivery of paperbacks sent in from my father.

When I was in the boys' wings I only ever saw a Mr Love, who was the deputy library officer. I had had to hand one set of books in before I could get a new set to read, so Pascall asked for the old set. I told him I had handed them in when I left the boys' wing. He was a grumpy bastard but turned out to have a heart of gold. He gave me my books and then told me that when he'd finished his deliveries he wanted to see me in the library, just across from the mattress shop. Thirty minutes later, he signed me out and took me into the library. There, with a 'red band' on his arm, was the silver-haired Quentin Crisp lookalike. Pascall took me into his office and told me that my application to join the drama group had been turned down. That was quick: I had only applied three hours before. Apparently there wasn't a vacancy, but I could join the stage management group, helping make the sets and setting up the shows or prison plays. Obviously, I said yes. And I'm glad I did, because Pascall then arranged for me to work in the library.

The following morning, as I went to leave the wing with the mattress shop party, I was told I was in the library now. The library 'blue band' came and picked me up. John, the silver-haired theatre aficionado, worked on allocating the prisoners' newspapers; several others managed the bookshelves. My job, however, was to help John. When he was eventually released, I was to take over from him. I also had to cut the corners of all prisoners' returned paperbacks, where the name and number was written. The pristine ones would be put in Pascall's office and the others would be sent over to the bookbinding shop, where they were unbound and given a hardback cover. I later found out that some of the pristine ones would be taken to a local second-hand bookshop, where they would be sold for a small fraction of their original price. The money received would supply tea, milk, sugar and biscuits for both the library and the stage and drama groups. My first day in the library was a Friday, so there were no classes that night. After association, which on a Friday finished at 6 p.m. instead of 8 p.m. as was the case Monday to Friday, you were banged up. Unless you had a prisoner visitor, you stayed in your cell until the next morning, your solitude broken only by tea and buns being delivered at supper.

Weekends were spent cleaning cells, unless you had a job that required you to work. The library was one of these, as was the skeleton staff in the laundry. Most prisoners had visits on Saturdays and Sundays, although it was better to have one during the week, because it meant you got off work detail. If the weather was good you could go out in the exercise yard and walk around, or play football, or cricket, or basically whatever you felt like doing, within reason, of course. But Mondays always came around far too quickly.

On my first night with the stage management group, I was asked to make the tea. Blimey, not only was I contributing to buying it, I was now making it and drinking it! The only thing I didn't contribute to it all was the growing of it.

No sooner had I made everyone a cup of tea, than I was ushered into one of the dressing rooms where the actors were. Doberman's *doppelgänger* had retired from his career on the stage. I imagine the abuse he had received on his last performance had probably had something to do with it. Soon after this, he was transferred out of Wormwood Scrubs, hopefully to somewhere he couldn't pass on any STDs.

Apart from the half a dozen prisoners sitting on chairs in the room, was a man in civvies, who introduced himself as Jon Haerem. He directed the plays. He was a lovely man, who chain smoked and seemed very nervous.

I tried to explain that I was only there to make the tea, but I was told that they needed people to read the plays, because they were deciding which play they were going to stage next. The two we read were *Dry Rot*, a very funny farce, and *The Anniversary* by Bill MacIlwraith, which had been also made into a film starring Bette Davis. The leading man of the drama group was off having electric shock treatment, and as Doberman had quit acting they were short of bodies.

The next evening I went back to making the tea. As the kettle was boiling and I was washing out the cups, I heard my name being called. It was Jon. I was told I was playing Tommy, the youngest son of a jerry house-building family, who was bringing home his girlfriend to meet his family on the anniversary of his father's death. It was a black comedy, very funny and very controversial. David, the leading man, who had been off having electric shock treatment, was there, and he was to play my older married brother. He was extremely ugly. The story went round that they showed him pictures of boy scouts and if he responded, they zapped him. How true this was I don't know. So because of a few volts of electricity I was propelled on to the stage in an acting capacity. Whether the electric shock treatment rumour was true or not, it certainly didn't seem to affect him or his acting. Read into that what you will.

I met him years later on the James Whale television show in Leeds, where he was now a fully formed she. I should imagine he was probably having treatment preparing him for his sex-change operation. Mind you, no matter what they took away to make him a woman, he was still very ugly.

9

THE SAME OLD ROUTINE

Life in the long-term wing, although a great improvement in many ways – mostly the food, the educational facilities and the fact we had a large shower area, so the weekly trip to the bath house was a thing of the past – was mundane and repetitive. When I had arrived, the wing had suffered several cases of blindness and one death, because certain inmates had been producing their own booze, out of wood alcohol and pineapple juice, salvaged from tins of pineapple chunks. Alcohol and tobacco baroning, as well as supplying pornographic material, seemed to be the only illicit things going on. Sure, there was homosexual activity, but illicit booze and tobacco undermined the system, which, in any case, worked only with the co-operation of the prisoners.

The pay in the long-term wing may have been more than in the boys' wing, but we never received actual money; it was logged against your name in the pay book, of which a copy was kept in the shop and what you spent was deducted. If and when you were released, you were then given the outstanding amount. But there were plenty of ways to supplement your income, all of them illegal, prison-wise that is.

If you worked in the laundry, you could earn slightly more by pressing someone's visit clothes, and selling tailored shirts (with slightly larger collars, as was the fashion) and trousers, all paid for with tobacco, or money sent into someone's account, or to someone's home. Tables made in woodwork would end up in someone else's hands for a few ounces of tobacco; some inmates made model stagecoaches out of purloined wood and prison work boots. So many boots were being butchered in this way that in the end the practice had to be stopped.

Nothing was for free, and tobacco was money. Extra steaks and bread and tea and coffee, plus other stuff from the kitchen, all cost money. If you didn't smoke, you had extra money to spend, and if someone came to you and asked to buy tobacco from you, you could charge a hell of a lot more. I saw men getting two thin roll-ups and having to pay half an ounce in return on payday. The tobacco was usually brought in by members of staff, in one form or another. If they ever were caught, it was always the most unlikely ones. One of the most notorious was a scruffy officer who looked as if he was on the bones of his arse; he retired to a very lovely house in Spain, having made a successful career out of such dealing. And obviously with the arrival of the train robbers and the Kray gang members, temptations for prison officers increased.

My cell was on the top landing, and apart from sleeping and Friday-night early bang-up, I hardly spent any time in it. We ate out of the cells and stayed out till eight o'clock each night. Once we had all left for our cells, the wing cleaners would clean downstairs, and then be banged up themselves. We were allowed radios in our cells, but not short-wave receivers. Ever since the spy, George Blake, had escaped with the help of a short-wave radio, they had been banned; although some managed to keep them. Obviously, there was always someone could adapt a radio so that it could receive short-wave. We were also allowed record players, but battery-operated, so music was plentiful, and mixed, and loud. This caused quite a few problems.

Whereas any violent exchanges in the boys' wing were school playground stuff, those in the long-term wing were heavy and quite bloody. Although razorblades had to be handed in each morning after you had shaved, plenty were still in circulation. Many an inmate had trouble sitting down after he was slashed across the arse. Razorblades were also broken and hidden in someone's soap, so when he washed he cut his hands to shreds.

Physical violence usually took the form of bursting into a cell, placing a pillowcase over someone's head and then punching him, although many were hit with jugs. The most disturbing and gratuitous violence I encountered was at the snooker table. A prisoner – who had killed two children – suddenly screamed and fell when a snooker cue, turned into a makeshift spear, impaled his chest. No one knew who had done it.

Punishment for misdemeanours usually took the form of loss of privileges, and closed visits. If it was a major offence, however, such as violence, theft or damage of prison property, extra days would be added on to a prisoner's sentence. Or he'd be sent to another prison. And only the lunatic would want that.

Nonces (rapists and child molesters) and anyone who resembled one, or grasses (people who were informers), usually had scalding hot water from the tea urn poured on them. How anyone knew who or what anyone else had done was always a mystery to me. Unless someone knew a case history personally, the information must have been circulated by the prison staff. I am sure that a lot of the nonces, desperate to hide their own crimes, and having ingratiated themselves with the bully boys, would point out innocent inmates (innocent in the sense they were not nonces or grasses), and these unfortunates would be victimized. The most notorious nonces were kept under what was known as Rule 43 and were segregated, and saw no one. There were also others who asked to be banged up away from danger. As a rule, though, no one in their right mind would want to be stuck in a cell 7 feet by 13 all day, every day.

The majority of prisoners just wanted to do their time and leave, yet still try and buck the system while they were in it. Alcohol was being stored in the fire extinguishers; the smell was overpowering as you passed them. What would have happened if the wing had caught fire? By now the prison population was beginning to change as more and more drug-related criminals came into the long-term wing, usually doing four-year stretches.

During my first year in the long-term wing, we had a very rich American come in. He had killed a girl on an LSD trip; he thought she was a dragon and had stuffed a sheet down her throat to put out the fire. That was his defence anyway. He was a multi-millionaire, and he joined the ever-growing list of really rich people who were in there. I am talking rich *before* crime, not rich *after*. We may have all committed crimes, but the clever thing to do was to circumvent the system, by making an appeal, and work on a defence. These blokes didn't have to work, but sat around all day supposedly studying law books and receiving lots of appeal visits, which meant they could carry on conducting their business interests from inside. If and when their appeals were turned down, they just applied to the House of Lords, and their sentences would end by the time it ever got that far. Obviously with the money they had they found it easy to survive.

The American, however, was not circumventing the system: he had lots of visits from the American Embassy, but he went to work like the rest of us. He did receive a lot of mail, mainly from Bermuda and the States.

At night, screams could be heard coming from a number of cells, and more and more inmates would be carted off to the hospital. At first this was put down to nervous breakdowns, or to alcohol abuse, but it wasn't either of these things: it was LSD. But where was it coming from? At last the authorities had a brainwave (though these were pretty thin on the ground): it was coming in on visits or in the luxuries the prisoners were allowed, such as radios, record players, handicraft kits, bedspreads or carpets, maybe even in the post, perhaps even via the staff. Searches took place every day, radios and record players were taken apart, carpets and bedspreads analysed. Eventually the culprit was found. It was the post room, although not intentionally: seemingly the LSD was put on the stamps of the letters being sent to the American. And apparently he was making money by selling these stamps to the more gullible inmates, who just wanted to escape the daily routine. Prisoners, being prisoners, refused to inform on him, but eventually one did, and the American was deported to finish his sentence in the States.

Food played a huge part in people's lives inside; sometimes the food was OK and sometimes it wasn't. If we had visits from magistrates or the Home Secretary arrived for a 'surprise' visit – as if it was a surprise – we had gammon steaks with fried egg and a slice of pineapple on top, peas and chips. Obviously extras were plentiful and appearing in the wing in various strange ways. False bottoms in milk churns, in tea towels – you name it, it was used. One day I was in the food queue when an altercation started, and as it was broken up I was told to get a move on and get my food, told there was nothing to look at, by this rather large northern-sounding prison officer. I did as I was told, but as I was about to get my food a voice shouted, 'Grab a loaf of bread while you're there, Les!' It was one of the blokes on my table. I reached into the basket, grabbed a loaf and stuck it under my arm. Suddenly the screw shouted, 'Stop right there . . .' He grabbed the loaf and exclaimed, 'I'm not stupid! Loaves don't bleed.' He thrust it under my nose. Well, I know loaves don't bleed, but this one did. It was soaked in blood, and when it was opened it contained three or four steaks. Obviously it hadn't been meant for me . . . and because of the fight I had grabbed someone's loaf, or was it meat loaf?

The drama group was now going from strength to strength. I had got through the first play OK, and people said I had a gift for it. In *The Anniversary*, we had all learned each other's lines. The ladies came in, one a mature lady who was to play Mum, and a younger girl who was to play my sister-in-law, but my character's girlfriend didn't turn up. The next evening this rather beautiful young lady arrived, and although she had tried to dowdy herself down, she had not achieved anything like the desired effect.

Her name was Pamela Salem. Years later, when I was in 'EastEnders', I suggested her for a part as the wine bar owner and she got it. In *The Anniversary*, she seemed very nervous, but after a while she relaxed a bit, and when it came to the kissing scenes, I just pressed my lips to hers. She quickly snatched hers away, and I whispered something about a hairy-arsed prisoner. Gradually, though, we began to get on famously. Pamela couldn't do the next play, as she was off to Chichester, but her replacement was just as stunning, an actress called Gay Hamilton. We also had a wonderful old musical artist called Ethel Revnell, who was part of the double act Revnell and West. One day, as we were leaving rehearsals, Ethel turned to me and said, 'You should give my agent a ring; he thinks you are brilliant.' I flippantly remarked, 'OK, I'll ring him . . . in 1990.' She looked at me and smiled. Obviously she must have then said something to Jon Haerem, who told her I was a lifer.

Pamela came to see our next play, and as we chatted afterwards I asked if she was going to come in and do another one with us. She said no, and when I asked why, she said it would mean she couldn't visit me. I told her that she wouldn't be able to do that while I was at the Scrubs, but she could if and when I moved. I was thinking, no way that is ever going to happen, this beautiful actress, visiting me. But visit me she did: all those years I was inside, she wrote and she visited me in every prison I was in. She really was a kind and generous person, and we are still great mates today.

I had also been asked to be part of the new prisoners' union that we were being encouraged to start up, mostly by the new wing governor. We managed to get extra visits, and an extra television so that those who didn't want to watch 'Top of the Pops' or 'The Big Match' could watch other things. The televisions were situated one at each end of the wing, but obviously you couldn't sit where you wanted; the top dogs had the front row, and the others seemed to be pre-booked with towels. It looked at times like the loungers in a Spanish seaside resort, which was funny really as there wasn't a single German in the prison. Things seemed to be going well until 'Angelface' Probyn arrived, and was elected into the union. Then it started to go wrong: he wanted to tear down the wire, remove the cameras and basically turn the place into a holiday camp. Meetings became more and more a waste of time. He had been a bank robber, and had a reputation for escaping. He had messed up a big escape from Durham Prison, in which he had broken both his ankles.

From the moment Probyn arrived life in the wing became strained. Tensions were high, and rooftop protests started to spring up everywhere. One night I was told by Freddy Forman to bang myself up, and also several others too. We didn't argue – you didn't with Freddy. Others had guessed what was going on and banged themselves up. As we did so, it happened that the remaining prisoners refused to go to their cells and barricaded the doors. There was no

My maternal grandfather: after a career in the Black and Tans, he went to America and lived for years with a Red Indian 'squaw'.

My mother in her father's car.

Dad at the outbreak of the Second World War.

My parents.

John and I.

John and I: slightly older.

At school: why was I smiling?

Philip.

John, his mates and me.

Me in army uniform at the Seven
Stiles pub: a boy in a man's world.

Just a number. NCOs' cadre, the Royal Fusiliers, Germany.

Philip in our back garden in St Mary Cray.

The Visitor at the Belgrade Theatre, Coventry: learning my trade.

Leslie Grantham Esq.,   August 28th 1984.
28 Sydney Street,
LONDON.
SW3

Dear Leslie,

    Many thanks for coming in to read on
Friday.

    I thought you might like to be put out
of your misery, so I am writing this brief note
to say that all being well and other things
being equal, I hope you will be joining us on
'East 8' to play the part of Den.

    As I said before, Jonathan, our booker,
joins us on September 3rd, so things should
start moving then.

                    Best Wishes,

                    Julia

                    Julia Smith
                    Producer, 'East 8'

Long live The W.D.!

Had I got the part, or not?

On the set of 'EastEnders' with
Pamela Salem.

A personal appearance.

violence as such, and eventually the Governor negotiated with Freddy and the protest was called off. When the prisoners were finally put in their cells, one was missing: Probyn. Now apparently everyone had been told it was to be a peaceful protest, but the reason loads of us were banged up while it went on was in case the prison authorities decided to use force. Freddy was aware of the volatile nature of some prisoners, and knew a peaceful protest could have turned into a full-scale riot. There was no way, though, that Probyn could have got out of the building. Eventually he was found, sitting in the Governor's office reading the prisoners' files. He had destroyed his own records.

Probyn was moved out and when he was released he was done for child molesting. And this from one of those who had had a reputation for attacking child molesters and rapists while he had been inside. Mind you, he did always hang around with very young prisoners.

While I was in the Scrubs no one escaped from the prison, although several didn't return from home leave and one escaped from hospital. The only attempt that was made ended in failure, although I was responsible for a false alarm. The officers running the works department had gone on strike, or work to rule, as they put it (prisoners went on strike, prison officers went on work to rule). The inmates of the works department had to be found other employment, so we were all allocated various jobs while the dispute went on. I ended up in the sock shop. This was nothing to do with the high street chain of the same name, but was a tailor's shop where you unpicked old socks and then remade them by putting the wool around a frame.

As I entered the place I saw an old mate from school, and sat next to him. We chatted; he was in for a short sentence and after lunch I gave him tobacco and a few other things. At the end of the day, as we were about to pack up and go our separate ways, I realized that I had made a huge sock, about 20 feet in length. I had just carried on feeding the wool into this frame as we were chatting about our schooldays and home, so I had not paid attention. I tore it off the spindle, went to the toilet and wrapped it around my waist. I then said cheerio to my old mate and walked back to the long-term wing.

As I walked around the exercise yard, I started to pull the monster sock out from under my shirt, rolled it up into a ball and then kicked it over the wall, or so I thought.

Within ten minutes we were all told to get into the wing and back to our cells. After about an hour, we were unlocked and could have our tea. Everyone was pissed off with being banged up, and so of course when I found out the reason for the bang-up, I kept quiet. Someone walking past the outside of the prison had seen this huge sock hanging over the wall, and thinking someone was trying to escape, had telephoned the prison.

The one failed attempt was a case of life imitating art. Two prisoners dug between their cells with spoons, taking out the cement between the bricks and replacing it with porridge. They then made false heads to fool the inspection, shimmied down the drainpipe and got on to the education block roof. There they picked up scaffold boards, and made it to the top of the inner fence, but the planks didn't reach the outer wall. Every time I see Clint Eastwood in *Escape from Alcatraz* I am reminded of this.

I was all too well aware that keeping a low profile and keeping my mouth shut were both recommended ways of staying sane for a Lifer. Every now and then, though, it was impossible to keep it all bottled up. One time in particular, my cell had been 'spun' in a random, spontaneous search. Although we were never told what the officers were looking for (and always had to tidy up ourselves) there was often a sense that the guards were acting, reluctantly, on orders. This one time, however, my radio was dismantled so carelessly that it couldn't be put back together again. Confronting the guard responsible I said: 'Tell me – if I called you a prick, you'd have to nick me, wouldn't you?'

Smiling his malevolent sneer, he confirmed that, yes, he would be obliged to charge any prisoner found using inappropriate or insubordinate language.

'But if I just *thought* it . . . you couldn't nick me then, could you?'

Becoming a little uncomfortable now, as he sensed himself being outflanked, he none the less grunted, 'No . . . s'pose not.'

My sneer must have matched his own for a second.

'Good,' I beamed. 'I think you're a prick.'

He nicked me.

I had by now moved on from the library to the works department, and had been shunted around from works party to works party, doing everything from welding to mixing cement, tiling and building partitions for welfare rooms, although mostly it was just maintenance work. Then it was decided that D wing was to be refurbished. The wooden floorboards were to be ripped up and concreted. Myself and three others went round cell by cell as they became empty and ripped out the floorboards. Another team would pour concrete in, and then they were screeded; the walls were sprayed with a base coat and then a fleck. The slate landing slabs were replaced with vinyl-covered boards. Inmates were being moved from their cells and rehoused, so to speak. Some were OK with this, but others were absolutely furious, and one in particular, who created such a scene that eventually he had to be shipped out.

He was a hoarder. His room was crammed wall to wall with newspaper cuttings and legal papers. Apart from his bed and washstand, his cell was just a depository for old papers. Accused of rape and sentenced, he was one of those who had elected to be banged up, because he was working on his case, attempting to have his sentence overturned. When we got into his room, it was really filthy. How he could have cleaned it was impossible to conceive, and why he was allowed to keep so many papers beggared belief, since it was a fire trap. He left his cell screaming and never returned. When the job was finished I was allocated it, but seeing as it was newly painted and tiled this was fine by me.

I had been six cells further down the hallway, and we were now working on those. The pressure was on, as C wing (the short-termers' wing) had to hold some long-termers waiting to get into D wing. It was therefore full to bursting, so extra help was needed to complete it on time. Not only were the cells and buildings being done, but all the furniture was also being replaced. Pinboards were being put up, so that nothing needed to be stuck to walls. Graffiti were banned, and there was no way that you could stash anything under the floorboards now, or in the bed ends. A constant check was kept on walls for damage.

Around this time I was beginning to get very depressed. I could see no end in sight to my sentence: it just stretched on and on. There was no point to my existence and I thought that maybe it was time to pack it in. I also thought about my family and the shame I had brought them; now they could get on with their lives. I decided that the easiest way to die was by hanging myself. So I gave away my bedspread, radio and record player to the guy next door, telling him to look after them for me for a couple of hours as I was going to clean my cell. I closed the door and put a chair under the window, but as I picked the tie up to put it around my neck, I suddenly thought, 'No, not the tie. I might need that for a visit.' The absurdity of the situation then hit me and I started to laugh and laugh, and in doing so fell off the chair and bashed my head. Luckily I had taken the tie from around my neck or I would have hanged myself. Later, when the cell was opened, I went next door, got my stuff back and settled down once more to a life of nothing.

Friday night was bang-up night, where if you were smart you cleaned your cell, allowing you to pretend on Saturday morning that you were cleaning, when in fact you could move around freely, as long as you had a broom or dustpan in your hand. The cells, having been freshly painted, were in pristine condition compared with before, so they didn't really need cleaning that first Friday. Nevertheless, I noticed that the window area was filthy, so I grabbed the bit of cloth with which I would normally have wiped the table and washstand. I was just about to get down off my chair, when I noticed movement in the building opposite, which was a fair distance away. To my left I could see the football pitches, which were jam-packed each weekend, but suddenly I could see into rooms opposite. I saw a young lady take her clothes off, grab a towel and leave the room. And to my right I saw a number of smaller windows, some open and some not. A light came on and the young lady with the towel started having a shower. No wonder the cell's previous occupant hadn't wanted to move; he had his own peepshow twenty-fours hours a day. It was the nurses' quarters for Hammersmith Hospital. Not all the nurses were as brazen, just the odd few. I am not sure they knew that they were being watched. Sometimes it wasn't just one in a room.

They would go through the motions of trying on clothes, sometimes they waved, and even those who didn't mean to inadvertently provided entertainment. I later found out that the previous occupant had paid fifteen ounces for the privilege of having that cell. Cheap at the price.

One of the prisoners I had been working with was a bank robber, a pretty serious gangster. He sat on the top table with Buster Edwards, Freddy Forman, the Lambrianous, Billy Curbishley and various others. Buster was fine; he did my laundry for nothing. But Frank O'Connell, with whom I ripped out floorboards, could be quite moody.

One day Frank and I were loading boxes of floor tiles on to a barrow, when one of the officers from the toyshop in the boys' wing went past. He was a Chelsea supporter, and when I was working in the toyshop he would bet me a Mars bar that Chelsea would beat West Ham. If Chelsea won, I had to give him a Mars bar, and he would give me one if West Ham won, but somehow I always got the Mars bar back.

As he passed me he stopped and said, 'You were lucky at the weekend.' (West Ham had drawn three all with Chelsea.)

I laughed and said, 'Saved you a Mars bar.'

He laughed and moved on.

Frank turned to me and said, 'What you talking to him for, you a nonce or what?'

'Oh, go away,' I said and turned away.

Suddenly I felt him rush at me, so I turned round, grabbed his arm, and threw him on the tiles. We were dragged apart, and when asked what was going on, we both said we were just messing about. We were told to stop fighting and to load the tiles, but as I started to obey I saw his face, and I knew he wouldn't forget it.

We didn't speak for the rest of the morning. At lunchtime I went to my cell and then to the toilet area and started to wash. The little light there was in the room suddenly disappeared as if the sun was being eclipsed. I stood up and made out four heavy heavyweights, staring at me. Shit. One of them was Freddy Forman. Standing in the middle of the room, I thought it was the end for me. He asked me what the business was with Frank, and I told him.

Frank had tried to mug me off but had mugged himself off instead. Freddy looked at me and said, 'Serves him right, he's been a right pain lately.' Then they all left. Frank, who up until then had been fine with me, obviously had a lot on his mind, and whether it was the sentence, prison, waiting for parole, or family, had just snapped. Luckily no blood had been spilled. The next day he came up, said, 'Let's forget it, I was out of order.' I don't know if Freddy had said something to him. We worked together for a few more days, until I was allocated to a civilian worker called Tom, who was tiling floors. I stayed with Tom until he left the service and started painting and decorating on his own, and when I was released I went to work for him. He was a wonderful guy, non-judgemental, hard-working, straight as they come. I was delighted when, years later, Tom was best man at my wedding.

When we worked evenings to finish the job, Tom would bring extra sandwiches and apple pie in, always with the explanation that his wife had given him too much, and so I'd best eat them. This became a running gag, and after about a week of this, as he dropped me back at D wing, I said, 'Have a good weekend, and could you ask your wife to make extra rhubarb pie for next week?' He laughed and off he went. Monday night: rhubarb pie.

I was still doing the drama group, and still playing the leads. When Tom was off or working on prison officers' houses, I was assigned to another party, another civilian worker. The second day his main man wasn't there and all morning he kept looking at me.

'Got a problem with me?' I asked.

'Yeah, I have,' he replied.

'With my work?'

He pulled me to one side and said, 'Would you do me a favour?'

'Depends . . .'

'Look, mate, there's some tobacco in it for you.'

Always interested in tobacco, I perked up.

'OK, what?'

'Take this here tobacco to . . .'

He proceeded to pass me four green bags pulled tight with a drawstring and told me to take my shirt off. I did this, and he hung one bag on each shoulder, so they hung down by my arms; the other two he put around my waist, so they hung between my legs, and he told me to practise walking. At first it was something out of *The Great Escape*, the scene where they are transferring dirt from the tunnel to the vegetable patch. Fortunately, I made it to the prisoner and got rid of the stuff. This went on for a few days.

One day I was standing in the works department, where we were being checked at lunchtime, when a lorry pulled up. This officer who was a right pig — no one liked him, least of all the other officers — looked at me beadily.

'Unload that fucking truck.'

'Did did you grunt, sir?' I replied.

'Unload that fucking truck!' he screamed.

'Why me?'

'Because I fucking well told you to, cunt.'

Naturally my first instinct was not to comply, so I said, 'Unload it yourself.'

He went ballistic and charged me with refusing an order, and I was taken to my cell. Luckily, I didn't have any tobacco with me — mind you, the amount I had been carrying the last few days it was a wonder that the tobacco companies hadn't run out.

When I went in front of the Governor, the officer gave his evidence. I had to look at him twice to make sure it was the same bloke, because his diction was perfect, there was no mention of the F or C word; he sounded like some voice coach at the Royal Shakespeare Company. I couldn't hold my tongue and launched into a tirade, said he was lying. He had never been guilty of speaking the Queen's English and what he said was bollocks. Don't know why I bothered . . . Three days' bread and water and loss of privileges, banged up.

As I was sitting in the empty punishment cell — the bed and bedding had to be taken out each morning and only returned at night — I could hear keys in the door, and there was Pascall from the library with my paper. I told him I had lost my privileges, and that papers were a privilege. Pascall said no I could have my paper. He left, and as I opened the paper five roll-ups fell out along with some matches and a piece of matchbox. Puzzled, I looked for somewhere to hide them, which in an empty cell was nigh impossible, so I put them on the window recess outside. I knew I couldn't smoke them during the day – too obvious.

Lunchtime came and I looked forward with relish to my culinary delight of bread and water: four slices of bread and as much water as you could drink. As the door opened I could smell real food, and when I held out my hand to get the bread I saw a tray of fish and chips being thrust at me. I queried it, thinking it was a ploy to get me more punishment, and told the officer that he had made a mistake. 'No,' he said, 'no mistake,' and slammed the door shut. I sat looking at the tray and, after a while, decided I would eat. All the time, as I put mouthful after mouthful into me, I waited for the door to burst open, but it never did. The next day was the same and the third day too. Apparently the Governor, who wasn't stupid, knew exactly what the officer who had nicked me was about, and if I hadn't have lost my cool, I would have got off with a warning. He had had to make a show of it for the officer's sake. He told the Chief to arrange it. I was living a charmed life.

Sadly, on Tom's return, he had decided to pack up working for the prison service, and started his own business. I stayed with the works department for a few weeks, and a mate of mine, who was the education department clerk, said the cleaner was leaving, and why didn't I apply for the job. The education department knew me because of the drama group and so I applied and was accepted. The education block was only used in the evenings, so it was pretty much of a doddle: sweeping, mopping, preparing the rooms for evening classes (mostly art and woodwork) and making tea. The chap in charge was an Irishman who had been there years; he had an assistant, a woman who was always suffering from migraines, and a resident member of staff of German extraction who really thought she was something.

After I had been there for a while, it was decided that the education system needed to be overhauled and full-time education started: English as a second language, O-levels and A-levels. A whizz-kid came in to run it and soon he was interviewing teachers.

A mixed bunch they were too. Laurence, who was the clerk, and myself had to show them around the education block and make them tea and coffee. These interviews went on for days. None I met stick in my mind, except for one young lady who sat on the floor, because of a lack of chairs. It was very hot and she had on a loose, summery skirt, and as I entered the staff room I could see right up it. As God is my judge, she was wearing no knickers. I asked her if she wanted a drink and she did, so I made her one and went to find Laurence, reported what I had seen, and returned to the staff room. I could see even more now. Laurence entered, looked, said, 'Got it,' and then left. Unfortunately for us, she didn't get the job, but she did fill in for the art teacher in the borstal wing – those lucky borstal boys!

By this time in my prison career, fresh evidence about my offence was beginning to emerge. Two prisoners, who had been locked up in an army cell with the main witnesses at my trial, had come forward with new information. This was handed to my solicitors, who had the appeal reopened. After examining the new evidence, a date for my appeal was set. The main witness, Kenneth Nelson, could not be located as he was working around the country roof tiling. So the judge, instead of making it the responsibility of the defence to ensure the attendance of witnesses, ruled that it was the prosecution's responsibility. The appeal was therefore adjourned until the witness could be found.

When Nelson was found, I returned to the Old Bailey in October 1969. As my escort handed me over, the person in charge of the holding cells told him to leave as I would be going home. Of course, my escort raced back and told everyone, including my Dad, who was outside. After all the evidence was given, the army's QC asked to talk to the judge in private. It was a different judge from the first adjourned appeal – he was dealing with the Krays' appeal – and on the judge's return from his chambers, the verdict was appeal dismissed; he would give his reasons later. About three weeks later, a five-page rationale, quoting cases going back to about 1721, appeared in a national newspaper. I wasn't appealing about the killing – I had admitted that – it was the severity of the sentence and its classification. When I got back to prison, inmates and officers couldn't believe it; they had been told I had been released. I don't think they were upset I hadn't got off; they were more upset that my cell wasn't empty. People were queueing up for it.

The education block in the summer break had been tarted up, with new desks and overhead projectors, and textbooks covering everything from maths to Spanish. With the new facilities came the new staff. It really was a new era in the education block; it attracted many pupils, some obviously to further their education, some just to skive or meet and impress new people from outside.

The staff seemed a great bunch and they really cared. They were mostly male teachers, though two were female. After one lesson, one of the female teachers came up to me.

'Les, could I have a word?' she asked.

'Yes,' I said.

'I just wanted to tell you that I'm leaving.'

'Oh . . . but why?'

'I don't know, maybe I'm not right for this job. You see, I've become very attached to one of the prisoners. But, please, keep this to yourself.'

'I'm not going to say a word.'

'Thanks.'

'Whoever he is, he's a very lucky bloke. Does he know?'

'No.'

'Well, do what you've got to do. By the way, who is it?'

'You.'

I nearly fell out of my chair. 'Maybe we should talk later.'

In the meantime, Laurence had moved to a new prison specifically for lifers who were in for domestic crimes, and as he had killed either his wife or girlfriend this was considered a domestic crime. So I was doing the clerking and the cleaning.

After this revelation from my teacher, I made sure that I was picked up early from lunch so we could have a clandestine meeting in the stock room or in an empty classroom.

Mind you, I was spending a fortune on mints and toothpaste. We nearly got caught once by the art teacher; although he never mentioned it.

I had written a play, called *As Trains Go By*, with another prisoner who was on the stage management course. It wasn't wonderful, but we put it on and it went very well, so we started to write another. By the time, I'd finished the play I was told I was being transferred. I had had a visit from my local MP, who was still with the Home Office, but moved up a notch. I was going to Portsmouth, Kingston Prison, where Laurence had gone. I was confused. (Which was pretty much the case with most of the decisions involving me while I was in prison.)

I knew that the majority of staff and prisoners in the Scrubs couldn't make me out: I was in the drama group and wasn't gay. I had in fact changed the drama group around; it was no longer a refuge for homosexuals, it was now a group where prisoners who wanted to act could do so, without being labelled gay, which in prison doesn't really have an upside.

I didn't conform to the prisoner stereotype. Each prisoner had to be angry when they arrived, then soften and then repent. Although I felt remorse for what I had done, in order to cope (as best as I could) I just got on with it as a job. Well, it was only the army without weekend leave. I also keep my feelings to myself, no way was I going to show any weakness, not to 1,700 prisoners, each and every one looking for a chink in others' armour. But what puzzled me was why I was being sent to a prison full of domestic offenders. Apparently it was an experiment. When I was told this I asked if it was a similar experiment to the time we were given cigarettes made of wood chip to smoke, or when the meat was substituted with soya.

I told my teacher friend, who was very disappointed, but she did promise to visit me. Fortunately, I didn't have time to dwell on our parting.

The journey to Portsmouth was like all the others: just a glimpse of the outside. I wasn't in one of those vans you now see transporting prisoners to and from court; it was a standard green coach. But although I was a windowpane away from the outside world, I couldn't touch it, despite having embraced it with our lovemaking sessions in the education block.

10

OH, I DO LOVE TO BE BESIDE THE SEASIDE

Portsmouth Prison was a refurbished young offenders' prison that had now been turned into a prison for lifers. But to placate the locals, after their protests about this unwelcome influx into the community, they were told that inmates would be domestic killers, who had killed wives, girlfriends, lovers, mothers, fathers, sisters and their kids – and cats and dogs too, I guess. My arrival didn't go down well with staff or inmates. The staff had basically to look after non-violent prisoners. Non-violent? Did they blow on their victims, then, to kill them? The prisoners thought that their easy lifestyle was going to change, with someone like me there. Like me . . . they really thought they were a superior breed, and that I was the scum of the earth. Yes, I had killed a man; the end result, though, was exactly the same: someone had died. And in some cases several had died, whether it was the girlfriend who had her head blown off with a shotgun, or the wife's lover who had been axed, the wayward daughter who had been cut to pieces, the children (all four of them) drowned in the bath, the mother and father hung upside down by their feet, and then systematically kicked to death, because they wanted their son to clean his room.

Portsmouth had an open-door policy. By that I don't mean the front door was left open, but the cell doors. It also had a policy of bringing in outside groups, such as darts teams, table tennis, badminton and football teams to play the inmates. Apart from the football teams, these were mixed, men and women. The drama group was thriving, and I was asked to join, which of course I did. The outside actors were from the local amateur group; they were so enthusiastic, and contained some great singers, so we did a lot of musicals. Whereas I had been the leading light in the Scrubs, here I was just a bit player. Which was fine by me.

Portsmouth had a great education officer, and Laurence was his clerk or orderly. The only other major work in the prison was the electrical shop, although 'electrical shop' was a slight distortion of the truth; the prisoners sat around a huge table and assembled dimmer switches, each prisoner assembling one piece. When the dimmer switch reached the end of the line it was checked and then passed back in reverse order until it was disassembled. When that was done, we started all over again.

On arrival at Portsmouth Prison, I had the usual medical, but no bath.

On my second day as an electrical genius, the prison psychiatrist came into the electrical shop and spoke to each prisoner individually. When he came to me he introduced himself and asked my name. Seeing as how he had my file under his arm, I am pretty sure he knew who I was, especially since I was the only new prisoner in the place.

'How are you getting on?' he said.

'I could think of better things to do with my time than this shit.'

'What do you mean?'

So I let him have it: 'What kind of work is this?'

'For rehabilitation.'

'Oh, really? Who came up with this crap?'

'I did.'

'Really? In that case you're as mad as your patients.'

(He had said he was the resident psychiatrist in the local mental ward.)

The only thing experimental about my being here was holding on to my temper . . . any more days in this shop would send me nuts. After breakfast, on my third day, I realized that I couldn't go back to the electrical shop, so I turned on my heel and returned to my cell, closing the door behind me.

Within five minutes the door opened and an officer said, 'Sorry, I thought I had unlocked you.'

'You did. I've banged myself up.'

'But why?' he asked.

'I'm refusing labour,' I said. Well, I might have said that I had just given birth to twins, he looked so gobsmacked.

'You can't refuse labour.'

'Why not?'

'No one has ever . . .' he stammered.

'Welcome to the latest entry to the *Guinness Book of Records*!' I shouted after him as he legged it down the landing, obviously going to ask someone's opinion on what to do.

I hoped they would quickly work out what to do and send me back to the Scrubs.

Within ten minutes an Assistant Governor arrived at my cell, and asked if it was true that I was refusing labour. I said it was. He looked at me with the same incredulous look as the prison officer had and after a while he too ran down the landing. Obviously the think tank was being assembled. Suddenly a huge amount of activity started up below; gates were slammed, keys were rattled and footsteps pounded up the stairs and made their way to my cell. I braced myself for the beating that might follow, but no, the Governor stood there with four officers. I was sitting on my bed, but stood up as he entered the cell. He sent the four officers away.

'What's the problem?' he asked.

'The only thing the dimmer switch is going to make dimmer is me,' I said.

He looked at me, and said, 'Yes, you're right. Wait in your cell, and I'll sort something out.'

I stayed in my cell till lunchtime and after being let out to eat made my way back to my cell, when suddenly I was called out and told to report to the education block. The education officer had an idea that, in conjunction with Portsmouth College, we would put together a slide slow and write the scripts for a learning aid. Great idea, and after a while the next new inmate arriving joined me.

The play I had co-written was being put on in the Scrubs, and I had to go back and watch it, so I was taken up in a car under escort but not handcuffed. On arriving back at the Scrubs I was put back in the long-term wing and even had a cell which had a better view than my old one. The play was well received; the audience laughed a lot. While at the Scrubs I had been allowed to borrow a typewriter from the education block and use it in my cell. After several days hanging around in the long-term wing, I was to be taken back to Portsmouth, not in a nice car but a prison bus. I was handcuffed to another prisoner and we headed towards Portsmouth, but instead of stopping there, we went on the ferry to the Isle of Wight and dropped some prisoners off. As we pulled into the prison, the reception officer came out, saw me handcuffed and said, 'Get those handcuffs off him,' and then launched a string of verbal abuse at my escorts: 'Don't you ever handcuff one of my prisoners again,' he said, and followed it with descriptions of their brains and anything else he could conjure up in his Scouse accent. I had to double check that I had been dropped at the right prison.

I had applied for, and received permission to have a typewriter sent in, but again, like the refusal of labour, no one had ever been asked for one before. After a while I was given permission, and I applied to do a playwriting course to justify having it. It wasn't sufficient to have written two plays that had been performed, albeit in prison; some obscure rule, buried somewhere deep so no one knew about it, insisted that you had to be registered on a creative writing course, so I had found one in a correspondence course booklet.

I also wrote to several television channels to see if they had a television script I could look at to understand scriptwriting. I was sent camera scripts of an afternoon children's show, so I used my afternoons watching the television in the education block and working out what the differences were between a camera script and a normal script. I also watched other dramas and wrote poetry, so the education officer thought it might be useful if I had someone look at my writing. I did get a certificate from the scriptwriting course, although I think because of my address they were being generous.

The first person to read what I'd written was a man who obviously came just to be nosey; we had nothing in common whatsoever: he was a deputy headmaster. The education officer admitted this wasn't going to work out, but he had another option: a woman who was teaching English as a foreign language, and was unsuccessfully trying to teach an Indian prisoner to speak English.

She arrived and seemed very pleasant, but our conversation always turned to sex, not directly, but in general chitchat. I asked if she had driven here, and she said no, she didn't drive, but came by bus, and she couldn't help noticing all the adverts on the way, of women eating bananas. Everything was so suggestive. We came to the end of the lesson and she went to see the education officer and obviously told him she liked my stuff and wanted to help, so he said she could visit me every Tuesday.

Either she was making innocent remarks, and I had read them wrong, or she was a wind-up merchant, and thought it clever to tease a prisoner. So I decided to play her at her own game. I wrote about a dozen poems, some ordinary and some with hidden, poetic sexual meanings. I prepared to watch her reaction.

The first play the drama group, KADS (Kingston Amateur Dramatic Society) decided to do was *Oh! What a Lovely War*. When I wasn't working on the visual aids and doing rehearsals, I was taking part in all the outside-oriented activities, because some of the inmates there had known me from the Scrubs, or because of my involvement with the drama group, I was invited to go and play darts and badminton when the outside teams came in. The people who came in were a mixed bunch, and came from all different walks of life. The drama group outsiders, as I have said, were very talented and the director was called Eric. Two of the members, Keith and Christine, still keep in touch, and come to see me whenever I am performing near where they live. The badminton was run by Joe Fryer, the gym officer, and during my time in all these activities I met Len Philips, who used to be centre half for Portsmouth. He and his wife were great champions of organizing activities for the inmates, and his son used to bring in a local football team to play the prisoners.

On the following Tuesday I handed the teacher the poems I had written. After she read each one, she would tell me where I was going wrong. As she got to the ones that had hidden connotations, I could see that she obviously understood them. She said that I clearly had a talent, and that she had thought a lot about me during the past week. What she meant I didn't ask and let it pass over, and she set me an exercise for the following week, about dreams. We went our separate ways. I was right: she was a tease, a wind-up merchant, because again she had made a few suggestive remarks.

Because of the relaxed yet contained environment, prisoners could go out on to the football pitch at breaks, and exercise was not just walking around a yard. The prison had been made escape-proof by a huge metal blanket curled over the outer walls which made them impossible to scale. The marines had been called in to see how long they would take to escape, and as it had taken a long time, what had been an experiment at Portsmouth became standard in most prisons. The inner buildings, on the other hand, had been designed so that the education and visiting areas could be monitored by the naked eye from any part of the prison. It was in effect a goldfish bowl.

The visual aid stuff was taking shape. We were starting with Crete and Mykonos, and it was great fun collating all the information, although it was pretty tedious waiting for new material to arrive. In my lull periods, I kept working on my next assignment. The teacher from the Scrubs had been to see me, and so had other friends and family, so things were back to normal.

There was a huge shower area and laundry room down below the ground floor, where we could do our own laundry. As I went down there one day to do mine, I came upon a sight that I still can't believe: one of the younger prisoners was having sex with this older Hungarian prisoner. As the young bloke saw me he stopped, and as he stood up, I saw stapled – yes, stapled – to his back, the centrefold of a *Mayfair* or *Penthouse* magazine. The Hungarian, by all accounts, was into pain and had been known to pay people to beat him with a coat hanger. Whenever I ventured into the shower area, I tried to make sure he wasn't there.

I remember once I was working in the kitchen, basically in charge as the chef had the day off. The chap who cleaned the dining area was butch, and very pleasant, but he did have a very short fuse, and many a time and oft, as William Shakespeare would have put it, he had been known to trash his cell and throw the tables and chairs around the dining area, just because of something trivial, like his mop string getting caught in a chair, or because someone hadn't returned his plate. So he was not one to annoy when riled. He was a compulsive obsessive: he showered six or seven times a day, and was continually washing his hands and pouring water over his head. I thought maybe he was an arsonist, or an ex-frogman. Anyhow, he saw me in the kitchen and asked why I wasn't playing football, because I normally was. I told him it was my turn to run the kitchen. I offered him a cup of tea as I was making one and we sat down on one of the tables in the kitchen – no way was I going to mess up his tables – and had a cigarette. I said I was going to my cell to have a doze until it was teatime.

I was lying on my bed fully dressed, apart from my boots. I had had a shower and changed into clean whites, when he appeared with a cup of tea and handed it to me. He made to leave, then turned back and made to grab my crotch through my white kitchen trousers. I jumped up and said, 'What are you playing at?'

'Ah, look . . . I'm . . . very . . . sorry,' he stammered. 'I . . . just . . . thought . . .'

I felt sorry for him, so I said, 'Look, don't worry about it.'

He now started to cry.

'Don't worry, mate, just sit there. It'll be all right.' I said.

I had my record player by the bed on a table and switched it on. Marvin Gaye's 'Come Get to This' blasted out. Uh-oh, wrong choice. Straight away, I switched it off and said I was going back to the kitchen, hoping he wouldn't trash my cell. As I was leaving the kitchen later, he grabbed my arm as I went up the stairs, looked at me and said with wide, staring eyes, 'You won't tell anyone will you?' There was no way I would have anyway, but with that look it was 200 per cent certain I wasn't going to.

At the next session with the teacher, I put plan two into action. I had completed the assignment she had given me, and had made it as sexually explicit as I could. When she asked me how I had been, I told her I had had trouble sleeping. Then I dropped my bombshell: I told her that I thought that this should be my last session with her. She looked shocked, and asked me why. I then did the whole number: I couldn't possibly tell her . . . I felt embarrassed about it. Bloody hell, I should have been an actor the way I was bringing her in. She told me not to be silly, that she was an adult, and that I could be honest with her. So I told her. I said I had been fantasizing about her and was embarrassed to admit it. She wanted me to go through my fantasies with her. So after a few rather good stuttering starts, I told her how she had invaded my night thoughts . . . how I had dreamed she had arrived at our lesson, wearing nothing on underneath her coat. She then told me how she had had naughty thoughts too, and would I write all this stuff down. I refused in case it was found and got us into trouble. As she left, I said I was sorry if I had embarrassed her, and would understand if she didn't want to see me again. 'Oh no,' she said, 'I am looking forward to next week, even more so now. But remember to write those thoughts down.'

I kept trying to see how I could reduce the goldfish bowl effect and I realized that if I moved each of the cupboards a fraction it would reduce the visibility from the outside, while seemingly staying the same. As I arrived for my next lesson, the education officer came out of his office and said, 'I am afraid that your lesson . . .' – my heart sank: she wasn't coming in – 'she's going to be a little late.' I said, 'Thanks. No big deal.' In the classroom I checked that the cupboards hadn't been shifted back and moved the table and chairs a bit so as to us give a bit more privacy from prying eyes. Not that I expected anything to happen, but as Baden Powell said, be prepared.

Eventually she arrived, looking as she normally did, and she apologized for her lateness. After the usual pleasantries and an analysis of my last week's work, she suddenly opened her coat and revealed that she was naked, apart from bra and panties. She had travelled on a bus dressed like that?! When I commented on this, she said she was really self-conscious and at the gate of the prison had panicked and nearly turned back. Thank God she didn't.

In the meantime the visual aids had come to a full stop as the college had decided that funding for the project would not be forthcoming. I was out of work as a result, but thankfully I wasn't going back to the dimmer switches. I was going into the kitchen to work, and after a while I started to make bread, biscuits and desserts. Although hard work, being the baker was the best job an inmate could have: you got up early and started everything off and when it was done, you had the rest of the day off. This allowed me to sunbathe, write or just chill out.

Also, being the baker suddenly made me a lot of money. Out of the blue, there was a national bread strike, and the prison department was in a quandary, not about whether to follow it – I am sure they knew that I couldn't go on strike – but obviously it would be odd if the prisoners had bread and the prison staff didn't. So, after a high-powered meeting involving the Governor, the officers and the chef, there was a flurry of activity. I was summoned to the Governor's office and informed, off the record, that I would be making extra bread each day. Would that be OK? I asked how I was going to be able to stretch the flour, and I was told it was in hand. No way were the prisoners going to stand for their bread rations being reduced, and obviously I would be under a lot of extra pressure if that happened. Extra flour was purchased, I made the bread and the officers picked it up. I forget how long the strike went on for, but when it finished I was called to the Chief's office and given a tin of money, which the officers had donated for each loaf. After the cost of materials had been taken out, I had £37, which was going to be put in my private account. I had also been dropped the odd packet of cigarettes along the way, so I was quids in.

Being in charge of the entertainment at the prison meant that you had to try and arrange variety shows to come in on a Sunday night. This was easy: the amount of talent around the Portsmouth and Southampton areas was phenomenal, so I would write to local entertainment agencies and they would help out, sometimes trying out new acts. We had a group called Buster, who were a cross between Slade and the Bay City Rollers, plus others like Shep Wooley, who was a navy man and very funny and sang great stuff. Trouble was that Portsmouth Prison was full of prisoners who had it handed to them on a plate and so lethargy was rife. In the end it was pointless arranging anything for them, as they were never happy. There wasn't a night when there were no activities going on, but even then the majority wanted just to sit in their cells or watch television.

One night I was lying in my cell learning my lines for the next play. In Portsmouth the light switches were inside the cells, so you controlled when you turned them off yourself. Suddenly the door of the cell opened and standing there was the man whose brilliant idea it had been to assemble and disassemble the dimmer switches: the prison psychiatrist.

'Lucky you found me in,' I said. That went straight over his head.

'Get dressed and come with me,' he replied.

I knew I hadn't been acting strangely lately but then again anything out of the norm in prison could be classified as strange. I did wonder if I was being nutted off, but as I got dressed and went outside the cell to meet him, I was relieved when I saw there were no men in white coats with him.

'Come follow me.' He made to close my door.

'Am I going to come back?'

'Oh yes.'

'Don't worry about closing it; no one's going to break in.'

He led me to the kitchen area. My first thought was that if he wanted a cup of tea he could have helped himself, there was no need to get me out of bed at nearly midnight to make it. As I arrived at the dining area, though, I saw a man sitting in a chair. The psychiatrist introduced him as Bruno. I was told that this man's wife had been having an affair with a wrestler, and he had been determined to kill them both. The police had found Bruno running through the streets with a huge carving knife looking for them, and had taken him to the psychiatric unit at the local hospital.

The psychiatrist, in his wisdom, had decided it might be a good thing if an inmate, who had killed someone, spoke to him and tried to talk him out of it. Why me? I could only hazard a guess, unless of course my light was the only one on . . . but I doubt it. So, I did my bit. I kept saying that it was a stupid thing to do . . . why would he . . . prisons are dreadful places . . . the usual banter. But Bruno kept saying he didn't care . . . he was going to kill them . . . and if he was locked up, he would do it when he got out.

Now Bruno was a pretty heavily built bloke, and the angrier he was the more animated he became. Trying to persuade him to stop being violent was ridiculous. This roundabout conversation went on for hours. I was becoming more tired while he seemed to be getting more alert.

Eventually, I decided that it was pointless talking to him, and just turned around and said, 'Oh for fuck's sake, kill them then. Stop talking about it – go and do it. In fact there's a whole bunch of sharp knives in the kitchen. Choose one and fuck off and do it . . .'

Suddenly, he stopped ranting and burst into tears, saying, 'No . . . no . . . I love her. I couldn't hurt her.'

Well, no way could I be a psychiatrist, or if I were I'd be a poor one. I'd actually wanted to tell him to do it about three hours before, but hadn't in case it wasn't what the psychiatrist wanted. No wonder they keep the sessions going for days and days; it justifies their fees.

As we both watched Bruno sob his heart out, I touched him on the shoulder and said, 'Good luck mate, I'm going to bed. Hope you and your wife can work it out.'

The psychiatrist looked at me and smiled and said, 'Thank you, well done, brilliant.'

'I'll see myself home.' Again, this went over his head. 'By the way, what's going to happen to Bruno?'

'Oh, he'll stay in the ward for a few days and then go home, once the police have decided what to do,' he replied.

Later, when I bumped into the psychiatrist, I asked him how Bruno was and he said that he and his wife had gone away on holiday to make up with each other.

I had made my parole application and went about my business as usual. Christmas Eve came; we had made the Christmas cake and puddings months before, and were getting the turkeys ready for the next day, when I was called to the wing office and told that my application for parole had been turned down. I was not to be considered again for seven years . . . A seven-year knock-back was unheard-of. I said fine, and made my way to the kitchen – not really comprehending, or maybe not wanting to show my absolute distress – where several others had heard that they had been granted parole, and were whooping with joy. What a Christmas present for them . . . still, hopefully, my star of the East would be there one Christmas.

I have no memory of anything that night.

After breakfast we were all banged up, as it was Christmas Day and, apart from those who went to church, most people stayed in their cells until lunch. No sooner had the door closed on me than the officer in charge of the sick bay opened it and told me to follow him to it. As we arrived he offered me a cup of coffee and asked if I was OK. I said yes and he asked if I wanted to phone my parents and wish them a happy Christmas. I said OK and when I did, I mentioned to them that my parole had been turned down, but made no mention of the seven years. 'Better luck next time, eh? Have a nice Christmas.' I hung up. The officer offered me a Scotch bottle and asked if I wanted some in my coffee. I said yes, all the time wondering what was going on. Was this a ploy to keep me out of the way while the prison officers went through my cell to see if I had a noose or a knife to top myself? He also showed me something very interesting: my medical reports, and, most important of all, the psychiatric report. Now that made interesting reading. The psychiatrist who had got me to talk a man out of killing his wife and lover felt that I was unstable and should not be released! I was furious, but the sick bay officer said, 'You can't quote this, you'll get me sacked.'

My cell was exactly the way I had left it, but the prison officers had been up to something. Although I was not their favourite prisoner, they had been upset that I had got such a huge knock-back, while one prisoner, who had killed his four children by drowning them, and had tried to blame his wife, had got parole first time; and another who had skinned his wife alive, or something equally horrific, was about to be released.

I thought that because I was not a domestic lifer, having a prisoner with such a huge parole refusal in the establishment might upset the status quo. But no, the prison staff had forced the Governor to come in on Christmas Day and, while the prisoners were banged up, had told him that it wasn't on, that he must try and do something about my situation. All this I found out later. Lunch was late that Christmas. Meanwhile, I had to get on with it and although I was bitterly disappointed there was nothing I could do about it. The Governor, prompted by the staff, had petitioned the Home Office, although they had not knocked me back; that had been the army's doing. Although serving my sentence in a civilian prison, I was still under the jurisdiction of the army, regarding release. It seems that, after all these years, the army was still intent on making an example out of me.

Unbeknown to me, all the staff had signed a petition, apart from the psychiatrist. A few days after Christmas, I was called to the Governor's office and told I was being moved. I knew it, back to London or even Albany Prison . . . but the Governor's next words shook me, as if someone had stuck a red-hot poker in my back: I was being moved to Leyhill Prison. That couldn't be right, I thought, Leyhill was an open prison, where prisoners went to finish the last part of their sentences, or where non-violent or non-security risks went. But no, I wasn't imagining it, I was to be moved as soon as the paperwork could be done, which might take a while as everything else shut down, but not the prison service. The Governor told me to go back to work.

As I made my way to the kitchen I suddenly realized that a whole new chapter was opening up for me. The next few days seemed never to come to an end. I was exhausted by the time I hit my bed, not because of the work – that hadn't changed, in fact I was doing less as I had handed over the role of baker to someone else – but by the tension of waiting to hear when I would move. All the inmates and most of the staff were pleased for me that I was going. In the end I found out who had been behind the move: it had been engineered by the chief officer and one or two others. Bloody hell, my breadmaking must have been good . . .

I was finally told when I was to move, and the night before, I cleaned out my cell, packed my stuff and said my farewells. As I made my way to reception, a few of the staff and the Governor came to wish me good luck. Apparently most of the officers had asked to escort me, probably to make sure I was gone for good. As I passed through one gate to the other, who should come in and say, 'Well, good luck!' but the psychiatrist himself. He offered his hand, and I looked him in the eye and said, quite calmly and collectedly, 'CUNT!'

11

WALLS BUT NO WALLS

After what seemed for ever we came off the motorway and made our way down a series of narrow country lanes between an endless stream of fields and stone walls. Suddenly to our right there appeared a large country house, and then what appeared to be row after row of army-style barracks. As we drew nearer I could see the sign, HMP Leyhill. We turned right and stopped at a barrier. There were no great wooden or iron gates, no barbed wire, just a fairly low wall surrounding the prison area. So it really was an open prison.

Once inside I went through the usual checks, but this time there was no bath; obviously no perverts working in this reception. From reception I took my own possessions and my bedding and with a prison officer was escorted up a long covered corridor past row after row of huts to the orderly room, where I was handed over and then shown to my hut. This was just like the barrack hut I was stationed in when I'd been a boy soldier at Oswestry. I entered the hut. Inside the main doorway there were three or four rooms with proper doors, and these, I found out, were occupied by long-term prisoners. As each one of these was released, the next one on the waiting list for a room would be moved in.

The hut, when full, contained prisoners serving various lengths of sentence, from three months to life. Several familiar faces from

Portsmouth had heard I was here and came over to say hello. Security was relaxed; many of the inmates attended local colleges, and there were groups that paid visits to various outside locations. The bird club paid two or three visits a year to bird shows; the drama group saw several plays a year at either Bristol or Bath; the literary society had debates and theatre visits. And at weekends a large number of prisoners did resettlement work in and around the surrounding area.

Apparently for the first few weeks after arrival at Leyhill everyone had to work in the garden party, which basically assessed you to see what form of employment you were suited for. This was done while you spent weeks picking up stones in the pouring rain and transporting them to a pile somewhere else in the prison. As the stones never seemed to get fewer and the prison – which had originally been built during the war as a hospital for American servicemen who had contracted venereal diseases – had had this stone ritual ever since it had been converted from military hospital to prison, some inmates thought the trainee prison officers went out at night and redistributed the stones. All this to keep the inmates on the stone detail gainfully employed. Rather fanciful, I know, but it did sound feasible to many of the boys in grey.

I must say that, having looked out of my cubicle window and taken in the grey, wet weather, the prospect of spending ten hours a day picking up stones didn't really set my pulse racing. Fortunately, the window I looked out of had no bars on it, and opened out like any normal house window. I wouldn't be working the next day, as it was a day for my guided tour and for seeing doctors. God, I have spent more time, healthy, seeing doctors in prison, than I have with illness in my life outside.

Amazingly, Leyhill's doors were not locked, although the inmates of the rooms in the hut locked their doors during the day, and unless there was an inspection they kept them locked. Strange, really, after years being locked in and being escorted from A to B, even if it was only fifty yards, to be in a prison with no locks or bars, being trusted to make your own way about the place. It really did seem odd that someone should want to do the prison officers' job for them and lock their own doors, but I guess that it was a property issue rather than

113

a prison security issue. Although since my release I have been back to Leyhill, when I was asked to launch some charity stamp appeal, and the huts have now been replaced by brick buildings which are locked.

That night, as was usual after lights out, a rather noisy night watchman came round and checked the numbers. Several inmates had decided they would hop over the wall and, being met outside by a mate, they changed into civvies and visited a local pub. As they ordered their drinks and sat down to enjoy them, they were interrupted by the arrival of two prison officers, who escorted them back in a minibus. Apparently they had made the mistake that many others before them had made: of popping into a pub that was owned by an ex-prison officer. The following day they were shipped off to a closed prison. I guess the moral of the story is: if you're going to drink while at Leyhill, drive to a pub well away from the prison.

After running the gauntlet of a guided tour, which entailed being shown the welfare office and main administration block, I was shown the sports fields, which included football, rugby and cricket and tennis facilities. Maybe I am wrong, but I am sure there was also a bowling green, but sadly no swimming pool. Some inmates had golf clubs, which they would take up to the playing fields to practise driving and putting. There was a church, where if you were a regular churchgoer, every month your family could go to church with you. This gave inmates another extra visit. I suppose the prison church at Leyhill had the best-attended services in the West Country.

I was told to report to the orderly room, where I was to be allocated work; and as I was told repeatedly on my first day by the inmates and all the next morning by the various prison departments, I would be on the stone detail. I therefore reported as asked to the orderly room, dreading the stone detail, when to my surprise I was sent to the kitchen, where I was put to work on the breadmaking. Obviously my breadmaking skills, forged at Portsmouth, had earned me a glowing report. No one could believe I had escaped the stone detail. But I fortunately had.

The kitchen job was a doddle. Bill, who was in charge, was an easygoing prison officer who also ran the officers' club. If you did your work and kept the kitchen clean and no one complained about the food, he was happy. The number-one inmate in the kitchen, who basically carried out Bill's instructions, also cleaned the club and helped out with the prison officers' kids' playgroup. We used to be at the kitchen at 5 a.m. to prepare the bread for the following day, while others got breakfast ready, then we'd do the desserts for lunch and buns for tea and supper. After breakfast, when we'd finished our jobs, the rest of the day was ours. In the good weather, this meant we could sunbathe all day. After a while, I became the number one and worked in the club and the playgroup. The wives seemed to like me, so I also helped with the kids.

Obviously, I was asked to join the drama group. However, everything here seemed to be run by committees. Each group had a council member who attended council meetings where the council chairman and his buddies okayed everything, although one of the Assistant Governors was officially in charge. As you can imagine, the councils were, more often than not, manned by budding future prime ministers and past government officials who had committed white-collar crimes. At the time T. Dan Smith was there, and he tended to bring in some of his old mates from his political career to give various talks to the groups he had set up.

T. Dan had been involved in a huge political scandal with John Poulson, and because of this, he was regarded by quite a few prisoners as the main man, although a lot thought otherwise. But his door was always open to everyone who needed advice. And T. Dan revelled in the attention he received. I can't actually recall if he did any work at all in the prison, but he was the theatre critic for the prison magazine, and also head of the literary society, and quite possibly also the head of the humanities group and the debating society. They sure loved a group and committee in Leyhill. After the disastrous prisoners' committee in the Scrubs I tended to shy away from anything like this again, but after a while I realized it was better to be on the inside than on the outside – committee-wise that is.

Mac, who had been in charge of building sets at Portsmouth, was stage manager in Leyhill. He was a brilliant carpenter, and his sets were superb. He obviously was one of the first to seek me out when

I arrived, and he demanded that I join the drama group. Like all the other drama groups I had been a member of, we had outside actresses coming in. An absolutely fantastic lady named Madge ran the group. At first she seemed very tough, somewhat similar to another great lady who was to shape my career and become a friend, the lovely Julia Smith.

Rehearsals took place in the evenings after work, and when the plays were performed they had the usual captive audience, as well as two nights of an outside audience, which included prison officers and their families. The visiting audience paid a small fee, and monies were also raised on the sale of tea, coffee and a raffle. This money would then be put back into the prisoners' committee main fund and each time a play was put on we had to apply to get money from this fund to stage it. Lights, costumes and furniture were usually hired from Bristol Old Vic.

The drama group was the biggest contributor to the fund, and after a while, it became harder to get the council to agree to fund our plays. Now, we are not talking thousands of pounds, possibly sums around the hundred-pound mark. As the council became more and more interested in its own self ('Hey, look at me, at how big I am', a type I had encountered all too often while I was inside), I decided to become interested, and was elected as the drama group's committee member. As I attended my first council meeting, I realized that, as I suspected, the prisoners' fund was being manipulated, not by the staff, but by the prisoners. In the first year at Leyhill, the prisoners received a new video, two new television sets and various other apparently impossible-to-obtain items, most of which had been purchased with money from revenue raised by the drama group.

I had regular contact with the hire companies we rented our stuff from. So when the opportunity came to get some equipment for peanuts – the lights we hired three times a year for something like £45 could be purchased for £25, plus a load of bulbs and other stuff thrown in – a huge saving was being made. On applying to the council, however, they couldn't see the sense of it, and were more worried about the fact that some inmate had taken a stroll round the grounds and had nearly fallen in the duck pond. Because of this nonsense, a vote of no confidence was called. After an election I was voted on to the council, and as soon as I had approved the purchase of the lamps, I resigned. Now, where there's a will . . .

The drama group flourished, mainly due to Madge, who had became more and more ambitious. We did *Look After Lulu* by Noël Coward, *Conduct Unbecoming*, *You Can't Take It with You*, *My Three Angels*, *Hot and Cold in All Rooms* and several others. Performances for outside audiences grew. And because of the quality of craftsman in the prison we were also able to sell lots of arts and crafts. The money was starting to roll in.

With working in the kitchen and helping out on the playgroup and cleaning the officers' club, my days were now pretty full, so I didn't have much chance to get bored. Three of my nights were taken up with the drama, and after a while I was asked by John Shergold, the liaison officer for the drama group, to join the literary society. When I asked why, he just looked at me blankly and said, 'More theatre trips.'

If you were a member of any group, there were several trips a year out of the prison, to university debating societies, or local bird shows and so on. Of course, if you were in the drama group you were allowed to go three times a year to Bristol Old Vic, or the Theatre Royal, Bath. Obviously any organization that had outside trips was oversubscribed, and the chairman of each group decided who went, usually his mates. In the case of the drama group, none of the actors actually went, but that soon changed when Mr Shergold was in charge. He had to vet and approve the final list. Prior to his taking over a list was submitted and approved without any real thought. I think on his first outing he actually did what others had done before him and simply said yes to the list of names submitted. But he actually had an interest in drama. By the time the second trip came around, he had worked out that none of the actors' names was ever submitted. So he changed that.

Shergold obviously knew I was deadly serious about acting, and that was the reason he asked me to join the literary society. The trip to the theatre was popular because you were allowed a half of beer in the interval. And it soon became obvious, as some people disappeared during the play, that they were only on the trip for the beer. I am sure Shergold knew he was missing half of the group during the show, but they always turned up to get back on the minibus at the end. In fact no one ever absconded. A lot of the prisoners who lived very close to the prison area tended to have friends pop in to see them – not that it was too obvious. One chap, in particular, who lived in Bath and owned several clubs, would disappear when the curtain went up and pop across the road to one of his clubs to see his girlfriend. Only once did I do it and it nearly went wrong.

Three of us had gone to the bar at the interval and found it closed, so we decided to pop across the road to the pub. As we walked in, who should be standing at the bar dressed in civvies, but the three most disciplinarian of Leyhill's prison officers, having a drink. Oh, shit.

They took one look at us and said, 'What are you doing?'

'The theatre bar is closed,' I said, quick as a flash. 'So Shergold sent us over to see if the pub across the road is half decent. But as you're here I'm sure it's not.'

They laughed and bought us a half each. Before they twigged that the other eighteen inmates weren't coming, we said something like, 'Well, the others must have found a better pub,' and we left. I don't know if they checked up with Shergold, but nothing was ever said.

My first trip to the theatre had been entirely different, and will always stick in my mind. We went to see *The Duchess of Malfi*. We had left the prison in a minibus, dressed in civvies. My brother Philip, who was my size, had sent me some of his old clothes. At first I had sort of balked at the idea, until they arrived and I then realized that Philip only ever wore something once – he really was a fashion slave – so the clothes that arrived were in pristine condition. I didn't look out of place, although I felt that everyone would know we were prisoners out on a cultural trip. As we arrived outside the theatre we disembarked, completely oblivious to the fact that there was traffic on the roads.

You have to realize that every time I had ever got off a prison vehicle it was always in a prison compound. As a car whizzed past me, missing me by inches, I realized just how much I had forgotten of the outside world and suddenly had a bout of agoraphobia and stood stock still, stuck to the pavement. Only Shergold's voice, saying, 'The theatre's over here,' woke me from my nightmare.

The world was a big place, and I had forgotten this, stuck in the small world of my own making for the past seven years. Once inside the theatre, there was another huge awakening. Never before had I been in a place so full of people who were not members of my school or regiment or prison wing. I was so in awe of my surroundings that I didn't take in much of the play. The interval came and we were all bought a drink by Shergold. Working in the officers' club I had had a beer given me by Bill, but this was unreal. The glass of beer in the officers' club was secretive and provided some taste of danger. This glass of beer, drunk while dressed in my own clothes surrounded by members of the public, although a great buzz, also made me realize what normality meant. In that brief moment, I sadly realized all those years I had lost by being stuck inside; I had lost my youth. But I couldn't dwell on it, or else I would have been driven out of my mind. Nevertheless, it certainly gave me something to look forward to.

We took our places for the next act, and I realized there were a few missing from our lot, and prayed that they returned so that the experience would not in future be taken from us. Prisoners are after all their own worst enemies. If anyone can fuck up a prisoner's life it's the prisoner himself. Thankfully, they returned and we made our way to the minibus and back to the prison. After changing back into our prison clothes, and not being searched, we went off to our huts after calling in at the orderly room to let the night patrol know we were back. As we made our way to our huts, various piles of contraband, tobacco and drink were unloaded from the other inmates' various pockets, and stashed in numerous hiding places.

Because I was paid half an ounce of tobacco every time I cleaned the club, I had a ready stash of tobacco, which I sold for inflated prices. This enabled me later to have cash to spend on shopping trips. The usual method was to have cash sent in to my own personal account in the prison, which could be spent only on things that were luxuries if approved by the Governor. Once the money was in I would hand over the tobacco. Also I would take part in other things at the officers' club. If they had a do I would help set it up and help Bill prepare the food for the event. These usually occurred every few weeks and this work was also paid in tobacco. There was a lot of ducking and diving going on. Obviously, it wasn't as heavy, say, as in a closed prison, but like anywhere where there were rules and regulations, someone always had to buck the system.

OK, so I was also part of that. But I only ever dealt with one chap, since it would have been fatal to branch out and become a sort of full-time baron. That would no doubt have aroused suspicion, and as prison is full of those who like to dish the dirt, it wouldn't have been long before I lost my little cushy jobs. When my tobacco stocks became too much I would ask Bill if I could have a packet of normal cigarettes, and to avoid suspicion I would purchase a packet of the same fags every week from the canteen.

When I first worked in the kitchen you were allowed extra milk, cheese, tea, sugar and coffee, but as is often the case, the system was abused. The kitchen staff sold their share and then got more, which had a knock-on effect, as more was going out the back door than was being served up. And portions became skimpier and skimpier. So it was rationed out in an attempt to cut out the trafficking. After a while it had to be stopped. Bill decided to have a purge and I was made the number one. I cut out the trafficking completely; the kitchen staff had the hump but the food improved, also I was able to supplement the prison-issue food with extras.

Some people were on special diets, due to health, weight or religious reasons. One chap, an Indian, who it seemed was a religious leader from somewhere in Wales, had a serious medical problem caused, I believe, by having worked in a birth control pill factory. He was supposed to be on a meat-free diet, due to his religion. Apart from a piece of fruit and cheese and an omelette, there wasn't much variation in his diet. He had offered to cook his own food, but that apparently had been vetoed. One day, I was in the kitchen at teatime when he appeared with his plate, on which was a very small piece of cheese and a bit of bread. He was obviously upset. Bill, who was hardly ever in the kitchen except at mealtimes, was blissfully unaware, so I made the decision to give Sandhu a yoghurt and extra fruit. I also couldn't understand why they wouldn't let him cook his own food. With a little persuasion, the Governor allowed the local Sikh and Hindu welfare officers to come in and liaise with Bill and Sandhu. Sandhu and the other Indian prisoners were soon very happy. And why not? If you have happy prisoners, the prison system runs itself. Years later, my good deed was to produce a very strange and mystical event.

My family came to see me on visits and, of course, I had various girls coming down, which kept me in touch with the outside world. Philip, my younger brother, was living in Bristol, working for Cosmos, but he hardly ever came. Not, I am sure, because he disliked me, but because he didn't want me to know he was gay. But he wrote, and always asked if I needed anything. Dad came down with my mother, and that was always an event. She would spend most of her time looking around the room, checking out who was there. When Dad came on his own, I always asked him not to bring her, but he felt that that was going to put a strain on their now broken-down relationship. My sister wrote regularly and came down with Graham, her husband, and the kids. Everything between us then was fine.

Resettlement now reared its ugly head. After a dress rehearsal for *Conduct Unbecoming*, I was approached by a woman who was the new welfare officer. In a broad Scottish accent, she announced who she was and said, 'I have a perverted interest in you; oh, I am so sorry I mean perverse.' And she told me to come and see her in her office some time. She had short, tight, curly hair and was very mannish. The next day at lunchtime she stormed into the kitchen and demanded to know why I hadn't been to see her. 'Uh-oh,' I thought, 'this one's trouble.' How right I was! After I explained to her that I had in fact been working solidly from five o'clock that morning and I hadn't had the chance to visit her, she then informed me that she would be in her office after lunch. I was to go and see her then.

I turned up at the admin block as requested. She demanded to know why hadn't I applied for resettlement, or shopping trips, or ever requested a talk with a welfare officer. I explained that I really had a full engagement diary and felt no need for those things. I don't think she got the joke, because she drove straight over my remark and informed me that I would be put on the list for resettlement and a shopping trip. I then said I wasn't interested in either and that as far as I was concerned I couldn't be forced to do what I didn't want to do, outside activities-wise. She told me to go back to work, which I did. That was the end of resettlement, I thought.

Tommy, the resettlement prisoner, was also a hut orderly, which entailed keeping the hut clean and secure. In reality it was just a job that took a few hours in the morning and then the rest of the day was his own. Each hut orderly was given a supply of tea and sugar, which had to last a week, so the hut residents could make their own tea in the morning or at night. He also received a small supply of milk each day. Each week the orderlies would come to the kitchen, usually on a Friday, and fill up their tea and sugar tins. On one of these Fridays Tommy seemed a bit down, and on being asked what was wrong he replied that the resettlement bird was leaving – his words not mine; nearly every woman in prison, or who was related to the prisoners, was called a 'bird'. A new 'resettlement bird' would be taking over in a few weeks' time. Obviously Tommy was worried that the new lady would not be susceptible to his charms. And that he would lose some of his power. How right he was.

Bescoby, the welfare woman, was in charge of resettlement in the meantime. On the following Saturday and Sunday afternoon, I had to go out, with a prisoner called Danny, to dig some old lady's garden in Wotton-under-Edge. Luckily for me, this happened after my stint cleaning in the officers' club. The garden was overrun with weeds and in serious need of attention. Luckily, the lady had a rotivator, which helped. Basically, I realized that resettlement was in fact slave labour in the main, although some prisoners travelled into Bristol and helped build playgroup areas, or worked in a local mental hospital. All this was unsupervised, although the people we worked for weren't slow in reporting any breach of discipline. Some inmates took the opportunity to phone home from a public payphone. The woman whose garden we were digging kept herself to herself, and after the initial introduction, we never saw her. Danny shot off and made a phone call, and was back within a few minutes, although it seemed ages. And as the minutes dragged on I was paranoid someone would ask where he was. This was repeated the next day. Much later, he was to be taken off resettlement when at a new place of work; the woman he was working for reported him.

Danny and I worked in the garden for a few weeks. One Saturday, we heard music coming from a bedroom, and much to our surprise saw a young woman, possibly nineteen or twenty, in the bedroom. Every now and again we would look up and see her wearing some new outfit. Alarm bells began to ring in my head. I didn't know if she was just trying on clothes she had bought on a shopping trip, or if she was posing. We hadn't seen her in the process of changing her clothes, just appearing in a new top every so often. So I made a decision that I wouldn't go back to that place again. Luckily for me, I had a weekend of visits lined up the following Saturday and Sunday, and events at the officers' club the weekend thereafter. So I couldn't do resettlement for a while. Danny, in the meantime, continued on his own, and came back full of stories that he had seen the girl half naked. Whether he had or not was a different matter. Most prisoners have more stories than 'Jackanory', so I took this with a pinch of salt.

Tommy came into the kitchen one day with a grin on his face like the Cheshire cat's, and he was wearing his best bib and tucker, his visiting outfit. Highly starched shirt, trousers pressed to the nines; even his glasses seemed brighter, and he had liberally applied the aftershave.

'Visit?' I asked.

'No,' he replied in his best Jack-the-lad manner. 'New resettle-ment bird . . . Going down to see her.'

'Poor woman,' I thought, 'does she know what she's let herself in for?' And at the same time, part of me thought, 'No doubt she's another one who's going to think she's the belle of the ball.' Tommy swaggered off to see her, no doubt practising all his tried and trusted lines and charm on the way.

Later that day, while lunch was being served, the Chief arrived, and I could see he had a young woman with him. She was attractive with a startled-rabbit look in her eyes and a slightly nervous demeanour. Apart from that initial observation, I dismissed her, as quite often lots of strange and varied people tended to visit the prison. How wrong I was to be proved.

Later that day, prisoners would come and go, saying, 'Have you seen the new resettlement bird?' I said I hadn't, but by all accounts she was some stunner. Again the thoughts that went through my head tended to be: avoid this one like the plague. Besides, in all the time I was in prison, never once did I hear tell of an ugly female. All 'birds' were stunners!

12

LOVE AND HATE

I had made friends with a few people, but had really got close to only one or two: a guy called Derek, who was in for drug smuggling, and a guy called Bud, who was involved in a major swindle stealing from Marks & Spencer. Bud had stolen stuff from shops all over the country and had taken them back either to exchange them or to get his money back. Aileen Bescoby, in the meantime, had managed to get a couple of lovely ladies from Bristol on to the resettlement list, and a fellow inmate and myself had been sent to help them refurbish their house. As I had been in Wotton-under-Edge, the new resettlement girl seemed to make that her last port of call. Her name was Jay.

Bescoby's ladies lived in the Clifton area of Bristol. One was a probation officer, the other a headmistress, and they were sisters, one a widow, the other single. Jean and Sheila were lovely; they fed us and just kept out of the way. Bescoby would turn up just to see how we were doing. Jean and Sheila used to pick us up from the prison and return us, although sometimes Bescoby filled in in their place. Jay had the habit of turning up at the house I was painting last thing, just before we were leaving. Now she truly *was* a stunner, absolutely beautiful – but I was still suspicious of many of the women who worked in prisons.

As I made my way to and from the club each morning I had to pass her office, and more and more I found myself catching Jay's eye as I went past. One day, I was doing the playgroup when she turned up. She said: 'I always wondered where you were going to.'

'Now you know,' I said, not rudely, but just matter-of-fact.

But I found myself thinking about her, not in the usual way I had about the teachers in the Scrubs and Portsmouth. I began to look for her, and wait for her to come to the house in Bristol so I could get a glimpse of her. Strangely enough, I would bump into her in the oddest places: on the top sports field, as I was having a walk spouting my lines out loud for the play I was doing. And I would feel cheated if I didn't see her as I made my way to and from the club.

Meanwhile, Bescoby had decided that she was going to take me under her wing. She had contacts with two well-known actors, a husband and wife, called Barbara Leigh Hunt and Richard Pascoe, who were at the Old Vic and stayed with her when they were in Bristol. And she was going to get them to come and talk to me about acting. Although I never did meet them, she did introduce me to Louise Jamieson.

She also decided that she was taking me shopping. I knew it was no use prevaricating and saying no, so I said yes, and a shopping trip was arranged. I decided that the first thing I needed was a proper haircut, as a few days before, Jay had asked me if I was all right, and when I said, 'Yes, why?' she said, 'You look drawn and haggard.' When I looked in the mirror I realized what she meant; my hair was long and straggly, and it made me look dreadful. The weekend before had been open day, and someone had taken a picture of me, which made me look skeletal. (That photo appeared in the papers years later when my past was revealed.) And having seen the photo, I did look dreadful. Bescoby kept trying to influence everything on that trip, from the haircut to what I bought. I wanted a pair of jeans and a decent shirt, plus a good pair of shoes – Philip's ones were clumpy, high-heeled and were not my style, and I don't think they were leather – but she kept on and on so I ended up with none of those things, but did buy a dreadful jacket. Bescoby had been making me shop quickly, and had made me very confused. I hadn't shopped for years and my trip was a disaster. We made our way back to her car, and apparently headed back to the prison. Well, I guessed I would have to wait another three or four months before I could go out again to buy clothes.

We didn't return to the prison straight away, but went to her flat, where she needed to pick something up. She made me a cup of tea and disappeared, and when she reappeared she was wearing stockings and suspenders, bra and knickers, but the stocking tops were so tight that they were cutting into her thighs. She looked not only ridiculous but also pathetic, tragic even. I said, 'I think we should be getting back' and with a face like thunder she disappeared and then returned, dressed. We went to her car and back to the prison, not speaking. I had tried to make light conversation, but she turned the music up on the radio, and dumped me at reception, where I changed back into prison clothing.

The next morning, as I made my way across the car park in front of the officers' club, I suddenly felt the hairs on the back of my neck stand up, and as I looked to my right I saw her car hurtling towards me. I jumped out of the way and she screeched to a halt, not on the tarmac but on the grass beyond it . . . no way would she have missed me if I hadn't jumped out of the way. She reversed the car on to the tarmac, got out and strolled off. Now, I had only ever had that prickling sensation once before, at Wormwood Scrubs: I had gone to reception to pick something up that had been sent in for me, and as I had passed this prisoner sitting in one of the cubicles, although he seemed like any other prisoner, not very significant, the hairs on my neck stood up and I felt myself going cold. At the time, I put it down to the fact that the wooden outer gate of reception had been left open, sending a cold chill through the barred gates. It wasn't until later that I was told that Ian Brady, the Moors murderer, had been in reception that afternoon. That insignificant prisoner had been Brady. He was evil, and so was Bescoby.

When I saw Jay through the window she called me into her office and asked how the shopping had gone, and that my hair looked better. I told her the shopping was a disaster, and asked her if she would return the jacket for me, but not to mention it to Bescoby.

127

She looked at me strangely, but said she would. I made no mention of the ridiculous scene in Bescoby's flat: no one would believe me anyway. I left and made my way to work. But no sooner had I left the resettlement office than Bescoby stormed in and demanded to know what I had been talking to Jay about. I looked at her, thought about it long and hard and said: 'Resettlement'. Then I went back to work. A few days later, Bescoby took some sick leave, and was working from home. It turned out she had leukaemia, and a few years later, she was to succumb to it.

During a rehearsal, Madge had said that she wanted to enter the Gloucester one-act-play festival, and what did we all think about it. We said we'd do it, and she said she would speak to Shergold about it. I decided to write a script called *A Reason to Live*, and when Madge read it she loved it and made a few alterations and we entered it in the original play section. It was up against a lot of plays, but it made the cut and we were invited to perform it, as Leyhill Amateur Dramatic Society (LADS). The play was about a woman dying, and in her last moments on earth, she was visited by people from her past. It was really about unrequited love – I wonder why I wrote about that?

We built the sets, or Mac did, and just as we were about to leave the prison in one of the lorries, the officers decided that they would not come and escort us. It looked as if it was all off; Shergold could drive the truck, but who was going to drive the minibus? Jay arrived, but neither Shergold nor she had an HGV licence. After a brief discussion, we worked out that we only needed a chair, so that was loaded into the minibus, which Jay drove while Shergold acted as escort. She had been a great supporter of the drama group, and watched rehearsals and shows, which she didn't have to do, as she was very much in demand from the single prison officers, who were always asking her out. When we got there she raced in and spoke to the organizers, saying we had no set, as it was stuck on a truck somewhere, which was true, but that we would do it with a chair. Luckily the play before us was using only a black drape backdrop. We checked the entrances and rejigged the action so it fitted the gap in the drapes. The actress playing the dying woman was brilliant, as were the lads. I wasn't in it. While waiting for the adjudication panel to make the decision, I got chatting to this bloke about the theatre. It appeared that the theatre had been awarded a massive grant and was to be refurbished, including the seating, which consisted of beautiful green velvet theatre seats. Our seats at the theatre were standard tubular steel and plywood, linked by u-clips. I asked what was going to happen to the chairs, and he told me they were being scrapped. I asked if he would sell them. He couldn't but if we wanted to make a donation we could have them. I asked, 'How much?' He said, 'Twenty-five pounds.' I took his name and said someone would get in touch during the week.

At last the winner was being announced . . . in third place . . . in second place . . . And the winner is: *A Reason to Live*! I felt my hands gripped on both sides, by Madge and by Jay. I don't know what made me feel happier, the winning or the squeeze of Jay's hand.

On returning to the prison, it was, award or no award, business as usual. I applied to the council for the £25 to purchase the seats, and strangely enough we were turned down. Now that the drama group had handed all its money into the main pot, and was funding nearly every new thing that was purchased, I went straight to Shergold. I told him the score, and he summoned the council to his office, and told them that unless they rushed the purchase through, he would suspend council. Within the hour we had the money, and later that week we had collected all the seats and fitted them.

I was asked by Madge to adapt a children's book into a play for the kids. It was called *The Scamp Family*, a sort of Famous Five adventure. I did it and it was performed. I had also written a script for television, which I sent to HTV, but heard nothing, not even the usual fuck off.

Jay's time at the prison was coming to an end, and when she told me, I was gutted. Although I wished her well, I said it was my loss. She just looked at me and smiled. She said that she would be popping back every now and again, as she was very friendly with the Chief Officer and his wife. Within a month she had popped in, and of course she had somehow managed to bump into me. She asked to write to me, but I said it might compromise her situation. So I gave her the name of a visitor who no longer came to see me, but whose name was still on my address list for letters in. We said goodbye. She was as good as her word and wrote to me every now and again. She would pop down to see her old landlord and landlady and the Chief. I would always know when she was around, because the Chief would suddenly stop me and say, 'Hey, have a guess who's popping in tomorrow?' If he knew anything about my feelings for her, he never let on. Every time I saw her, I realized how terribly I missed her.

Bill in the kitchen had moved on, and a new kitchen officer arrived from Dartmoor. Unfortunately, he was the exact opposite to Bill: he didn't want anyone helping in the club, he used his wife. And he didn't like the fact I was doing the playgroup. He was a stickler for the rules. With his attitude and the lax regime at Leyhill, something was always going to give. Suddenly I was told that I couldn't work on the playgroup any more; it wasn't correct form, or good for discipline or security. So he set about having me removed. He had the backing of a few officers, but he didn't have the backing of the wives, and when they heard they stormed off to see the Governor, and then they gave their husbands a hard time. Guess what? I stayed in the playgroup. But he was not to be outdone; he didn't like the way the kitchen ran smoothly, and changed it so that we were there all day. Something had to give, and it did: I quit, although that didn't stop me doing the playgroup. When I applied for a change of labour, the Chief said, 'Yes, fine, go in the library for a couple of days and watch what happens on the *Leyhill News*.' This was a weekly paper printed on A4. It contained reviews of shows performed, minutes of council meetings, information, cartoons and prisoners' letters, and was printed in the library, but the Chief vetted it and had the final say as to what went in it. Shortly after I had left the kitchen the new number one started running the kitchen the old way. Food was being sold and going missing, and was getting worse (and less). I had also become friendly with an Indian called Moussa, and he was in a desperate state about the food. More and more letters to the *Leyhill News* complained about the food. They were okayed by the Chief and I printed them in the *News*. Well, I paid for it: one teatime, as I queued for my food, I received very small portions.

'Could I have a bit more?' I asked.

'Fuck off!' said the guy in charge of the hotplate – not the officer, who was standing well back.

'Pardon?'

Suddenly the officer rushed over. 'What did you say?'

'I said "Pardon?" '

'No you didn't,' he said.

'Oh, Steve Austin, are we? Bionic ears?'

Fatal: he nicked me, and I was on Governor's report the following morning, sentenced to seven days in a closed jail. I was sent to Gloucester Prison. I was having a visit that afternoon, but I had asked them to ring and cancel it, which they said they would do, but they didn't.

On the second day of my time in Gloucester the door opened and two Leyhill officers stood there and told me to get my kit packed. I did, and followed them. They signed for me and we made our way to the Leyhill minibus and back to Leyhill. 'More trouble,' I thought, and prepared for the worst. When I returned, I was taken to see the Chief.

'You are a silly boy; go on, go back to the library, but not in the post of editor.'

'What's the kitchen officer going to say about it?' I said.

'Nothing. He's suspended, and won't be back.'

Obviously, he hadn't really fitted in at the place and had caused grief, too much grief. He didn't know how lucky he was. I hope when he was back in that cold dark place in Dartmoor he realized what he was missing.

The library was an easy job, and the library officer left us to it and we used him to take us in to get props and suchlike for the plays. Obviously, we popped into a restaurant in Bristol for lunch. He also took over the running of the club, and I was reinstated.

When the drama group ceased for the summer months, other ways were found to fill the evenings, and Derek, who was a gifted painter, got me involved in the art class, just for the trips, same as I had got him and Moussa involved in the drama group. They ran the front of house for me, and made the tea and did the raffles, so it was all right that they went to the theatre. I had been spotted in a play or rather someone had brought the head of Bristol Old Vic in to see a play, and he had offered me a summer school place, but the Home Office had vetoed it. So I was enrolled at Filton College doing English literature and film studies instead. The reason I had been vetoed for the summer school was that it was going to be full of young women, or so the Home Office thought. Well, Filton Tech was heaving with them, and obviously on the first day, we were all asked to introduce ourselves, and I did. I didn't tell them where I lived; when pushed I said Leyhill, and then why, and after a while I told them; one person didn't come back the following week.

The art teacher, who was half American Indian, arranged for us to visit the Arnolfini Centre. We had all come out with money, but getting it back into Leyhill was a problem. So we asked her to and after a short think she said yes; but she was as nervous as hell when she did give it to Derek on the inside. She loved talking about America and American Indians. One day, she showed us some pictures of her back in the States, and one, I saw, was of her naked, taken by her ex. You could see everything, but I noticed that no one else had seen the picture. As I was helping her clear up, I asked if she wanted to meet for a drink.

'Where?' she said.

'I go to college one day a week and we could meet,' I replied.

She agreed and we did.

At college I told the tutor I was going to do some research in the library. After popping into the library briefly, I slipped out and met her at a pub not far from where Jean and Sheila lived. After a drink, we went for a stroll, and we ended up having sex on Clifton Downs. Soon after, drama resumed and I had to leave the art group and its attractions.

A few of the men had worked in a psychiatric hospital, and it was their open day, so everyone on resettlement was roped in to help. Derek and I had drawn the short straw of walking around with animal heads on us. The place was full of visitors; there were stalls, bingo, a tombola, coconut shies. Derek and I got chatted up by two women, both in their thirties, both attractive, and we arranged to meet them, me while I was at college and Derek on an art trip. Again, my excuse was to work in the library and I would then disappear to a prearranged spot and we would drive to Tintern Abbey and have sex there. No wonder I got an O-level instead of an A-level.

Not one of these women did I want for anything else but sex. There was a woman out there I thought I loved, but she sure as anything wasn't in love with me. I eagerly awaited her letters, and devoured their contents. Although hers were just friendly, talking about college etc., I thought they were just wonderful. My letters to her were just straight boring everyday accounts. And I was frightened that if I told her how I felt I would scare her off; also there was the fact that I was in prison and had several more years to do before I could even think about applying for parole.

By now, Derek and Bud had left, though Bud would turn up at football games or cricket matches, and Moussa was on his way. Although I had always been a bit of a loner, I was really on my tod.

My father had bought me a watch and it was an exact copy of the one he had been given as a retirement watch. One night, while I was asleep, it went missing. No one had seen anything, but my thoughts had been that the night patrol had done it. But, after a while, I had narrowed it down to two people, the night patrol and one inmate, a Welshman. Both had seemed overly concerned about my loss. The first few days after the watch went missing were unbearable; it was as if a black cloud had descended upon me. I was gutted and depressed, unable to leave my room.

Eventually, when I had just given up on getting it back I was told that someone had been offered a watch, and wanted twelve ounces for it. I told the informant to set up a meet in the greenhouse and the exchange would be made at lunchtime. I got there early, and waited. I was hidden behind a large bush, and I heard my name called. I looked up and it was two officers. They asked me to describe my watch, I did so, and they handed it to me, and told me that the culprit had been caught and was being moved. I raced to reception and there in front of me were loads of prisoners all hurling abuse at the culprit. It was the Welshman.

My Indian mate Sandhu approached me and said, 'Mr Les, would you please take this and keep it in your pocket, the left one, for ten days?' It was a black-and-white bead-type thing. I said yes and put it in my left pocket. I didn't see him around. I was curious to ask him why he was making me do this, but of course not seeing him meant I couldn't.

On the tenth day, he approached me and asked for the bead, which I gave to him. Later that day, he approached me with a piece of paper. Written on it were the numbers: 27 3 78. I looked puzzled, but he smiled, said nothing and left. Shortly afterwards, I was down at the playgroup, when I was told that the Assistant Governor wanted me. As I went into his office, I was asked how I felt about going back to London. Obviously, I said I didn't want to (as I had not wanted to go to Portsmouth) but felt I had to comply. My heart sank; obviously I was to be returned to a closed prison. But no, I was to be put on the hostel scheme at Wormwood Scrubs and I was to leave the next day. The Home Office had overruled the army. I was on my way home.

That night I was told to report to the orderly room and as I waited outside I was suddenly drenched with fire buckets and the hose was turned on me. The officers had got their own back. I made my way back to my room, but my door was locked, the key wouldn't work, the keyhole was blocked up, and when I cleared it all my furniture was gone, save for a mattress. I lay down and tried to sleep, so excited about the next day. The night patrol kept waking me up to see if I wanted to buy a battleship. In the morning, when I returned from my shower, my clothes had disappeared, so I made my way to reception dressed in a white sheet, looking like the Emperor Nero. I got through reception, changed, and made my way to the main gate to catch the bus to Bristol Temple Meads. Before leaving, I was ushered in and told to open my suitcase. As I did so, the officers took everything out, which I had to put back in, which they then took back out again. I was going to miss the bus. Suddenly the Chief arrived and said, 'Take care, good luck, the place won't be the same without you,' and handed me a card from the playgroup girls.

So I eventually left Leyhill and walked the few yards to the bus stop. It was 1977. My old journey had nearly finished; a new one was about to begin. I hoped it wouldn't be as rocky as the last one.

13

HOMEWARD BOUND

As I stood outside Leyhill at the bus stop waiting for the bus that would take me into Bristol for the last time, I pondered as to what the future would hold. I knew that I wouldn't be coming back. I had my plans and ideas as to what I might do and the £17.11p in my pocket seemed like a fortune. I glanced down at the floor to see if anyone had dropped any money for the prisoners going to college, and realized it was me who would be dropping the money. I put £5 in a cigarette packet and threw it on the floor as I saw the bus approaching. As I got on and ordered my ticket, not one of the passengers paid much attention. This for them must have been an everyday occurrence.

Even though I had made the journey on numerous occasions, it felt like the first time I had been on a bus since I was sentenced. The journey to Bristol seemed to take an age, but eventually we arrived at Temple Meads Station. Suddenly the world got larger. Here I was about to start a new life and catch a train, when it dawned on me that I didn't know what to do, which platform to go to or which train to take. I queued up at the ticket office and as I reached the window, the clerk behind the glass looked at the railway warrant I had thrust through the window, glanced up at me and said, 'It's your ticket; London trains go from platform one.' I thanked him and turned to leave. As I did he said, 'Good luck'. I made my way to the information boards, wondering, what he meant. Then I realized that he must have seen thousands of warrants and thousands of ex-prisoners go through the same routine every day. Or maybe I had the look of a prisoner. I hoped it was the former, not the latter.

I had a while to wait for the train so I popped into the newsagent at the station and bought some writing paper and envelopes and a book of stamps. After years of writing on lined prison paper with a rubber stamped address on, I never realized how difficult it would be to purchase something so simple as writing paper. I settled on good old Basildon Bond, and after paying for it, I made my way to the platform and waited for the train. The platform was filling up, and I prayed that the train wouldn't be too crowded, and that I could get a seat. No one on the platform paid any attention to me, although I still checked to see that no one had followed me, to make sure I was not up to no good. Old habits die hard.

The train arrived and I got on and grabbed a seat in the smoking compartment. I had managed to get a window seat and there was a table as well. Trains had changed since I had last been on one, in 1966. After taking in the scenery from the window, I started to write some letters, one without an address on the top, as if it was one of the illicit ones I sometimes sent out. And after half a page or so I put in how I was on a train and even wrote the sentence upside down that I was out. I was out! How long had I dreamed of that? I knew that the letters wouldn't get there until the Saturday at the earliest, or Tuesday at the latest, and I didn't know what the reaction to them would be. They were just matter-of-fact letters saying I was out and could be contacted at my parents' address and I would get in touch once I had got settled.

I arrived at Cove. I asked for directions and made my way to my parents' house. It seemed to take for ever. Finally I arrived at this huge estate of houses all identical, all with a patch of lawn at the front, and after finding the right one I rang the doorbell. I knew my father wouldn't be there, as he was at work. Dad had said he would take the day off but I had said no, I would see him when he got home. John would also not be around, as he worked nights.

I rang the doorbell and after a while I could see a shape making its way to the door. The door opened and my mother was there.

After a certain silence she said, 'Come in,' led me into the living room and plonked herself back in her chair. The room was cluttered with a mish-mash of furniture, the floor was strewn with what seemed to be bits of cotton and there were a lot of magazines by her chair. The silence between us was deafening, and after what seemed a very short time, she asked if I wanted a cup of tea. I said yes and followed her into the kitchen.

As she filled the kettle, I took in the kitchen and noticed that it was not very clean, and as I glanced at the sink and the cups on the draining board I realized that cleaning was not high on her list of priorities. Of course she covered it by saying she had a bad hip and couldn't get to do it all. As only my father and she lived there, and he was at work all day, it seemed to me that she wasn't overdoing it with the housework. I told her to go back in the front room, and that I would make the tea. I scrubbed the cups, and after making sure they were scalded with the water from the kettle, I took her her tea. She made some comment about having to hoover in a minute, and after telling me about what she did all day, and how lovely the neighbours were, and how she missed the old place, I realized that she hadn't once asked me how I was or how the journey had been or even was I pleased to be home.

After a while I asked her where my bedroom was and she told me. It was no bigger than my cell in the closed prisons I had been in. She had put the bedding on the bed in a pile and as I made it up I was glad that I would be using it only at weekends. Hours passed without much being said between us and after several repeats of 'I must get on and hoover,' I took the hint and grabbed the vacuum cleaner and started to clean the front room. During the first few hours back with my mother, every time she got up from the chair, she made a big thing of standing up, as if to underline her statements about having a bad hip. As I started to clean, she made a comment about having to pop out, and told me she would be back soon. Did I need anything, she asked. I said no, although I wanted to say something like, 'Three gallons of bleach.' But I held my tongue. The more I cleaned the more I had to clean. I hoovered the whole house, scrubbed the kitchen, disinfected the toilet and bathroom, and anything else that I thought looked iffy. Eventually she returned, with a plastic bag with some groceries in and a pile of women's mags. She plonked herself back in the chair, and began to read. Not once did she comment on the tidiness of the place. Each magazine, when she had finished reading it, was dropped on the floor and sometimes a page was ripped out and put on the side: a knitting pattern or something else of interest, I guess; it sure wasn't going to be cleaning hints or recipes.

All I had done since I been in the house was make tea, make my bed and clean. She did offer to make me a sandwich, but I declined. I asked how everyone was, and she gave me a potted run-down.

John had a new girlfriend who obviously wasn't my mother's cup of tea, but then I had forgotten how she believed she was a cut above everyone. 'He really could do better for himself,' she said. The way my mother described her, the poor girl seemed to have been dragged through a hedge backwards.

I kept glancing at the clock, hoping that it would soon be time for my Dad to arrive. Never had time dragged so, not even in prison. The phone rang, and as she made the struggle to get up even more dramatic than the last time, I grabbed it and answered. It was Dad, checking I had arrived safely. He told me that he would be home around six and looked forward to seeing me then. I asked my mother if I could make some phone calls, and with the rather curt reply of, 'Of course, you live here,' she went back to reading *Woman's Own*. I phoned my Aunt Joan, my Uncle Danny and Tom in Wembley. I also phoned my sister. She said she would come over as soon as she could, which would be sometime over the weekend.

Eventually Dad arrived and was so pleased that I was there. My mother suddenly sprang into life and was about to start on Dad's tea: the usual Friday-night fare, poached eggs on toast. In the paper I had noticed that 'The Professionals' was on that night and that Pamela was in it, so at least I would get a glimpse of her. After tea, Dad and I settled down to watch it, but no sooner had the programme started than John arrived with his girlfriend, who was absolutely lovely, not at all as my mother had described. Then my mother started to make a big fuss of her and produced a pair of earrings that she thought would look lovely on her. Wow what a turnaround. John kept asking if I wanted to go to the pub, and I said, 'No, not tonight' as I really just wanted to have a quiet time. He looked disappointed, so I said, 'Let's do it tomorrow instead.'

Dad commented on how lovely Pamela was and how good 'The Professionals' was. I agreed, and added that I had missed much of the plot with the arrival of John. Not at all bitchy, just a comment. Well, suddenly the door flew open, and my mother raged at me: 'What did you say about me?' I told her I hadn't said anything, and my Dad confirmed it, but she was raging on and on. She had obviously not been making a cup of tea, as she'd pretended, but had been listening at the door. I tried to placate her by saying I thought she had misheard, and went to put my arms out to give her a cuddle. Suddenly she screamed, 'Don't you threaten me, I'm going to call the police.' With that Dad went ballistic and grabbed the phone from her. I said, 'Look, obviously I'm not wanted. I should go.' Dad went white and said, 'Oh no you won't. If anyone goes it's her.' And with that, my mother went off up to bed.

Dad and I had a beer and sat chatting until he went to bed, and then I sat up a while longer. As I made my way to my bedroom, I saw the big bedroom door was shut. Suddenly I heard my Dad's voice say goodnight from across the landing. I saw a door open and there he was in bed, alone. I realized then they didn't sleep in the same room; she had the big bedroom, he had one no bigger than mine. My God, what had I come home to? My first day home and I was in the middle of a minefield.

My weekend at home went by quickly; Dad and John made sure of that. My sister and her family came over and, at that time, Angela and I got on well. My mother acted as if nothing had happened, although she was decidedly quieter than before, and came to life only when other people were there. When one of her friends popped round to have a natter with her, you would have thought I was the prodigal son who had returned with the fatted calf.

I kept my date with John at the pub, and was surprised how much he drank, but I guess I put it down to the fact that I had been away and wasn't really aware how much people now drank. But Dad had assured me, as did John, that he was over his drink problem.

The first time I saw my brother John on a visit to Portsmouth I was shocked. He had put on a huge amount of weight and had started chain smoking. When I had mentioned this to Dad, he said that John had had a bit of a drink problem, but was getting over it. Obviously I thought I was to blame, as perhaps John had started to drink as a result of the shame he felt at my going inside. At closing time he wanted to know if I wanted to stay for afters, and I just said, 'No, I had best get back home.'

Sunday was the usual Sunday fare. John and I went to Dad's local pub at lunchtime, after which it was back to the house for Sunday lunch. The longer I stayed the longer I didn't want to be there. Was it me, I kept asking myself? Had my years away in the army and in prison made me unfit for human company? These anxieties and doubts had reared up before. I had blamed myself for Philip becoming homosexual, for John and his drinking condition. I knew that the breakdown of my parents' marriage was nothing to do with me directly, although I am sure that I was a contributory factor, as were all the kids. Or was this part of my conditioning as a failure?

Monday came and went in a flurry of washing and cleaning my clothes and packing my bag ready to leave early on the Tuesday morning to report at the hostel at Wormwood Scrubs, where I was to spend the next year. My next weekend at home wouldn't be for a month or so. I was glad to be on that train to London and glad to be out of the house, although I knew I'd be back soon. I wasn't looking forward to my next weekend at home.

The hostel building was directly at the front of the prison, a big house, separate from the prison, although it was run by a prison officer. Having checked in, I was shown my accommodation, and was immediately set to work in the kitchen.

My job entailed feeding the prisoners breakfast and supper, although any of the prisoners around during the day, either looking for work or cleaning the place, also needed to be fed. But the majority usually went off to the pub or a local café. My first week flew, and I was not let out at the weekend as I was not yet fully entitled to the privileges that came with being in the hostel.

Basically the hostel scheme lasted six months to help you assimilate back into society, by getting a job and making sure that you had a safe environment to return to. At weekends you were allowed to go home to an approved address and you had to return on the Sunday evening ready for work the next day. Any breaches of these rules were met by a warning, and any future breaches could result in your being returned to prison. The majority of prisoners were in employment. Mac was there: he was a carpenter working on a building site. But most prisoners, though, seemed to work in a windscreen-wiper factory somewhere out in Ealing.

Breakfast was up and running from six o'clock and usually lasted until every one of the workers had left at various times according to their jobs. The rations came from the prison, and were allocated according to how many prisoners were in the hostel. Obviously not every prisoner had an evening meal cooked, as they didn't have to be back in the hostel until late at night. So at the end of the week there was always food left over, which would be taken into account and taken off the next week's rations. So it was always essential that you cooked it all, although the previous cooks had made extra money by selling chickens and other stuff on a Friday night to prisoners going away for the weekend. The prisoners also left money for the cook at the weekend, which was his wages. Once it came nearer the time for your employment period to start you were sent to the unemployment office to register for your national insurance and social security number. And the hostel officer had a list of useful numbers for companies who took ex-prisoners and, if suitable, employed them. You had to pay for your keep out of the money you earned, and this went into the hostel fund. What happened to the money I was never really sure, although I think it paid for the television and telephone, light and electricity.

After a while, I was allowed out at weekends but only for the day. I had to return to the hostel every night. The addresses I visited had to be cleared by the officer in charge of the hostel, usually by means of a letter from those you were going to visit, detailing their relationship with you. My sister and aunt wrote, so that was OK. And as my sister was married to a policeman, that was deemed a good environment. I was allowed out on a Saturday afternoon prior to this to go shopping. Usually I popped over to see some of the people I had kept in contact with, just for an hour or so.

Working in the hostel and being in such close proximity to the Scrubs, it was inevitable that I would bump into Jon Haerem, and we always had a brief chat when this happened. He was pleased for me, and gave me his address and telephone number so I could keep in touch.

Pamela and Mike lived in Earl's Court, so I could pop round for lunch or an evening meal. But again this was only for a few hours. It was interesting listening to the working prisoners talking about how much they were earning. It certainly motivated me to get a job that paid. When I went off to see my sister I took her the chickens and whatever else was unused from the hostel fridge, and she always seemed grateful. One Saturday evening, after seeing her, I had had permission to stay at my aunt's for the night. The rest of the prisoners were away for the weekend and I was the only person left in the hostel. When the officer, who had an office just inside the front door, realized this, he said to me that I could have a break from Saturday lunch to early evening on Sunday. This meant that I had to be there to cook tea for anyone who felt like it and also breakfast on the Saturday morning for those who were leaving. The officer had decided that he didn't want to be popping in to check on me, so I could have a night out.

I hadn't seen my aunt or any of her family for years, but the moment I walked through the door it was as if I had never been away. She looked the same and, although her movements were restricted by the cancer, she insisted on cooking me tea. Ernie, her husband, did odd hours at work, here and there, so he could spend as much time as possible looking after her during the day. My cousin Carol was also there. She and I had always got on well, and she had written to me lots of times during my sentence, and had never once forgotten my birthday. After we had eaten Carol suggested we go for a drink. She took me to a really nice quiet place on the Camberwell

New Road and we just sat and chatted over a couple of drinks. Suddenly a bloke went past and stopped and turned and uttered the word 'Lionel', which I hadn't heard for years.

It was a name the other inmates called me after my first stage appearance in the Scrubs, as they said I looked like him – I thought more Harry Fowler. It was Dickie Moody, one of the guys in Wormwood Scrubs and, according to prison folklore, a hard man and a gangster. When I told him I was at the hostel, he wished me luck and told me to get in touch if I needed anything; he then stuck a piece of paper in my breast pocket, which I took to be his phone number. Off he went. As Carol and I left the pub, I took the piece of paper out of my pocket and couldn't believe my eyes; it wasn't a telephone number but a fifty-pound note. Thank you, Dickie. I never saw him again and, as I hadn't got his number, I couldn't thank him.

Carol and I walked back to her house and we sat up talking for hours, catching up on all the gossip. And when I told her about the reception I had received at home on my first day out, she was furious, and said, 'Wait till Joan and Ernie hear about it.' There had never been much love lost between my mother and my aunt's family, due to the arguments and rows they'd had over the years. Sure enough, when Carol told her Mum and her Dad they were furious; they wanted to ring my mother up and have a go at her. But sense prevailed, and they didn't. They were adamant I wasn't to go back home at weekends, and I was to stay there with them. But that would only have caused more grief for my Dad, so in the end I convinced them that I would find somewhere else to stay. As it happened my sister thought it would be better to stay with her, as the best way of pleasing everybody concerned. How wrong she was.

By this time, I was starting to look for work, and after signing on at the social security office I was sent for an interview at a painters and decorators in Kensington called Callinghams, where I met the man who hired and fired. He asked me a few questions, said that no one would know I was an ex-prisoner, and that it would be better for me if I didn't tell anyone. We agreed this was the best thing to do. I was to start the following Monday, to report at eight o'clock.

I couldn't wait. I was so excited about the prospects of a proper job and a proper wage in a proper world.

My first day for work arrived and I caught the bus to the office. I was given a pair of overalls and told to clean the garage out, burn out the paint kettles and clean the brushes. It was a real family–run business. They took pride in the work they did. After a few days, I was given a set of brushes, a paint kettle, scrapers and fillers and a bag to carry the stuff in. I was then told on the next day to report to Regents Park, make myself known to the chaps there, and start work.

During a lunch conversation the other men told me that the man who had hired me had had a son who had been murdered a few years back. I had no idea that the man had had such a terrible tragedy happen to him, and yet he knew my case and circumstances. What a man he was. How many other people would have done what he had by employing me?

My time at Callinghams was happy. I was now applying for drama schools and many wouldn't look at my applications because of the address. Nevertheless, a few people were giving me a real hand: Louise Jamieson and her partner Bob Ashby, Pamela and Mike, and a friend of theirs called Jeremy Young.

One day I received an amazing phone call. Having been brought up on a diet of classic Hollywood movies, it was understandable my heroes were John Wayne, Humphrey Bogart, Robert Mitchum and others. Above all though, I idolized Jimmy Cagney – so imagine my combination of terror and sheer, unbridled excitement when I picked up the phone to be told by a friend, who was filming in a studio, that one James Cagney Esq. was working on the next lot! Armed with a flask of tea and enough sandwiches to last a week, I arrived early and sat it out. I was not going to move until I'd met him. The day dragged on with neither hide nor hair of him, and I was starting to think about packing up when a blacked-out limousine glided up outside one of the sound studios. Two *huge* men got out, disappeared inside the studio and re-emerged pushing an old man in a wheelchair. It was Cagney – much older and frailer than you could ever imagine from his screen roles. I hastened towards him, calling out his name. One of his minders stepped forward to block my path, while the other informed me Mr Cagney was very, very tired.

I just blurted out 'sorry' and said, 'I am a drama student.'

'Drama student, eh,' came the reply from the legend in the wheelchair. 'Acting's about walking through the door, planting your feet and telling the truth . . . good luck.'

What a man! Obviously tired and in poor health, he still had time for a fan. I learned more in those few minutes than in all my time at drama school.

It's something I've tried never to forget when it comes to making time for my own fans. The Cagney incident came to mind one time when we were shooting in Rotherhithe. We were just about to turn over (i.e. start) when an oldish fellow attracted my attention and told me that his wife was a huge fan and she'd come out especially to see me. Could I just spare a moment to say hello? I was just about to say, 'Wait till there's a break in filming and I'll come across and have a little word,' when I looked up and saw this woman standing there. She had a big, radiant smile on her face, and waved across to me – she looked cold and ashen. She'd seen us filming from her tower block flat and nothing was going to prevent her from coming to meet the people she admired so. Straight away, I asked the director for five minutes while we all went to say hello. I know that for this small consideration we gave the old lady something to remember. It also transpired that she had been on her dialysis machine when she had heard we were there and had stopped the treatment to come down. It may sound a bit gooey, but it costs nothing to be nice. I've always tried to find time for my fans, always been approachable – though sometimes to my cost.

I had managed to change my weekend address to my sister's house, and this arrangement worked out very well for a few weeks. Then suddenly I got a letter from her suggesting that perhaps it might be better if I went back to my parents'. I phoned her and asked her why. She made some excuse about spoiling the kids, or something. So I said OK, I would arrange for my stuff to be collected, not that there was much. Later I found out that pressure had been brought to bear on her by my mother and as she had a huge hold over my sister, my sister didn't want to fall out with her.

I phoned Dad and explained the situation. He was pleased, as he had been getting grief from my mother and this would make his life easier. I went back that weekend, but spent no time there at all. I stayed at Pamela's and Louise's. But it was at Louise's that I met a Canadian actress, a friend of theirs, who was an aspiring writer. After an evening out, we popped into a big London hotel and had breakfast. Somehow the actress and I ended up back at her hotel and I stayed there. She was living in a hotel because she had a very rich, old boyfriend. I think he was about eighty; she travelled the world with him. I would go to the hotel every night after work, but I had to be back at the hostel by 10.30 p.m.

Eventually one of the drama schools I had applied to said I could have an audition. Excited, I told Pamela, and thanked Mike, as it was the one he suggested: Webber Douglas. Trouble was, the audition was on the Saturday, only a few days away. Pamela and Mike were brilliant. They arranged for Jeremy to go over my pieces in preparation for the audition, and the night before the audition Jeremy came over to give me my final run-through. As I was going through the Porter's speech, I was just about to utter the line, 'Knock, knock!' At that precise moment, there came a knock at the door and in walked Pam and Mike. An omen, or what?

Jeremy arrived early the next morning and had me running around the square reciting my pieces. What must the neighbours have thought? I was nervous about the audition and hadn't really slept well the night before, but the worst was yet to come. I lost my voice. No matter how hard I tried I couldn't speak. Jeremy grabbed some port and black pepper and made me gargle with it. Thankfully my voice came back. We set off in Jeremy's car to Webber Douglas. Mine was to be the second audition in. On arriving I was led to a huge room where I was told to put my name and address on a small brown envelope and wait to be called. A few interviewees were already there; they all seemed so young compared to me. Eventually I was called and shown into a room where four people were sitting behind a table. The panel included the principal, the secretary and two visiting directors. I introduced myself and after a few questions I was told to do my pieces. I started with a Pinter speech and then went into the Porter's speech. I was oblivious to the fact they were there, although I panicked when suddenly in the middle of the speech I had a coughing fit, which nearly threw me. Fortunately I had the presence of mind to incorporate it into the speech. I went back and sat in front of the panel at the end and after a few questions I was told to leave. I would be hearing either way in the next few days.

As I left the building, feeling good but still very nervous, I saw Jeremy standing by his car. He asked me how it had gone, and I said, 'I think I did you proud.' He smiled and said, 'Just as long as you did Shakespeare proud.' With that, we headed back to Pam and Mike's. Pamela wanted to know everything about the audition. How lucky I was to have friends like them! What was it someone had once said? You can choose your friends, but not your family.

From the highs of auditioning for the drama school, it was soon back to the day job and earning a crust. I had called it a day with the Canadian actress, as I was concentrating on work. She was also trying to start a second career as a writer in her native Canada. One of her books, I was told by Louise, contained a character based on me: he went through the book breaking the heroine's heart. I was apparently portrayed as a dark, mysterious stranger with a past that captivated every female I met and subsequently ruined their love for any other man. Artistic and literary licence, I am sure!

On returning to the hostel one night after work, I found a thick envelope waiting for me. It had 'The Webber Douglas Academy of Dramatic Art' written on the cover. I dreaded opening it, as every other letter I had had at the hostel had contained bad news. I stared at it for a while and then decided I would read it in the toilet. Nervously, I made myself open it and, not believing what I was seeing, I had to read it over and over again before its news sunk in: I had been offered a place at Webber Douglas. Written in ink at the bottom was a note from John Malpass, the secretary: 'Obviously subject to your release, we will keep a place for you. Please get in touch.'

I phoned Pam, Mike and Jeremy and told them the good news. I also phoned home to tell my Dad.

When my mother answered the phone she said, 'Dad's not in.'

'Mum, I've got some great news.' I said, 'I got into drama school.' All she said was, 'I'll tell your Dad.'

Here I was on the first rung of the ladder that led to the place I wanted to be. All I had to do now was to get the money to pay for it. Always easier said than done.

14

TOMORROW NEVER COMES

Once the news had sunk in, it was hard to concentrate on anything but going to drama school. Nevertheless, that was still some time in the future. In the meantime I carried on with my painting job, and spent more and more time seeing friends and family. Although registered at home, I was hardly ever there: I was catching up with old friends, having fun and making up for lost time.

I used to go down to Bristol to see Sheila and Jean, and even stayed there for the weekend. I went to see Louise in *A Midsummer Night's Dream* at the Bristol Old Vic.

I was seeing Derek and Moussa a lot and also Mary, who lived a few houses from where I used to live in St Mary Cray. She invited me over to see her parents, both of whom I knew well. They were a lovely couple and made me feel welcome: they even got the best china out for me. Unfortunately the handle of the cup I was holding, as I lifted it to my lips, broke. I felt bad enough about the cock-up, but when I was told it was their wedding china, I was absolutely mortified. In fact I felt so embarrassed about the whole thing I was too ashamed to get in touch with them again. Well, I suppose that's my innate insecurity coming to the fore again.

At the time, I was in touch with Tom, who suggested that when I finished on the hostel I start working with him. By now, he was in business with another civilian worker from the works department at the Scrubs, and had someone with the improbable name of the 'Vicar' working for him.

I was allocated a probation officer to whom I would have to report once a week. A meeting was set up at the hostel and he duly came to see me. Unfortunately, he seemed to be of the opinion that no prisoner was to be trusted and that ex-prisoners, in particular, we to be viewed with suspicion. Of course he was entitled to this opinion. When he asked me what I intended to do – even though he had my letter of acceptance in front of him – and I told him I was going to drama school, he laughed and in no uncertain terms told me I was barking mad, and made me feel like a liar. In similarly robust terms I thanked him for his time and left.

After a discussion with the hostel officer it was decided that another probation officer might be more helpful. I was introduced to Andy Marlin, who seemed completely on my side. He was worried, however, about my future address, as I really didn't want to go back home; so I assured him I would find somewhere to live. After a discussion at Tom's place one night, Tom suggested he talk to the family across the road, as they took in lodgers. I thought this would prove handy as I could travel in to work with Tom each day. My probation officer was happy with this set-up; he worked out of a probation office near to where I was to be living.

I continued to see my sister and her family, and at Dad's request I made the occasional trip to the family home. My mother was becoming increasingly difficult to talk to; she was terrified the police would turn up and find out I wasn't living at home. But that was a stick she continually tried to beat me with. The hostel officer knew exactly where I was, as I always informed him, and he knew the situation at home. As long as I was at work, wasn't committing a crime and was back in the hostel at the required time, then he was happy. The sad thing is that if it hadn't been for Dad – and for the fact that he was trying to keep the peace and give himself a quiet life – I would have stopped having anything to do with my mother years before. Sad state of affairs really and quite tragic.

My mother's support, or lack of it, was very much in contrast to my aunt in America, to whom I had written to say I was out, and thanked her for all the support she had given me while I was away. Immediately she sent me some clothes and various other little American treats like Hershey bars.

At last the time came for me to be released and Tom picked me up. He took me to his place and helped me settle in across the road. Anne and John were a lovely, generous couple with a young child.

As I left resettlement, I realized that the date was Thursday, 23 March 1978; I was being released four days earlier as it was Easter weekend. My official release date on licence was 27 March, but because no prisoners were released on bank holidays, I had gained a few extra days. Suddenly I thought of Sandhu and the scrap of paper he had written 27 3 78 on all that time ago. How could he have possibly known? No wonder the Indian prisoners looked on him as a god-like figure. Thank you Mr Sandhu.

Working with Tom was hard work. We painted the German Embassy by day and the VD clinic at St Thomas's by night. I informed Webber Douglas that I was out and they immediately said I could start straight away. When I told them I hadn't got enough money to pay the fees, they offered me a scholarship. I said it would be better if I started in the summer, so that I could earn enough money to pay for it.

In order to get the German Embassy job, Tom had to submit our names for a security check. I was surprised that I wasn't turned down: so much for German efficiency. Usually, after finishing work at five o'clock, we made our way down to St Thomas's, where, after a bite to eat and after the clinic had closed, we were allowed in to paint. I was walking from Waterloo Station early one evening, when I was suddenly bundled to the ground. Thinking I was being robbed, or worse still, being arrested, I rolled over ready to fight and curse my way out. I saw that it was Buster Edwards. From his flower stall down the road he had spotted me, and decided I was in need of a rugby tackle. After a five-minute chat, he asked if I wanted a cup of tea. I had to explain that I was on my way to the VD clinic, to which he said, 'All right, but have a drink on me,' and pressed something into my hand. I thanked him and said that I was in the area most nights but maybe next time. Once out of sight, I opened my hand to see a fifty-pound note. Blimey, I had now met two ex-cons, both notorious criminals, and each had given me fifty quid. And they said that crime doesn't pay, as well!

I had been working at the clinic only for a couple of nights when I came out in a dreadful rash. My first thought was that it might be the white spirit I used to get the paint off my arms, but then I thought about the clinic. I couldn't have caught something, could I? When, by the next night, the rash had spread to my stomach, I decided to visit casualty. I might as well have asked what the square root of four million and fifty-six was. The doctors and nurses were perplexed, and made an appointment for me to see a skin and allergy specialist. The next morning was a Saturday, so when I got up I explained to Anne and her husband that I had this rash and maybe I should move out for a while. Anne laughed and said that she had been waiting to tell me that her daughter had also developed a rash, which turned out to be German measles. I had caught it off the child. Thank God I hadn't gone to casualty with pains in my chest or something equally serious.

By now I could do what I wanted, though of course within reason. I still had to report to Andy once a week. This entailed a visit to his office, but after a month it became once a fortnight and then once a month, and finally just a quick phone call. Andy even found some work for me painting his windows when there was no work with Tom.

At the time, I was still madly in love with Jay, the resettlement girl from Leyhill. We wrote and spoke often, but I knew my feelings were unrequited.

While life may have been getting better – a hectic social life, a decent wage and a place at drama school – pressure was being put on me by Dad to go and see my mother. To keep Dad happy I went to see her, but I spent more time cleaning than communicating. The final straw for me – and I am by no means a squeamish person – was when she expected me to help her dress. I refused point blank. Well, I suppose I would have done it if I truly believed she was incapable of dressing due to her hip. But as I had seen her walk normally to the shops, I realized that she was playacting. One day I had turned up with Louise, who at this time was Leela, Dr Who's assistant. I asked my parents to keep it to themselves as Louise was doing me a favour, and anyway she didn't want all the attention and people staring. I guess that was too much to expect: as we pulled into the square and parked the car, half the neighbourhood was standing outside the house waiting to see her.

My mother denied telling anyone, which is as likely as the Government not raising taxes. Louise was obviously upset, but didn't comment about it. Here was yet another straw that, added to the others, would eventually break the camel's back. Strangely, everyone who ever met my mother thought she was odd. Louise, however, ventured the opinion that she was a bit eccentric. If by eccentric she meant barking mad, then eccentric she was.

I saw Jay, who I thought was the love of my life, several times, and she even came down to London once or twice to see me. She seemed interested in everything I was doing. She was now at university and I said I would visit her. Unused to travelling about the country by train, I made the mistake of catching a very slow train from Watford rather than from Euston Station, so by the time I arrived it was nearly time to come back. Poor girl, she waited and waited, and after a quick coffee and a quicker tour of her university it was time to go back. We kept in touch and continued to see each other, but it was the same old story: she obviously liked me as a person, and was interested in my progress, but not in the way I wanted.

Although I had had lots of other offers, it was decided that I would go home for Christmas. I bought presents for everyone in the family and rushed over to Angela's on Christmas Eve to drop them off. I then went up to see my aunt, who had also invited me over for Christmas lunch, after which I travelled to my parents' to stay for Christmas. But I knew I would be back in London as soon as the first available train left Cove Station.

I shouldn't have bothered: Christmas was a disaster, ruined by my mother and Dad arguing, and when John came round it descended into a heated slanging match. John left as quickly as he could after finishing his lunch.

I couldn't wait to get out. Boxing Day came and went; it was a day of silence punctuated only by the odd solemn visit to the pub. The next day I set off for London, and went straight to Tom's.

15

MATURE STUDENT

As I made my way to the main entrance of Webber Douglas, having summoned up enough courage to go in, I was suddenly panicked. Was I doing the right thing, or had I made a huge mistake? Perhaps if I had slept the night before; or had I not arrived so early and spent all that time in Dino's, there might have been less time to think? Looking back, though, I am sure that every other student was going through that same inner turmoil.

Out of the corner of my eye I saw other students arriving, mostly on foot, although one or two arrived by motorbike or in cars. All had large bags, similar to mine, crammed full with all the items we had been asked to buy. I had the completely ridiculous idea that I might see someone from my audition, but no familiar face greeted me. As I finally plucked up enough courage to darken the main door, making sure that I was with other students so as not to look too out of place, my panic was replaced with a feeling of nervousness. We were led down to the basement area, where I had sat on my audition day. Most of the other students were dressed in jeans, though one or two of the girls must have thought that it was a fashion parade.

After a while we were allocated our groups and given a guided tour of the school. The building, which at first had seemed huge, was in fact quite small; every available space had been put to use. The school also had several other rooms (i.e. church halls), widely scattered in the surrounding area. Like everything else the layout of the school would take some getting used to, and for several days most of us would often walk into the wrong classes at the wrong time.

After lunch we had our first lesson, entitled 'Improvisation', in the crypt of the church hall. As we all congregated until it was time to make our way to the crypt, the other students arrived. It was strange seeing all these people greet each other after their long summer holidays, and I saw what it must be like at university or boarding school. But, as soon as they saw us, it dawned on me that no matter where I had been it was exactly the same: whether it was school or the army or prison, the older kids, the old soldiers, the old prisoners, all liked to show off and impress the new ones. Amazingly, you could tell who was in which year: the final-year students were far more theatrical, in their dress, language and even in the swagger in their walk.

Several people asked me if I was a new teacher, and seemed surprised when I said I was a student. After a while I realized why I was being asked: I was the oldest student there, and this made me very apprehensive. Was I going to stick out like a sore thumb, not only in age, but in everything else I did at drama school?

The students in my class were a very mixed bunch. Tall, short, fat, thin, good-looking, frumpy, blonde, red-headed, they came from London, Portsmouth, Leicester, Leeds, Manchester, Finland, Iceland, Australia, Sweden, Holland and South Africa. Some of the girls were beautiful; I felt like a kid in a toyshop – plenty to look at, but no money to pay for anything.

While I tended to be accepted as one of the group – and several became great mates, though over the years I lost touch with a few – they all seemed so much more confident and accomplished than me. I later found out, however, that they had felt the same way about me. I never talked about my past, and when asked why I had become a drama student late in life I just said I had been in the army and left it at that.

There was certainly no time to relax, what with classes in movement, make-up, tap dancing, fencing, speech, voice, singing, text, and of course acting. Most of these were self-explanatory, apart from the acting lessons, which seemed to be based on the Stanislavsky method that focused on something called 'circles of concentration'. We all seemed to reach this point at different times in our training, though for the life of me I am not sure how we got there.

The teachers were, like the students, a very mixed bunch in age, dress and sexuality. Teaching methods also varied enormously. For tap and jazz dance we had Roy Riches, who had taught at several drama schools and loved to talk about how he had choreographed a Disney cartoon. For those of us who had two left feet or who weren't familiar with tap, there was no real opportunity to progress, so we just stayed in the back row. Some of us even ended up going up to Covent Garden in order to have private tuition, we were that hungry to succeed as actors. Roy also taught jazz, which at least got him out of the chair and to be fair his jazz dance routines were dynamic. Obviously I had to work hard just to keep up, but later on I realized that my innate lack of confidence had not helped.

For 'movement' we had Robin Winbow, who also taught dance. Robin lived and breathed dance and exercise; he also taught at dance centres in Covent Garden and was able to help me by allowing me to attend his evening classes. Most of these were attended by those who were preparing to audition for West End shows. Robin had such an enthusiasm that he didn't believe in no-hopers; he thought everyone was worth the effort. He always encouraged us to try and never thought to humiliate anyone who couldn't learn the routines. With the fear of failure looming over us, and knowing that people would be kicked out at the end of each term, we were desperate to succeed. Drama schools tend to strip you of your confidence and then build you up again – if you survive, that is. With so few people having either the talent or good fortune to make it in the profession, these schools are great money-making ventures. No one can teach you to act, though drama schools can go some way to develop talent. I still believe that there are great actors who have never graced a stage or film set just because they had little faith in their own ability.

After one of Robin's evening classes, he invited me out for a drink. I wasn't paying for my lessons so I didn't want to cause offence by turning him down. We popped into a place on Shaftesbury Avenue, which happened to be a gay pub, and then went to a little place he knew for a quick snack. We made our way up a narrow flight of stairs, at the top of which a spy hole in the door clicked open and shut. Oh no, I thought, not prison all over again. We were let in to what was a key club, full of gay men. God knows what everyone must have thought. Years later I met Robin when he came to see me in a play. He is now a psychic and travels the world giving lectures, though why that surprises me I don't know, as astral projection always seemed to crop up in his dance classes.

Fencing was taken by Roy Goodall, who always had his dog stretched out at his feet. We were expected to learn this art, with a view towards obtaining a certificate in stage fighting. After an introduction to the history of weapons and armour, we got on to the fun stuff. Kitted out in face masks and white tunics, with broad-swords, foils and daggers at the ready, we looked like a scene out of *Spartacus*. Unfortunately, I never did receive my fight certificate, as the chap I was paired with, and rehearsed with day and night, didn't turn up for the exam. He supposedly had tonsilitis; his tonsils, according to his girlfriend, weighed two pounds each. How someone could have the equivalent of two bags of sugar in his throat worried me slightly then, but I realized soon afterwards that he was rather off-the-wall.

The fight we he had rehearsed, and perfected so well, was according to Roy Goodall a dead cert. When the examiner came in, and Roy explained the situation, I was told that we could rearrange it, but the other chap never could be tied down. Strangely enough, never in my professional career have I once been asked in any fight scene – with or without swords – if I had a certificate. Maybe my unreliable partner knew that it was a waste of time.

Text was taken by the most exquisitely beautiful lady I have ever laid eyes on. She was seventy, if not older, and immaculately turned out. If someone were to ask me if I have ever met a real lady, then Judith Glick would be the first name I would come up with. I often wondered how she must have been at twenty, given that she was this beautiful at seventy. She knew Shakespeare backwards and had the most amazing memory, though she had a penchant for dozing off in the middle of her own lessons. Nevertheless, those two hours were a joy, even to someone like me, whose only acquaintance with Shakespeare was O-level English and the Russian film of *King Lear*. I regret to say that I hadn't a clue what Shakespeare was about. Judith, though, made me persevere, and she was right: one day, quite suddenly, I grasped it. We all had to work towards doing a one-man show, where we took a character from a Shakespearean play and told the story from his or her perspective. I chose to be Kent from *King Lear*.

By all accounts my performance was very good, as I was then chosen to be Orsino in a platform performance of *Twelfth Night*. Judith was also insistent that I would be a wonderful Vashinin, whoever he was. Loath to show my ignorance, I thanked her for her support, and then scurried off to find out who the hell Vashinin was. Thank God she didn't ask me if I had read Chekhov.

Raphael Jago, the principal, was a man of extreme vision who always embraced the ever-changing nature of acting. He put on the majority of the plays in the Chanticleer Theatre, as well as a Shakespeare play in the grounds at Cliveden every summer. When pub and studio theatre was in its infancy he took over the top of the Draycott Arms in South Kensington and staged productions there. With prompting from Patsy Rodenburgh and me, he took a production about environmentally friendly witches and warlocks around several primary schools in south-east London.

He obviously chose his staff with care, although not all were suited to the task of teaching students. He brought in different styles of directors, who would put on the productions from which the staff would carry out assessments. By the final year, though, productions were more geared to impress agents and producers, who might have work for leaving students, and, of course, enable them to obtain that added bonus of an Equity card.

Jago was ably assisted by the man who did all the hard work. John Malpass may have been the secretary by title, but he had the incredibly difficult task of working out the most complicated timetables. And then he always had a word of comfort and advice for all the students. Sadly, he committed suicide several years ago. On reflection it is ironic that a man that everyone poured their problems out to clearly had no one to listen to his.

As well as Robin Winbow, we had a female movement teacher, who was also a talented singer, actress and musician. She was like a young Jane Fonda, stunning in her leotard, tights and leg warmers, and she worked us hard. Although her classes were physically draining, just watching her made the lessons fly; and when it came time to leave I just wanted to stay. Her name was Caroline. When one of our improvisation teachers saw her, he was like a dog with three tails, but she didn't seem interested.

All the students tended to hang out in the Denmark Arms, just around the corner from the drama school. After one of her late-afternoon classes, Caroline joined us there. She seemed very nice, and asked me about myself. Fortunately I told her I did a bit of painting and decorating to help pay my way through drama school. A few days later I bumped into her in the street, and she asked me if I was interested in painting her flat. Bloody hell, of course I was; I fancied her like mad. She only wanted a quote, but I was over the moon. When I looked up in class to see her eyes on me − even though it was probably just to see if this old student was doing the exercises properly − I had a sneaking feeling that maybe she had a soft spot for me.

I eventually went round to her flat. She wanted the ceilings in standard white, but the walls had to be an ever-diminishing shade of purple, which was her new colour (her previous phase had been black and white). As soon as term ended and Christmas was over, I would start on it. By the time the job was finished, which with the added distractions took longer than I had imagined it would, the flat looked pretty good, if somewhat strange. Nevertheless, the distractions were well worth it.

I had decided to hold a party at my place in Wembley, and invited all my classmates. Obviously, everyone had someone to bring, so I asked Caroline, who sort of promised to come, although she had a lunch do to go to. The day of the party arrived, and most of my classmates made it, though there was no sign of Caroline. Now it seemed that I would be the host with the most, but without. When she arrived late bearing some home-made sweets, I was thrilled.

When friends asked me what the party was in aid of I flippantly remarked, 'It's my twenty-first.' Well, I hadn't had a proper one when I was twenty-one, so why not, eleven years later? The sweets were my twenty-first present. The party was a great success and everyone enjoyed it except for me. Someone at the party had lit a joint, so having never had one, I decided to take a puff. No sooner had I inhaled, I felt violently ill and ran to the toilet. That's all I can remember, until I woke up and Caroline was sitting on the edge of the bed watching me. I felt like a complete idiot. Once I had showered and gone downstairs, I found that she had cleaned up. After walking her to the station, I went back to the house and spent the next few hours kicking myself. I felt that if I had ever had any chance with her, I must have blown it by now.

I had settled down to look at what I had to prepare for when I went back to college, when the phone rang. It was Caroline. She said if I was at a loose end that night why not pop over and we could share some spaghetti. I tried not to sound overly enthusiastic as I said yes, and casually made my way over to her place, picking up a bunch of flowers on the way. She seemed very pleased to see me when I arrived, and loved the flowers. It suddenly dawned on me that I should have brought some wine, and so I offered to get a bottle. As I walked down the street with her it felt like the most natural thing to be doing. After dinner, as we were washing up, she turned to me.

'Do you know what an affair is?'

'Yeah, lots of coconut shies and dodgem cars,' I replied in my usual fashion, not believing what I was hearing.

'Because that's what it would be, but we'd have to keep it secret. No one, but no one must know. The school would go ape shit. Also it would compromise our relationship as student and teacher.'

I don't think I even replied. We did become lovers, but I became paranoid that our secret would come out. At school we carried on as if nothing had happened: not a word escaped my lips, nor hers for that matter. Although a year later, while I was helping the 'improvisation' teacher paint someone's house, he kept asking me if

Caroline and I had had a fling. I just laughed it off and carried on painting. But for some reason I was sure he knew.

It was fascinating, watching teachers and students vying for her attention, while all the time I knew that she was interested only in me. Obviously class work became a strain, as whenever she came near me I wanted to touch her. Now I look back and think how ridiculous it was that two adults, who were obviously so much in love at the time, had to stifle their feelings. Shades of being back in prison in more ways than one.

At the end of the first term came our chance to be put through our paces, in Louise Dunne's production of *Tales from the Vienna Woods*. After we had performed, the staff got together over a light meal at Dino's in order to assess our term's work. I had a key for Caroline's flat, so made my way there after a quick drink in the Denmark Arms. Apart from one or two of us, we all thought we had been terrible, and the doubts began to creep in; most of us thought we would be kicked out. As I waited for Caroline to come home, I began to wonder if our relationship was about to come to an abrupt halt. What if I was crap, unsuited to being a drama student and ultimately an actor? If this was the case, would Caroline's feelings for me change?

She arrived carrying a bottle of wine, and when she saw me she threw her arms around me, and said, 'I hate staff meetings. They just don't have any idea what you people go through.' I didn't ask her about individual students and she didn't give anything away. She said she couldn't be stuffed to cook anything, so why didn't we just grab a takeaway and relax? As we walked home she seemed to be holding on to me very tightly, as if afraid to let me go. Was she hiding something that meant this would be the last time we were together? Back at the flat, as we ate and drank, she suddenly looked at me and said, 'I know . . .'

'You know?' I replied.

And the bombshell I thought was coming came, but it wasn't about our relationship, it was my past. One of the members of staff had looked through the students' files and had come across my application. At the meeting at Dino's my past was announced to the table, though to this person's credit, I found out later, the announcement was made once they had all made their assessments.

Wasn't it amazing how well I had done considering where I'd been for the past twelve years? And when they all enquired what was meant, this person told them I had been in prison. At that moment, I gather, there was a stunned silence. Although Jago had obviously consulted the staff about admitting an ex-con, before offering me a place, he had not mentioned a name. The funny thing was that the staff thought the ex-con in question was another student, he of the two-pound tonsils, who although born in the UK, was a former member of the Australian SAS. The way he swaggered about the school seemed to confirm their opinion that he was the student with the criminal past. I was told by an American girlfriend of his that he talked about 'gooks' all the time, having served in Vietnam. Several Australian students thought he was a bullshit artist *par excellence*; they even doubted he was Australian. When we were preparing for our one-man shows with Judith Glick, he could be seen prowling the classrooms at night dressed in black with a hump attached to his back and a dagger fixed to his leather glove; he even wore a stone in his shoe to give him a limp. He never managed to turn up for that role, either.

Caroline asked me if it was true about prison and when I said yes, she said no more and we had another drink and went to bed. I remember, just before being kissed goodbye in the morning she said, 'See you in school, and see you tonight.'

When I arrived at the school, I made my way to the note session, dreading what the reactions were going to be. Caroline was the first teacher I had to see. She had a student with her, but when she saw me she ended that session. Once I had sat down opposite her, Caroline looked me up and down, and with her serious face on flicked the pages of her notebook and said very quietly, 'You know what I think. I will tell you tonight.' And added in a slightly louder voice, 'A good term, made a lot of progress, keep it up.' As for the other teachers, no one mentioned anything about the bombshell until I got to our acting teacher, Hilary Wood. I swear she had a tear in her eye when she leant forward and said, 'I love you even more now.'

So that was my first note session: now only the principal remained to be seen.

Jago was in his office and everyone was in and out in a flash, unless you were to be kept down a term or leaving. (Two were kept down and one was told to leave.) As I entered all he said was, 'A good term, keep building on it.'

The aftermath to my past being made known was that all references to my prison past were confined either to the bin or to Jago's office. Someone – probably Hilary – had seen to that.

I spent the Christmas break working with Tom, while Caroline went up north to see her family. I went to see my family, but as per usual Dad and my aunt were the only ones who really bothered. After Christmas, Jeremy Young phoned me and said he had been offered a job at the school directing. He was going to do *The Kitchen* by Arnold Wesker.

The day before term started we all had to go in to pick up our timetables for the first day and to see what groups we were in. It would be good to see some of the faces again. I travelled in from Wembley to Webber and as the weather was bad, it took a lot longer than usual. Snow was falling thick and fast. I picked up my timetable, said hello to a few friends and made my way home again. Caroline was still away so I spent some time at Tom's and prepared myself for the start of the new term.

The tubes, because of the weather, were up the creek, so I decided to walk in. The next day I got up disgustingly early and set off for the Cromwell Road. I arrived at the room where the first lesson of the new term was taking place be. It was rehearsals, and who should be sitting on the stage but Jeremy Young. As I walked through the door I glanced at my watch and it said three minutes past nine. As I opened my mouth to apologize, Jeremy boomed out as only he can, 'YOU'RE LATE! If you want to be taken serious in this industry you have to be on time.' He added a number of other platitudes, then said, 'Make sure you are here five minutes early tomorrow.' Bloody hell, he was a mate, as well, but even if he had to keep our relationship as mates separate from the business at Webber Douglas, I still thought it was a bit strong.

The next day I arrived at school at 8.30 a.m. and, as I approached the main door, who should I see getting out of his car opposite the school but Jeremy. As he was locking his door he saw me and bellowed, 'Why were you late yesterday?' When I told him I had walked in, he seemed mortified. We went to Dino's for a coffee, where he admitted that he had screamed at me because he didn't know if the other students were aware of our friendship, and he didn't want to be seen as having favourites.

The trains were becoming more and more unreliable, and I found myself walking back late at night, reciting my lines, after working in the evening on another year group's show. After doing some studying when I got in, I grabbed a few hours' sleep and then walked back in to school. Perhaps when Caroline came back I could stay at her place.

After a while it became obvious that she was having difficulty going out with me at night and teaching me during the day, so we decided to call it a day. Every now and again we would meet up to try and get back together, but that usually lasted a couple of days. Finally, it got to the point that she lost her rag in class and threw me out. What for, I wasn't sure. That evening I found a note on the school message board addressed to me; it just said 'Ring me.' We sat up all night talking, and she admitted she had no idea why she had thrown me out, other than the fact that I was distracting her and she couldn't concentrate on the job in hand, as she was spending the lesson thinking about me. We remained friends and every now and again she will turn up somewhere to see me in a play, though sometimes she just leaves a note.

I was still keeping in touch with my probation officer, although by now it was by phone. And after the tube and weather incidents, and with the ever-increasing workload, it looked as if it might be time to move on from Wembley and find a place to live nearer the school. With Andy's help, I scoured the local papers from several areas surrounding South Kensington, and finally settled on a choice of two places. There was a room to rent in Ladbroke Grove and another in Fulham. We checked out the one in Ladbroke Grove first, and as soon as we arrived at the front door we both knew it wasn't for me. The one in Fulham was perfect, a nice house occupied by a lovely theatrical man.

Sad as I was to leave Wembley, and the added bonus of having Tom and his family across the road, it really was more practical to be nearer the school, and of course it also meant I had a little more money in my pocket each week, as my travel costs were much lower.

My new landlord was incredible: he always had a meal ready for when I got in, and I always let him know what time I would be back. Whatever time it was – within reason of course – food would appear. He was delighted to have me staying there, perhaps only because I was a drama student. He was theatre mad: he had the most amazing music collection, of all the Broadway shows, sent to him from a friend in the States.

Drama school, however, was becoming more and more intense, and it was certainly a relief to be only a short distance from Fulham, which meant of course I had more time to study. I was still in contact with Jay from Leyhill, who was now living in the north, and out of the blue I was invited up there during a break from school. She was as beautiful as ever, and had exactly the same effect on me that day as she had had the first time I realized that I had fallen in love with her. After a pleasant day with her and her family, looking at all the sights, they departed for home and Jay and I toured the Lake District together in her car. I finally decided that, although my feelings for her were still very strong, nothing would ever come of it. And so gradually I distanced myself. She really was a special person, and without her help and support I'm sure I would have cracked up.

As I progressed through the school, my class was slowly being whittled down, as people were being discarded. I was earning money now by cleaning the school during the mornings, and on audition weekends I would be paid to help process the auditionees. On the first day of a new term I would show the new students around the school. Our class work, meanwhile, became more and more geared to performances and the plays became more and more varied, tragedy, comedy and the classics.

After my fifth term notes' session, in my interview with Jago I was told that I could leave if I wanted to. I felt as if I had been hit in the stomach by a sledgehammer, and burst out that I wanted to stay.

'Fine,' he said. I thought that I was being rejected, and as I had set my heart on being an actor, I was devastated that I was a failure. My insecurities again. I wanted that diploma so badly and I wanted to do the three years. Jago was apparently unaware of the turmoil and disappointment I was going through, because he said, 'I think you're ready to enter the profession, and need to get experience in the proper world, but if you feel you want to stay, I am going to bump you up into finals.'

I spent the next three terms in finals, instead of the usual one, so I missed pre-finals, which took up two terms. Finals consisted of working towards plays performed for the benefit of agents and outside contacts, so final-term students didn't have many classes to attend, and usually turned up at the school much later in the day. Because of my naïveté and the doubts as to my ability as an actor, I asked Jago if I could turn up to several classes as an extra body. He thought this would be fine.

Not everything at drama school was hunky dory, and not all lessons were a joy to take part in. One chap, an American called Andy Harmon, used to work from a box of cards with certain programmes included. One of these involved walking around the room for an hour, 'feeling the space'. After about eight weeks of this, twice a week, he turned to me and said, in this whiney, grating New York accent: 'Leslie [although it always came out as Lesssleeee], you're not enjoying this, are you?'

'Andy, if I wanted to walk in space I would have become an astronaut,' I said.

'Well, you have to do it.'

'Really,' I thought.

After the lesson I went to Jago and said, 'Look, this guy's nuts.' At the next Andy-Harmon-first-man-on-the-moon session, Jago popped in and left after five minutes. Andy Harmon's lessons became non-compulsory after that.

I only ever lost my temper once at drama school, and that was out of real frustration. We were doing *The Maid's Tragedy*, affectionately known as 'expanda dress', as five girls, all of various shapes and sizes, had to share the lead role, but had only one dress to wear. So when the thinnest girl had it on it fitted her perfectly, and as each girl took over the role, and they got larger, so did the dress. I was playing the King of Spain, who opened the play with an enormous three-page speech, or so it seemed, and it was a pig of a speech to do. We were being directed by this American chap, Robert, who had an opera background. He was very good-looking, five foot tall, boyish-looking, and dressed head to toe in leather. He obviously had not directed at a drama school before. Rehearsals came and went and he seemed to concentrate only on the two main leads; and we would all be sitting there in rehearsals, never getting to the play or the other actors. Dress rehearsal came, and I looked like a Mars bar, as I was dressed all in brown, brown boots, brown corduroy trousers and brown rollneck sweater.

Each day Robert assured us all that he would get to us, but never did. The night before we were due to perform it in front of the school, when it would be assessed by the staff, we all sat watching the two leads, who were good, but then anyone would have been good with the amount of rehearsal time they had been given. Rehearsals were now over and the rest of us, apart from the very first read-through, had not even opened our scripts. We all voiced our displeasure, and the director must have suddenly realized his mistake, and stuttered a reply, only to be cut off by one of the leads who said something to the effect of, 'Just because you don't have a big part.'

Well, I flipped. 'We'll see how big your part is after I throw you out the bloody window.'

At that they both ran out of the room.

The next morning we had a note session with Jago, which was strange as he used to see us only after we had finished our performance, on the last day of term, but this time he was going off to New York to attend auditions, and wanted to see us before he went. I had, as usual, in the morning been cleaning the school, and had then shot back home to have a shower and then returned to do my day's work. I was early, so I was sitting in the area near Jago's office waiting to be called. Suddenly the two leads in *The Maid's Tragedy* appeared together and said, 'Can we go in first because we have tutorials?' I said, 'Yes, go ahead.' Anyway, they both went in, and when they came out I went in. Jago was sat behind his desk with a big grin on his face, and when I sat down he just laughed. Then he asked about the incident the night before, and of course it dawned on me that the two blokes had got in first. I told him the score and thought I'd blown it. He just said, 'Well done, they need shaking up.'

Because the girls had never had any rehearsal in getting in and out of the 'expanda dress' it suddenly all went haywire. The first girl playing the maid was great, but as the play progressed you could hear swearing and cursing as each girl struggled to get the dress on and off in quick succession. After a while the dress was appearing unbuttoned and unfastened and sometimes just being held together by the actress's hands.

We also did things called student productions, where one of us would direct and the others would do scenes from plays. But as we were only students, we rarely made the right choices, according to our tutors. But that was, I guess, the standard reply to everyone, all part of keeping us in our places. But no matter how hard the work was, and juggling all the little jobs to help me through, I loved it. After the life I had had, I was just glad to be there, plagued as I was by the fear of being kicked out.

By now I was in finals, although there would be some crossover into pre-finals, and I didn't have to be at school so early. I used to clean the school the night before, so I could have a lie-in. I was also still doing the auditions, and some of the auditionees were hilarious. One chap will always stick in my mind; he was Welsh and was going to do a speech from *Richard III*. He had, I swear, a hump on his left shoulder, which at the time I thought was part of his preparation. He went in and came out after doing his pieces. I then took in cups of tea for the panel, who were in hysterics. When I asked what was so funny, one of them showed me. The poor chap had said, 'I'm going to do a speech from *Richard III*,' and they, seeing the hump, had thought the same as me, that he had something stuffed up his shirt. Well, he stood up and faced the panel, when suddenly he dropped his left shoulder and raised his right shoulder, which now became the hump.

Several faces from my past also turned up. Sharon, one of the girls from the Portsmouth drama group, arrived to audition and when she saw me she couldn't believe it. When she realized that I had been there for a while, she was thrilled. She hung around after her audition and during lunch break we shot off for a coffee. She couldn't wait to tell everyone back in Portsmouth about me. She asked if people knew about my past, and I said, 'Some do but the majority don't,' and she said, 'Well, they won't find out from me.' She got into Webber Douglas and went on to have a brief but very successful career, tragically cut short by cancer.

About this time I started to become more and more aware of this one Australian girl I kept seeing around the school. She was stunning, like a very young Vivien Leigh, and she was always the centre of attention, always laughing or making the people around her laugh.

I had become very friendly with a student in my year called John Lee, who was renting a room in the house that Jane owned – so now, at least, I knew her name. Jane's crowd seemed to play an important part in my life. I was on the stage management side for one of the shows in her year and it seems that one of her crowd had commented, 'Check out the guy on lights.' None of them knew me too well, so Jane offered to investigate on the girls' behalf. After the show, as usual, we all went for a drink in the Denmark.

Now Jane's year group were a bunch who were slightly rebellious; they were forever winding each other up, and indeed others. So when Jane introduced herself – and began peppering me with questions – I took it that this was just another wind-up. So I played along with it, and I asked to go for a drink with her on the Friday night. Deep down I was thinking, 'Yeah-yeah, I'll turn up like a lemon and you won't be there. And besides, why would such a beautiful girl want to have a drink with me when she had the pick of the school?' So I didn't turn up. Part of it was a genuine belief that Jane hadn't really been serious about the date – part of it my own fear of rejection. The next day John Lee, her housemate, told me that Jane had come home furious at having been stood up. She said that if John saw me before she did, he was to warn me she was after my blood. I sought her out and after a little while I managed to convince her that it had all been an innocent misunderstanding. She accepted my apology, and we made a date for the following Friday.

I was at this time, because of my army experience, teaching the other finals group how to march and do rifle drill for their production of *Sergeant Musgrave's Dance*.

On the afternoon of the rearranged date with Jane I had been sought out by the school secretary and told that my elder brother had phoned and I was to ring him urgently. He told me my Dad had been rushed to hospital that morning, and seemingly was in a bad way. I wrote a quick letter to Jane explaining the situation, and gave it to John asking him to give it to Jane as soon as he could. Then I made my way to the hospital where Dad was laid low. On reflection I couldn't have made a worse decision about the letter, as John, a great bloke but totally unreliable, tended to go off on a tangent. (His pet routine at that time was to stand in front of a mirror re-enacting scenes from *Taxi Driver*.) He never did pass on my message. He himself ended up taking my place and joining her for a drink.

I arrived at the hospital and Dad looked terrible. He was bright yellow and looked as if someone had covered him in gallons of that fake tan. He had yellow jaundice, but was not as bad as my brother had made out. He was pleased to see me, but as he was very tired I didn't stay long. After talking to the doctors, and being told he would be all right, I made the trek back home, secure in the assumption that John had delivered my letter.

Next morning, as I was making my way to the theatre to put the *Sergeant Musgrave* lot through their paces, who should I see but Jane. I crossed the road to talk to her, but she was annoyed with me, and told me to go away. After some persuasion, I managed to find out that John hadn't given her the note, and obviously her class had sent her up over my non-appearance. Eventually I managed to make her see sense about my Dad. She could see I was telling the truth, and calmed down. We agreed to a drink some other time.

I arrived at Jane's on the Saturday night and she looked absolutely stunning, not overly dressed, but wearing a pretty skirt and top. Off we went, and got on the tube and then a train. As we settled down in the carriage, I looked up and across from me was a familiar face, a corporal from my regiment in Germany. He looked at me and sort of half recognized me, but obviously couldn't place me. I nodded and said, 'Hello Ron.' We got in conversation, then he said he was sorry but he couldn't remember my name. So I told him, and we carried on chatting. Suddenly it must have dawned on him who I was; he went quiet and just stared at me, then hesitantly resumed the conversation. As we approached the next station on our journey, he quickly jumped up and got off. I wasn't sure if it was his station or not; or maybe he thought he was in danger, being in the same carriage as me.

Eventually Jane and I arrived at our destination: a party at a friend's flat. The party was great fun, but because the flat was small, it became impossible to walk, talk, or breathe. After a few drinks, Jane and I decided to clear off, and made our way back to her place.

Soon we were enjoying each other's company, and it wasn't long before we were an accepted item. One day after class I met up with Jane and she said that she had been picked on non-stop by this movement teacher. She couldn't understand why, but then when she had said that the teacher's name was Caroline I put two and two together. No one, not even Jane, had known that I had had a relationship with Caroline. Even the improvisation teacher, who also taught mime, made some comment about how lucky I was. I certainly seemed to get up his nose as far as women were concerned.

While I had never forgotten that I was a prisoner on licence, I had tended to forget how fragile freedom was, and how easy it would be to be hauled back in. This made itself clear one evening just as Jane and I had started going out. Several of us, including Jane and Jeremy, decided to go to a disco. After strutting our stuff on the dance floor, we decided we had had enough and would grab something to eat. I popped into the toilet, and when I came out I saw that Jane and the girls were being chatted up by a group of blokes. She was telling them that she was waiting for me. They, on the other hand, had other ideas: ditch the boyfriends and go off with them, as they were off to Belfast the next day. Shit! Squaddies on leave. Of course, they were drunk, and wanted to beat us up. As they tried to pick a fight with me, it flashed through my mind that this was the last thing I needed. I certainly didn't want to be arrested for a fracas as that might get me whisked back inside. Luckily Jeremy took control, and as he started to try and placate them, he whispered, 'Run.' We all, bar our hero, legged it out of there. As we waited for him, we all started to worry; but there he was walking down the road as if it were a Sunday stroll. This incident made me reluctant to got out to places that were a possible source of danger.

Jane was one of the first to get a job in her year, and had lots of agents after her. She went off to do weekly rep in Southwold to get her Equity card, and although it was hard work she loved it. I went up several times to see her and one evening we went out for dinner. Jane volunteered to choose the wine. Although my own experience of wine was extremely limited – Blue Nun was Premier Cru, vintage tipple as far as I was concerned – I still chortled at the idea of an Aussie knowing anything about wine. In those days, the only wines taken seriously were French, along with one or two marques from Italy and Spain. As for Australian wine, it was unheard of, apart from the obvious jokes in Monty Python sketches. Yet here was I, at the mercy of an Antipodean wine fancier. What was I doing, delegating such a key decision to somebody who was, fundamentally, going to take a look at the relative prices and guess? How wrong can you be, though! Not for the first time and by no means the last, I was to be put in my place by Jane's good taste and finesse. She came from a renowned family of vintners, and her grandfather had been influential in transforming winemaking into a science.

The first time I met her father was after a trip when he and his wife had taken Jane off to Scotland. I was to meet them on their return. Jane phoned me and said would I come over one evening that week. As I was shown into the kitchen, I couldn't believe my eyes; I had never seen so much wine stacked up, not even in an off-licence. Berry Brothers and Rudd, the very upmarket vintners they'd just visited, must have thought they had had all their Christmases come at once; there was, or so it looked, thousands of pounds' worth of wine just piled there from floor to ceiling. He had tried to get his wine into their shop, but they weren't interested, as they felt there wasn't a market for it. Later he and Jane would seek out Hugh Johnson and he was so impressed, he took it into the Sunday Times Wine Club. Jane would man a stand for her father at the annual wine fair and I would help; the wines always seemed to get the judges' and public's vote. So I guess Jane's family contributed to the beginning of the invasion of Aussie wines over here. Her father, who is a very generous man, has opened up new avenues for me – wine, food, travel and of course even financial help.

Jane's sunny and generous disposition made her a joy to be around, and after our first few dates I realized I wanted to be with her all the time. We started off socializing with the rest of the gang, and a great time it was, too – but more and more, we were sneaking off on our own. Jane had a house in Sydney Street just off the King's Road, and before long I moved in with her. At that stage thoughts of marriage had not entered my head. It wasn't that I had any doubts at all about Jane, more that I was still quite insecure myself. Let's not forget that it wasn't so long ago that I was a detainee at Her Majesty's pleasure, and the role models of my immediate family had not exactly sold the institution of marriage to me. I was happy to take things slowly on that front.

My time now at drama school became more and more intense. Although the sword of Damocles was no longer hanging over my head, a whole new dimension was suddenly added to the pressures. Everyone became very competitive, and the girls would get bitchy about the other girls, even if they had been close. The boys would also become secretive, reticent about giving anything away. And if someone suddenly started to get called for an audition or an agent was interested in them, they would be cold-shouldered. As the performances became showcases for their talent, agents were encouraged to come in, either by the school or by us writing to invite them. As the casting was announced for each play, those who didn't get leads were vitriolic, bitter and sometimes tearful. Obviously not everyone could play the major roles, although I do think that the school could have sometimes not pushed the same people to the fore. However, I was to find that a lot of those who had had the big parts at school didn't make it. Mind you, you also realize that some actors shouldn't be allowed near a theatrical bookshop, let alone a stage. Sadly, it's that type of world.

Around this time, Julia Smith, who was later to play a huge part in shaping my career, came into my life. She took the television course. Both she and Tony Holland came in after an initial introduction to television acting by Patrick Tucker. This basically entailed telling us the difference between a close-up, a mid-shot and a long-shot. Pretty mundane really, but when Julia and Tony turned up it all changed. We had scripts called 'Cherubims', which were in fact scripts from a hospital series they had conceived called 'Angels'. I was not given a part, but was the floor manager and the lighting operator. Others who didn't have parts played technical staff, and to be honest it was a great way to learn the business. As I was the oldest student, it was deemed right that I should run the show, as it was a complicated job. Rehearsals went fine; we spent the night before the performance setting up the studio as a hospital wing, and during rehearsals, we borrowed and begged stuff from chemists and hospitals to make it look as much like a hospital ward as possible.

I arrived early and was making the final checks on everything, when I was told that the leading man wasn't coming in. My immediate reaction was, 'Oh no, he hasn't got two-pound tonsils again.' (It was my fencing partner.) But no, he had heard that a theatre company was holding auditions, so he decided he would go off and attend them instead of the television class. So I was recruited to play his part, as well as doing the lights and running the show. The next lesson, we would see what we'd done, and Julia would give us her notes. We saw the show and although it was rough, it looked OK. Julia went all round the cast and gave them her notes, but didn't say a word to me. 'God, I must have been crap,' I thought. When the staff gave notes at a later date, though, nearly all said that television was my forte.

I was also rehearsing a new play written by the director, a man called Adrian Rendle. It was set in Russia, and called *Exhibitions at a Spa*. I was playing this war-weary and slightly deranged old soldier who, thoroughly depressed about war, decides to play Russian roulette with a single-shot pistol. Luckily it misfires. It was a cheerful little piece.

One evening I was coming into the main school building and I bumped into Julia Smith, who looked at me and glared, and then said, 'Have you got an Equity card, yet?' When I said no, she said,

'Pity, let me know when you do.' Apparently there was a part in 'Angels', but it was not to be. She employed many ex-students in that series, so hopefully if ever I got one, I could work with her again, only this time in the professional world. Little did I know how much my next call from Julia would change my life.

In my final term I was spending my time having photographs taken and sending out hundreds of requests to theatres, agents and casting directors, trying to get someone to come and see me in shows at the school. After *Exhibitions at a Spa*, I would get out of my costume and, after getting back into my normal clothes, I would start to clean the school, to save me getting up early in the morning and doing it. The other actors would go into the bar at the school, where they would mingle with family and agents. No sooner had I started to clean than the girls' toilet door burst open and Jago was standing there. He laughed.

'What are you laughing at?' I asked.

'Only you could be cleaning the toilets when there's a load of agents down in the bar and some are asking to see you,' he replied.

I was sweaty and smelt of bleach.

'Could you say sorry on my behalf, and get their names. I'll get in touch,' I said.

He laughed again. 'All right.'

I subsequently followed up their enquiries, and although all seemed interested, they obviously would rather I had an Equity card. I promised each one that if and when I did get one, I would be in touch.

My first break was not too far away, though. Jane had read a PCR (Professional Casting Report) breakdown for a BBC2 drama in its planning stages. She was very excited – one of the characters sounded like it had been created just for me. She found out the name of the director and left several messages at his office. Eventually his curiosity was pricked and he called back, inviting me to come in and see him. Jim O'Brien was the name of the director and the producer was Michael Wearing, both huge names in British television drama. Michael was the man responsible for dramas such as 'Boys from the Black Stuff'. Jim would go on to do *The Monocled Mutineer* and *Jewel in the Crown*.

Once again, there was that powerful combination of fear and sheer excitement as I went in to see Jim. This could be big. Sitting there in his office, the more I spoke with him, the more I realized I was desperate to work with him. He was absolutely brilliant, not at all like the stuffy theatrical types I'd envisaged, and Michael was the same – a breath of fresh air. Both men liked me and, subject to my getting an Equity card, wanted me for a major character in the production, entitled 'Jake's End'. The downside was that getting an Equity card was as likely as finding one of Willy Wonka's golden tickets. It was the eternal Catch-22: you couldn't work without an Equity card and you couldn't get an Equity card without a good body of work to your name. Many of the specialist unions at the time operated a similar 'closed shop' policy, but at least with Equity there were loopholes. For example, if you could get yourself three stand-up or variety gigs (with the contracts to back them up), you were in. The trouble, however, was getting the three contracts in time to be able to accept the role on 'Jake's End'. Michael Wearing pulled strings and whispered in the right ears, but not even he could magic up an Equity membership in time. The BBC had to recast, and that particular role went west.

While I was waiting to hear from people I had contacted, I was auditioning like mad. I auditioned for Alan Ayckbourne's company, and got a recall, to be seen by him. As always, I arrived early, and sitting down in the foyer of the Roundhouse was this middle-aged man. After getting into conversation with him, he asked me what pieces I was doing, I told him, and he replied, 'A bit one-dimensional.'

'Well, the same could be said for Ayckbourne's work,' I replied.

He left, and five minutes later I went into the audition space. My face dropped when I saw my earlier companion sitting at the table, and then he completely blew my mind when he introduced himself as Alan Ayckbourne. Suffice to say I didn't get the job, but years later he asked me to play the lead in his West End play *Man of the Moment*. I declined because I felt my playing an ex-con who was a huge star, and being confronted about it on a television show would have detracted from the play, with the media hysteria that would have no doubt surrounded the production. Peter Bowles did it instead, and when he was leaving, they asked me again, but I still felt that the production would have suffered from my involvement in it.

John Lee, who had left Webber Douglas early, had got himself a job with the Stirrabout theatre company and, after auditioning for them, they offered me a job. However, they rescinded it when they did a security check, and my past was revealed. Stirrabout was a theatre company that visited prisoners, so you can fully understand the logic of not wishing to employ a character who might give inmates the crazy idea that you can move on successfully after prison!

I was auditioning a lot at the time, just eager for a paid gig. Commercials were seen as a good way into screen acting, in that there was a regular supply of opportunities and it wasn't badly paid. You'd see all the same faces turning up for castings, often several per day. The advent of the answerphone became a blessing to aspiring actors, as it wasn't unusual to get a phone call last thing at night telling you to be at a casting first thing the next morning. I got home one night to find just such a message: 'Get to Covent Garden at nine-thirty tomorrow morning and come dressed as a cowboy.' What? How on earth was I going to cobble together a cowboy outfit at such short notice? But that, in essence, was a crucial part of the brief. If you didn't have the ingenuity to find an outfit, you probably weren't right for the part – or so we all thought! Between Jane and I, we rigged me out as Wyatt Earp (Wyatt Twerp, more like – I was stiffer than Woody off *Toy Story*) and off I lumbered to the tube station. It was agonizing – the longest train ride of my life – as people nudged one another and stared at the freak in the ten-gallon hat. Eventually I got to Covent Garden but, as I waited for the lift, I noticed I wasn't the only cowboy awaiting his ride to the First Chance Saloon. And as we got outside the station, all of a sudden there were more cowboys and cowgirls than there were regular punters, all headed in the same direction. Were we auditioning for a Village People video, perhaps? Thronging the waiting room were perhaps fifty cowboys and almost as many Shotgun Annies. One lone fellow sat in his civvies, eyes glued to the floor as he waited his turn. Needless to say he got the job.

After auditioning for the Belgrade Theatre, Coventry, I was offered a contract for three plays there. No sooner had I accepted, than I had another call from Jim O'Brien's office asking if I had got my Equity card yet. I told them about the Coventry job, but my contract wasn't due to start for another month yet. I asked them what it was all about, but they told me not to worry, it was nothing that important. Somehow, though, I sensed another opportunity slipping away. People like Jim O'Brien didn't just phone to check how things were going. I was starting to despair. But then, at long last – the break I'd been praying for. A club owner of Jane's sister's acquaintance gave me the three contracts I needed. So, at last, my Equity card was within touching (and kissing!) distance. Straight away, I called Jim O'Brien's office with the good news. Jim was delighted for me, and was now able to tell me what his earlier call had been about. He had saved a smaller part for me in 'Jake's End', and although it was nothing like as substantial as the original one they'd offered me, he said he'd be thrilled if I would consider it. *Consider* it? Bloody hell, I would walk on broken glass to do it! Only now I had to ask Jago if I could leave early, as it was to be filmed during the three-day period that would mark my final showcase performance, when for the first time I had the lead part. When I made my request to Jago, he just said yes, and so I left drama school a day early. I was elated, as I was near going into a profession that I had set my heart on. Thank you, Jago, thank you, Webber Douglas; and thank you Jim and thank you the Belgrade. And of course thank you Jane. I was now on my way, I supposed, to the life of a jobbing actor.

16

AT LAST

'Hi-diddle-dee-dee, an actor's life for me.' Like Jiminy Cricket, I was elated as I left the house and made my way to Southampton, to start my first job in the professional acting world. Although I had only one scene – I was to play a bookmaker who helps launder the money of the bank robbers in the play – I had read and reread the script and of course I knew the lines back, front and sideways.

On arriving at Southampton Station, I made my way to the hotel that I was to stay at. I checked in and prepared myself for the next day's filming. As I was unpacking – not that there was a lot to unpack – the phone rang. It was Jim O'Brien, the director. Everyone was down in the bar, he said, and he told me to come down. As I entered the bar, I could see a lot of faces I had seen in various television programmes, although I couldn't remember their names. After a while Jim came over and introduced me to everyone. The cast included Alan Ford, Derek Martin, Maurice O'Connell, Eric Mason, P. H. Moriarty, Richard Ireson and John Bindon. As Bindon left the bar, I was informed that he had a fourteen-inch collar. Seeing as he was a huge man, well over six feet and very well built, I remember thinking at the time that this was surely wrong; my collar size was sixteen and I wasn't as big as him. Subsequently I discovered what this reference to his collar size meant.

After a short while, I went back up to my room, to try and get a good night's sleep prior to my filming the next day. I was as nervous as hell, but I hoped that would disappear once I was on set. My call was set for 10 a.m. the next day.

I slept on and off, the lines going round and round in my head. I had breakfast in my room, as I didn't want to miss my call and be late. Ten o'clock came and went, as did every hour until six o'clock, and I couldn't leave the hotel room in that time in case my call came. Eventually it did, just after six, and I was driven to the location. On arrival, Jim and the production manager were very apologetic, and the reason for me being called so late became apparent. Apparently Bindon had performed his party trick to a member of the hotel staff; this entailed hanging several pint mugs on his penis à la Errol Flynn, and then wandering up to this young woman and showing the result to her. This was obviously distressing to the female concerned and when her screams had died down, several hours of hard negotiating by the producers saved everyone from being kicked out of the hotel. In addition, another member of either the crew or cast had tried to break into the bar to get a drink. The film unit had also lost one location, and had had to find a replacement. Meanwhile, Bindon, who was either filming a scene in a sex shop or just browsing, had asked the assistant if they had something suitable for his girlfriend. After a few minutes of showing him various things – none suitable – the assistant asked if he could be more specific, as they might be able to satisfy him. Bindon whipped out his penis and said, 'Something like this.' As he was very well endowed (hence the fourteen-inch collar remark), the assistant fainted. My first day's professional work, and so far nothing had gone right.

Eventually, I was to do my scene, and after a rehearsal we filmed it, from all angles. At the end I got a round of applause, which seemed to me to be a bit excessive, as I was only speaking while handing over keys and money. But apparently I did everything they wanted and they were pleased. The next day I left the hotel and went back to London, still on a high, yet at the same time thinking I could have done better.

Back in London, I started doing the usual rounds of the casting agents and auditions. I also got a call from Webber Douglas, asking if I would help out on the stage management side for some pre-finals shows. I jumped at the chance. I also did a commercial for cider, playing a bloke at the bar; we were told to have a conversation, nothing to be heard. This myself and the other chap did, and a few weeks after the filming had finished, I got a call to do some dubbing on it. Puzzled, as I hadn't spoken on camera, I went off to Soho to do it, and was given a piece of paper with some dialogue on. This I needed to match to my own lip movements on screen – easy enough, you might think, and you would be right. If only the scripted words had borne any resemblance to what I was saying to the other chap at the bar, which was a conversation about West Ham United. The script extolled the virtues of cider.

Another commercial followed, for Pearl Assurance. This was an all-singing, all-dancing one, although when I had got the job, no one had mentioned anything about either singing or dancing. After a tricky first few rehearsals, I had managed to get through the routine, choreographed by a huge Scot. The commercial ran for about a week, and with the cider commercial, money was starting to roll in. So far my career as an actor had started very well.

Soon, it was time to make my way to the Belgrade, Coventry. I travelled by train, and on arrival, made my way to the administration offices to pick up my accommodation key. The theatre had flats attached, and they were issued on a first come, first served basis. Simon Dunmore, whom I had auditioned for, had one permanently. They were brilliant little flats, if a bit cold in winter. But as basic as they were, they were heaven-sent to a poorly paid actor. Each of the flats had an electric meter, which you fed continuously with fifty-pence pieces. And if you put the electric fire on, which was built into the wall, it was a battle to keep up with it financially. Once settled in the flat, I made my way to the rehearsal rooms. The first play I was involved in was *Whose Life is It Anyway?*, about a terminally ill hospital patient. I was playing a young solicitor. The cast was a very mixed bunch: very experienced actors and actresses, some of whom had been at the Royal Shakespeare Company, and of course myself, who had had no professional stage experience at all.

Rehearsals were fun and, being in only one scene, I had a lot of time off. Once I had circumnavigated the town, and seen the sights of Coventry, I tended to spend my off time either in the flat or in the theatre restaurant, which was called the Stage Bite. I had teamed up with one of the other actors, a lovely chap called Raymond Bowyers. He too had a lot of time on his hands, as he also didn't have a huge amount to do.

Although the flat had a small kitchenette, apart from breakfast I tended to spend my time in the Stage Bite. This seemed to be open from early morning till after the show, and it was always packed, whether for morning coffee, lunch, afternoon tea or evening meals, although for meals it did just posh burgers. The actors were supposed to pay discounted prices, but once the staff knew who you were, you tended to pay for only one coffee, while the rest were free. But it was a life saver for me, as it broke the boredom factor of rehearsals, and also kept me fed. The play opened and went very well, although I don't think I was very good. I also learnt a lot of things, not just stagecraft-wise but also how actors built up their parts. Until, of course, it came to Saturday night's performance, when they had to make a mad rush to the station to catch the last train home.

When I'd arrived at the stage door on the Saturday night prior to the show and had seen a load of suitcases all piled up just inside the door, I really hadn't given it much thought. I changed into my costume and prepared to go on stage. I did my bit and then sat in the dressing room waiting to go on for the curtain call, after which I was going to walk back to the flat and then pick up my little bag with my dirty laundry in and stroll to the station to catch a train. While I was in the dressing room, listening to the show over the relay system, I couldn't help but think that we weren't getting as many laughs as we should. And suddenly it was the interval. I had the same thoughts in the second half; again, the second act went very quickly. We did the curtain call, and no sooner had the tabs closed than everyone suddenly ran off. As I left the stage door to make my way to the flat, I noticed that all the suitcases had gone. I went to the flat and picked up my bag and made my way to the station. After a while the train came, and it wasn't until I was on it that I realized why the rest of the cast had disappeared so quickly and had raced through the play. The train I was on, although London-bound, was a stopper. The one they had rushed to catch was the last non-stop one.

Once *Whose Life* was up and running, we were rehearsing *A Little Night Music*, and other actors joined the company. The cast of *A Little Night Music* was huge. We had Kenneth Nelson, Virginia Stride, Iain Laughlin (who would go on to create 'The Tweenies', a huge children's show whose success was only ever paralleled by 'Teletubbies'. The multi-talented Ian was also Fingermouse on kids' TV!). There was also Susannah Fellowes, Jill Benedict and many more besides, but for me the most important member of the cast was the wonderful Pip Hinton, who I remembered from 'Crackerjack'. I was playing the Butler, Frid. Pip's character was in a wheelchair. Well, somehow between us we managed to steal the reviews, and we became good friends.

Kenneth Nelson was a very good-looking American actor, with a wonderful singing voice. He'd been in the original cast of *The Boys in the Band*, as well as having done many West End musicals. Sadly, he was to die years later of AIDS.

Because we were doing a musical, we had an extra week's rehearsal, which meant that a touring play would come into the theatre. It was an Alan Ayckbourne, starring an actor who in the 1950s and 1960s had been a huge television star: Dave King. (I had been a huge fan of his shows.) I was sitting with Raymond Bowyers in the Stage Bite when suddenly Dave King arrived and sat himself at a table in the centre of the restaurant, and the little student waitress scurried across to take his order. The place was filling up, and apparently she was the only one on duty. When I saw Dave King arrive I said to Raymond, 'Do you think he would mind if I asked for his autograph?' He said something like, 'I am sure he would be flattered.' I left the table and went and grabbed a publicity flyer with his picture on it advertising the play he was in, and then went and sat down, waiting for him to finish his meal, before approaching him. As he did so and as I started to rise from my chair, he suddenly looked up, spied the young waitress and screamed, 'Where's my glass of fucking water?' I sat straight back down and let the flyer in my hand drop to the floor, vowing that if ever I got to his position as an actor I would never be knowingly rude to people.

I only caught a train to London once or twice, and after that long, lonely experience on the stopper, I got into the habit of making sure

I caught the fast one. One Saturday, when rehearsals had finished early and we didn't have a show in the evening because of the touring production being in, we all caught a train to London, and for an extra pound we had been upgraded to first class, where we found Roy Hattersley. One of the actresses made a beeline for him and said something along the lines of, 'If you were the leader of the party, I'd definitely vote for you.' She spent the whole trip deep in conversation with him.

After one show on a Saturday night, Iain Lauchlin said he would be driving back, as he had to do some removal work. He'd hired a light van, so if I wanted to get back to London he said he would take me, but he did have his agent in, so would be leaving a little later. That was fine by me, and eventually, after he had eaten with his agent, we set off for London. I asked him how his agent had enjoyed the show, and Iain said, 'He loved it but he spent most of the meal talking about you.' Iain then asked me if I had an agent, and I said not really, but someone who had expressed an interest in me while at drama school, although her books were full, did some negotiations for me. In any case, I really didn't rely on her to get me work. Iain said, 'Well, write to my man.' I made a note of his name and said I would.

On the Monday night after the show I was sitting in the Stage Bite when I saw Jill Benedict come in and sit down at a table with a man. I looked up as she entered, and I had a funny feeling that I had seen the man she was with before. He was her agent, and his name was Bryn, and I had met him when I had been doing the wine and food after a show at Webber Douglas.

I was sitting on my own, when she came over and said, 'Why don't you join us? You look very lonely on your own.'

I laughed and said, 'Thanks, but I don't want to intrude.'

She said, 'It's only my agent and he's a mate anyway, so just come over.'

'All right, I'll join you for coffee.'

After a short while I said goodnight and went back to my flat. I was rehearsing the next day for a new play I was going to do in the studio theatre, just behind the main theatre. It was called *Visitors* and took place in a house in Twickenham, and Papua New Guinea. Although my character, who was the lead, never actually left his front room, through some device on his head he could be instantly transported to the jungle, while still sitting on his sofa. The device consisted of the inside of a builder's hard hat with a few feathers stuck in it. One scene entailed me having nothing on but a pair of Y-fronts, which also housed the radio mike, which would make my voice do strange things. During one show, I felt an excruciating pain in my genital area and the sound effects stopped. On inspection afterwards, I found that I had burnt a hole in my penis. The director, however, was concerned only with why the sound had gone dead and a lot of vocal effects had failed to materialize, thus ruining the play. Sod my agony – save the play.

After rehearsing, I had a short break before doing *Night Music* in the main theatre and I popped into the Stage Bite to grab a coffee and a snack before getting dressed for the evening's performance. Jill sought me out and said that her agent had been very impressed with my performance, and thought it might be a good idea if I got in touch with him. So within a space of three days I had two very high-powered agents interested in me.

Meantime, though I had been contracted only for three plays, the pantomime season was upon us, and some of us new bods were being asked to stay on. The studio was doing a new adaptation of *Lady Chatterley's Lover*, adapted by a local writer. And I was asked to stay on and be in it. I was to be playing three parts: an Irish poet who had had a fling with Lady Chatterley before Mellors, a Welsh mine manager and finally Lady Chatterley's Scottish father. This obviously enabled people to make, 'There was this Irishman, Scotsman, and Welshman' jokes; the trouble was I was dreadful in all three parts, so the joke was on me.

Because I wasn't in the pantomime, though, I had a short break back in town, and went to see the two agents who had expressed an interest in me. They were very similar, young guys, but both very knowledgeable. After a lot of thought I decided to go with Jill Benedict's agent, Bryn.

★   ★   ★

Jane and I had been living together for a while now. We were head over heels and, regardless of my earlier and general wariness about marriage, we simply decided to do it one day, a spur-of-the-moment thing in a register office in Fulham. And then off I went to Coventry to rehearse *Lady Chatterley*. I told my Dad, who was pleased, and Jane informed her parents. They were happy for us, but insisted we must retake our vows under the auspices of a proper church wedding. After some to-ing and fro-ing, we settled upon a blessing at the Boltons Church, a place we often used for rehearsals. I spoke to my Dad about it and he thought the best thing to do was not to tell my side of the family as my mother tended to ruin everyone's great day. I obviously didn't have too many friends, so I invited people from the theatre. Tom was the obvious choice as my best man. The further behind I left my troubled past, the more I came to appreciate the way Tom had just taken me at face value, as someone who was ready to learn from his mistakes and work his way to better things. Everyone deserves a second chance and Tom, more than anyone at the time, is the guy who gave me mine. I'll always be thankful to him. I invited Andy Marlin, my ex-probation officer, although I didn't have to see him any more as I was no longer on licence. My flamboyant old landlord in Fulham was also invited – I still missed the five-star meals – and of course Jago, the head of Webber Douglas, so I had a lot of people on my side of the church. Myself, Tom and Jane's brother David were all kitted out in morning suits.

The morning of the wedding came and I was as nervous as hell. I think I either had drunk too much the night before, or hadn't slept at all well, so looked as if I was in serious need of a blood transfusion, I was that ashen. Tom and his wife drove me to the church and everyone I had invited had turned up. Nervously waiting out Jane's arrival (she *would* come, wouldn't she?), I noted how beautifully the church was decked out with blooms and bouquets. Tom gave me a reassuring wink. Of *course* she was coming!

When Jane arrived, she looked absolutely stunning, wearing a really beautiful dress, with her mother's old wedding veil. I remember nothing at all of the ceremony, I was in too much of a state to take it in properly. All I knew was that I was in this most beautiful of churches, being married to the most beautiful of women, surrounded by people who were happy for us. Just a few short years before, this would have been a mere fantasy, an impossible dream. Now I was living the dream, and we'd only just begun.

After the ceremony, we went back to Sydney Street to change. We had booked a restaurant for the meal after the ceremony at a great place in Walton Street called San Martino's. David supplied the wine, and the meal was very Italian, with an Italian wedding cake. After the meal we went back to the house and then Jane's brother told us to put some overnight things in a bag, and whisked us off to a mystery destination. As we trawled up Piccadilly, we couldn't believe we were pulling up outside the legendary Ritz Hotel, where David had booked us a room for the night.

When we awoke the next morning in this fabulous hotel room, we ordered breakfast from room service – very decadent. Jane and I hadn't a penny between us as we had left the night before in such a rush. Thank God that, in an innocent world that pre-dated identity theft, David had guaranteed all incidentals at the Ritz with his credit card. And while we both felt it'd be cheeky to go ahead and charge all sorts of extras to his card, we did enjoy breakfast in bed. Our honeymoon night at the Ritz gave me a tantalizing glimpse of the world of luxury that lay in wait for the rich and famous.

I returned to Coventry to start rehearsing *Lady Chatterley*. Mellors was played by Conrad Asquith and Lady Chatterley by Maureen Beattie. To give the stage setting some woodland authenticity, the director, with the set designer, decided they would hang dead pheasants and partridges and various other game around the set. Whether this worked artistically or not, I wasn't sure, but it certainly stank. There was talk of the play going out on tour; it did very well in the studio, and once word had gone round that it involved full frontal nudity and simulated sex, you couldn't get a ticket for love nor money. If it did go on the road, I certainly wouldn't be playing three parts; I most likely wouldn't even be in it, as I was wrong for all the three parts I was playing.

One day I was by the stage door when I was handed a message telling me to ring Susie Bruffin at Granada. I rang her number and spoke to Jim O'Brien, who had directed me in 'Jake's End' in Southampton. He was in Manchester, working for Granada Television on something called *The Raj Quartet*.

'What are you up to, at the moment?' Jim asked.

'I'm just about to finish at Coventry, although there's an outside chance of going on tour with *Lady Chatterley*,' I said.

'No you're not, you're coming to India with me.'

He was creating a little part for me, as the series was full of big names, but he definitely wanted to work with me again. Susie Bruffin was the casting director, and she said that she would sort everything out with my agent and looked forward to meeting me. Wow . . . Off to India; I'd never been outside Europe. What a first job to have for my new agent!

Part of me was sad to leave Coventry, as I had really enjoyed working with the people there, yet at the same time I felt that I hadn't really had the greatest of starts to my acting career.

Back to London and the usual rounds of casting agents. I had heard nothing further about the Indian job, and I began to think that maybe nothing was going to happen. Webber Douglas phoned to ask if I was around for a few weeks, as the bursar was in hospital having a hip replacement, and they needed someone to check on the last batch of auditions and get the students organized for the following term. This entailed going through the list of applicants and starting from the highest grading, phoning them up to see if they were accepting a place at Webber Douglas. That year Webber Douglas had held their auditions slightly later than usual, and this had obviously put them out of kilter. As I phoned round and went down the lists, starting at the A marks and moving downwards, it soon became evident that because of the competition with other drama schools, and as most applicants tended to apply for all or most of the drama schools around the country, many of the successful students had either been offered or accepted places at other schools. As I made my way down the list, being told that people had accepted places at RADA and others, it soon became apparent that in the end all I had to do was find X amount of students who had the money to pay. In some cases it was tragic that someone whom the audition panel felt had potential couldn't accept a place because they either couldn't get a grant or just couldn't afford to go to drama school.

While I was in the midst of sorting out the students for Webber Douglas, the call from Granada came, and I was given flight dates for my departure to India, and an appointment to have my jabs. My flight was ten days away. I had nearly finished the work at Webber Douglas, and all I had to do was send out all the information packs to the successful candidates. As I was doing this, I got a phone call from my agent to ask me why wasn't I at the airport. I told him that I wasn't flying out till the following week. Luckily, I had the confirmation letter with me, and I faxed it to him from my office. Apparently because everyone who was involved with the show was already in India, there had been a communication problem, and the travel and filming days information had got muddled between India and Manchester, and this had then been passed on to my agent.

This cock-up, although not my fault, did make me nervous, and I began to feel that I had messed up and would not be able to do the job in India. Luckily, Granada was flying people out all the time, and another flight was fixed for two days' time. To make sure there weren't any more mess-ups, I was biked my airline tickets and flight information. I stayed at Webber really late that night to get my work all done, and after a few hours the following day making sure everything was in order, I packed and prepared to leave for India. As yet I hadn't had a script, but I had been told that that would be forthcoming once I arrived.

The flight to Delhi was uneventful, and although I tried to sleep, I couldn't. I tried to imagine what it would be like in India. My only experience had been from books and films: I knew it was a huge country and that they ate rice and spicy food. You're probably thinking: 'What an ignoramus.' But you have to remember that even at the age of thirty-five, I had never even had an Indian meal. So everything about this trip and job was going to be a new discovery for me.

As I emerged from the plane at Delhi, it was early morning, but you could feel the heat smack you in the face. As it was still dark, I couldn't get a true perspective on my surroundings as I was taken to my hotel, although it was a shock to see cattle roaming the streets. The Taj Hotel was in a modern style, typical of any large hotel in any major city in the world. After a good sleep, I ordered a light breakfast, showered and waited for the car that was coming to take me to filming – or so I thought.

When I had arrived at the hotel there had been a note waiting for me to say a car would be coming at ten o'clock to collect me, so when the phone rang to tell me my car was downstairs I grabbed my suitcase and made my way to the foyer. An Indian gentleman approached me and asked if I was Mr Grantham, and then informed me he was my guide for the day. Oh, so I wasn't off to the film unit. He took my suitcase and gave it to the concierge and it was returned to my room. Off we set to see the sights of Delhi. I saw the Red Fort, visited the numerous temples, saw the site where Ghandi was assassinated and had several hours of running commentary about the history of India. Then my driver returned me to the hotel in time for lunch and said he would return later. I entered this huge restaurant area and saw the most incredible layout of food. As I entered I was shown to a table, and after a brief discussion with the waiter, he brought me a selection of the food that he felt was suitable for someone who wasn't sure what to ask for from the menu. It was very nice, and I was sure that I could get to like it. After lunch I waited in the hotel foyer for my guide, who had up until last year been a headmaster of a school, but because of some policy of Mrs Ghandi's he had been employed as a tour guide, welcoming foreigners to India.

While I was having lunch it had dawned on me that I had seen only the good side of Delhi, the sights, so as I entered the car I asked the driver if I could see the other side of Delhi. After a lot of hesitation, he reluctantly gave me a tour of the underside of the city, and what a side it was: beggars, cripples, filth and pure degradation. Although he seemed happy to drive me around, he wouldn't stop the car and wouldn't let me get out. Eventually we returned to the hotel and went our separate ways, but he did ask me not to tell anyone that he had taken me to the slums that afternoon, or it would go badly for him.

Upon my return to the hotel, there was a note waiting for me: I would be picked up after breakfast in the morning and driven to where the filming was taking place. I spent the rest of my afternoon by the pool and after a light supper tried to get some sleep, ready for the next day. My sleep was disturbed, as I kept seeing those poor sods in the slums of Delhi, and it was something I found hard to shake off. After breakfast I checked out of the hotel and waited in the foyer for my transport. As I was sitting there, I was approached by an Indian-looking gentleman, and when he asked me if I was with Granada I took it that he was the driver. He introduced himself as Albert Moses, and he, like me, was waiting for transport. He seemed a really nice guy, and had arrived the night before. We were to share a car up to Simla, where we would meet up with the rest of the cast and crew.

Our car arrived and we set off by road. The driver had collected two packed lunches from the hotel as we wouldn't be stopping to eat on the way, although we did pull in to stretch our legs later in the day. The traffic, even that early in Delhi, was absolutely phenomenal, the driving a combination of stock-car racing and land rush stampedes, only instead of horses and wagons it was cars, motorbikes and cars that were half motorbikes and half cars. Apparently whoever was bravest or maddest just commandeered the best spot on the road, and the sound of horns and hooters filled the morning air; the smell of fuel was stifling. If ever they put speed cameras up in Delhi, with the number of vehicles on the road, they will make a fortune. As we left the city and made our way north, houses and villages became few and far between, and after what seemed an eternity of fields with one or two people working on them, we came across a small town or village with various shops and markets, and always someone selling Coca-Cola, or fruit produce and bottled water. Our driver informed us that the bottled drinks were not the genuine thing, and would more likely lay you low than refresh you.

Eventually we arrived in the hill station of Simla. It reminded me of something from a scene in *Kim*, the film with Errol Flynn set in the days of the Raj. My impression was right. Simla had been the summer retreat of the Raj, used when Delhi became too hot, and once you had gone past the crowded district that was downtown Simla, you arrived at cottages and houses that wouldn't be out of place in Sussex. They all had names that were quaintly English, such as Rose Cottage, Buttercup Lodge and various others, although I didn't see any called DunRoaming. But I am sure there probably was one.

I was staying at the Woodville Palace Hotel, above the main area of Simla town. Jim O'Brien was also staying there with his family. We were met at the door by Billy Ram, who ran the place, and whose main claim to fame was that he had been taught to play snooker by Trevor Howard when he had been there a few years before, filming another of Paul Scott's books for Granada called *Staying On*, which had reunited him with Celia Johnson from *Brief Encounter*. The rest of the cast and crew were staying further down in the town, at the Obleroi Hotel.

The chef at the hotel I was staying at had cooked for various heads of state and dignitaries over the years as the establishment belonged to a Maharajah who owned huge apple orchards further up in the hills, and had turned one of his beautiful houses in Simla into a hotel. I was in the mother's room, so obviously it wasn't a hotel all year round. Billy Ram slept on the veranda outside, and whatever you wanted he could get.

There was to be a party that night, paid for by Granada, for the cast and crew and all the local dignitaries. It was held at a rather grand-looking establishment. Jim was pleased to see me, and introduced me to various people. Before I had left London, Pam and Mike had told me to send their regards to Geraldine James, who was playing the female lead in *The Jewel in the Crown*.

Because India is such a huge country and each state is very territorial, Granada had to spend a small fortune on smoothing the way to get around various rules and regulations. Hence the parties for local dignitaries in every region they filmed in, as well as the need to get documentation to allow the same drivers to travel with the props, costumes and equipment across the country.

As I entered the party area, I spied Geraldine, and after a while she came and introduced herself to me. During our conversation I gave her the message from Mike, and after a few speeches from the local dignitaries and the producers, I asked Geraldine if she wanted another drink, she said yes and went off to the loo. As I got her a drink, I was approached by two of the lead actors, Charles Dance and Tim Piggot Smith, and they both seemed to be of the opinion that I was a pushy minor actor. I had no idea what this was all about, and after a while Jim came over and basically told them to leave me alone. I realized afterwards that they were both flexing their muscles and were a bit peeved I was talking to Geraldine. And to make matters worse, when Geraldine reappeared from the loo she continued to talk to me. I had a rehearsal the next day, so long before the party was over I left and went back to the hotel to learn my small scene. I had the part of the signal sergeant who has a conversation with Charles Dance's character as he is being discharged. And a nice scene it was too.

We rehearsed in this army barracks, not far from Simla. The rehearsal was for the camera crew, and obviously for Jim to see what problems he might have. Once rehearsals were over, it was back to the hotel for lunch, costume fitting and then a look around Simla, which was as small as Delhi was large, but just as populated. That evening there was a barbecue at one of the hotels, and since we had all been introduced to each other the night before, this was to be a relaxed affair, without all the stuffiness and starch involved with being in the presence of local dignitaries.

The food where I was staying was absolutely fantastic, not at all hot or spicy, but subtle, sophisticated food. But apparently the crew, who had been out in India for a while (although they had trips back to England every so often, when someone else would replace them for a few weeks), were becoming disillusioned with Indian cooking. Not that they were eating it non-stop: the caterers on location were actually English guys who had been on another job in India prior to *The Jewel*, and when they were approached to do the location catering, had been experienced enough to provide various typical English vegetables, meats and other produce, so that everything was like English cooking back home.

Granada's crews had, however, a reputation for being picky. When *Brideshead Revisited* was being filmed on the *QE2*, they insisted that their caterers be taken on board. Now, in Simla, they were demanding that hamburgers, fish fingers and the like be flown out.

I arrived at the location, having been made up in an old school building that had been taken over by Granada for the purpose. The location was busy, as the crew made ready for the day's filming. After a quick rehearsal to refresh what we had walked through the day before, we prepared to shoot the scene, which entailed Charles Dance leading me around the corner of a barracks building, crossing the parade ground and then entering another building, where he meets Geraldine James's character. I had nearly all the dialogue. The first assistant director was getting everything ready and waiting for Jim to start the action, and as I stood there Charles Dance said, 'It would be better if you led.' Thinking that he obviously had some inside knowledge and was relaying something Jim had said, I agreed, and we set off, me leading and him following. No sooner had we turned the corner of the barracks and were about to set off across the parade ground, than I heard the word 'CUT!' Jim came straight over to me and said, 'No! Do it as we rehearsed.' I apologized and we went back to our start positions. Again we waited for the magic words 'Turn over' and 'Action', and again Charles leant towards me and said, 'Why don't you wait until we are in the open before you speak.'

Suddenly I saw Jim O'Brien storming into view. He marched straight up to me, and then wheeled around to Charles and said, 'Just let him do as he did it in rehearsals; that's what I want, that's what I cast him for and I didn't have him flown out all this distance to play second fiddle to you in this scene. This is his scene.' After a few moments, we shot it one way and then shot it from the other way and it was soon done.

At lunch I apologized to Jim and he said that it wasn't my fault. To be fair, though, I think I had arrived in India at a very tricky time in the filming. All the leads knew that this series had the potential to turn them into huge stars, and household names, as *Brideshead* had for Jeremy Irons and Anthony Andrews. So they were obviously becoming more and more nervous, uncertain and paranoid about failure as the filming months went on. Of course, it's so easy to fall into the trap of thinking that you are wonderful, when you are in an environment that is totally false and you are waited on hand and foot. Nevertheless, there is no doubt that Charles Dance *is* superb in the series.

Because of something that had happened to a film being made in India years before (a remake of *The Lives of a Bengal Lancer* had hired the film equipment in India and, after shooting for days and days, had had the rushes developed, only to find they were useless), Granada had insisted on bringing their own camera equipment and filmstock with them. This meant that I had to wait in India until the rushes report came through (rushes being the exposed filmstock used that day in filming). So my days were filled with exploring the local countryside, and taking afternoon tea on the lawn with various members of the cast. Judy Parfitt was one, as was Rachel Kempson, and a lovely actor called Nicholas Le Prevost. And obviously Billy Ram wanted to play snooker. As he was so proud to have been taught by Trevor Howard, I said I would play him. Once we set up the table and started to play, one or two things were obvious: either Billy Ram had completely forgotten what he had been taught, or Trevor Howard had been so drunk that he had made it up as he went along. The game resembled no snooker game I had ever played, but I went along with it and Billy Ram was happy as Larry.

Eventually, it was time to leave Simla and make the descent back to Delhi, where I had an evening and a morning back at the hotel. Then it was back on the plane and heading home. On the flight back I realized that I had been out of drama school for just about a year and had in fact achieved quite a lot in a modest sort of way. I had managed to get my Equity card, an agent, and had done two television dramas, several commercials and four plays in the theatre. I had also, of course, got married. Not bad, seeing as I had only been out of prison about four years. What next for me, I wondered as I gazed out of the aeroplane window high in the sky.

17

THE NEXT STEP

On arriving back in London, I found myself a little job in the evenings (keeping my days free for auditions), working behind the bar at a bingo hall next to Fulham Broadway station. After several days there I realized it wasn't for me, a conclusion confirmed when I saw my pay slip. I then spent several days walking the surrounding areas of Chelsea and Fulham trying to find a part-time job that would allow me to go off and audition. I had plenty of offers but once I had told prospective employers that I would need time off for auditions it became obvious that I might need to register for unemployment benefit. As I was just about to give up, I passed a greengrocer in South Kensington that was being stocked but not as yet up and running. I asked the chap inside if he was looking for part-time staff, and as luck would have it he was. Even when I explained to him that I would need some time off, he seemed to understand. I started the next day, and soon I was unlocking the shop early in the morning and locking up late at night. The pay wasn't great, but it was only a five-minute walk from where I was living and, at the end of the week, I could take whatever fruit and vegetables I wanted, free of charge. It was a strange shop, full of normal fruit and veg and flowers but also health foods. The shop was booming, and after a while we took on a young girl who would concentrate on the flower side. The owner, Peter, had been an accountant, but had decided to chuck that in and be a shopkeeper instead.

I served tennis players and famous actors such as Theresa Russell, Barbara Parkin and Lorraine Chase were regular customers. Every Friday, a very tall, elegant man with an Italian accent would come in, and spend an absolute fortune on flowers. I thought that perhaps he was a restaurateur or ran a hotel, as we did have several customers who owned hotels and restaurants in the area. One Friday evening he came in as he had done week after week, and wanted to purchase the huge margarita plant outside. He asked if we could deliver, and after finding out where he lived, which was only ten minutes' walk away, I said yes. After locking up the shop, I carried the large, heavy, potted plant to where he lived. After inviting me in, he asked me what I was doing working in a greengrocer's. I explained that I was an actor and was working there between jobs. He then told me he had a clothes shop in the Fulham Road and to come and see him the next day. He gave me his card and I left. He was Piero de Monzi, who had a very exclusive Italian designer clothes shop, not three minutes' walk from where I was living.

The next morning I opened the greengrocer's shop as usual, and told Peter that I had to go home for half an hour and would be back. I ran home, put some smarter clothes on – not that I was scruffy, mind you – but thought it better that I changed out of jeans and into something more appropriate.

I presented myself at Piero's and, after meeting his manager, was offered a job. Piero wanted me to start on the Monday, but I said that I had to give my boss some notice. On the Monday I told Peter I would be leaving, as I had a new job. Although upset, he understood; though I felt I'd let him down, as he was a lovely man who had certainly helped me. We parted on good terms and he said I could go back and work for him any time.

When I arrived at Piero's the next morning, the first thing he did was to tell me to select two shirts and two pairs of trousers and shoes from his racks. Within twenty minutes I was serving in the shop, wearing some of Italy's finest clothes. The shop had a client list that was something out of the *Tatler*: Lady Di, Bob Geldof, Billy Connolly, Nigel Havers, Eric Estrada, Tony Curtis, Dustin Hoffman, Greta Scacchi; you name them, they came to the shop.

Piero's importer was a chap called Cuomo, who was related to the then Mayor of New York of the same name. He also imported for Herbie Frogg and Cecil Gee.

Of course I had time off for auditions. I had an interview with the producer of my first job on leaving drama school, Michael Wearing. He was producing a one-off television drama set in an auction house, which was being directed by Richard Wilson, of 'One Foot in the Grave' fame. Michael said he was considering me for two parts, one older than my actual age and one younger. After an initial meeting with Michael, where I had read both parts for him, he said that with some jiggery pokery I could play either, but it was up to the director; a subsequent meeting was arranged. Michael was his usual happy-go-lucky self, but Richard Wilson, after the initial hello, sat quietly in the corner. I read the older part, with Michael reading the other parts, while Wilson sat there impassively. The next day I got a call, just as I was serving Eric Clapton with a pair of white cotton trousers, to ask me to go back and see them again. Only this time I read the younger part. The reception was the same: Michael was his usual open self and Richard Wilson didn't say anything. Michael showed me out and said he would be in touch. I had a funny feeling that I wasn't going to get the job, as I thought that Richard Wilson was only humouring Michael.

When I finally got the call from my agent, to tell me I didn't get the job, I wasn't that disappointed; yet, at the same time, I wondered what I had done wrong. Some time later I was sitting at home when the phone rang; it was my agent, who told me to switch on BBC2. It was the play I had been interviewed twice for, with Peter Vaughan, who was Grouty in 'Porridge', playing the older part. My agent said that I should be flattered to have lost out to someone like him, but to be honest I would probably have not enjoyed it, as I was really not right for either part.

After all those years of dreaming about being an actor I still wasn't sure if it suited me. I, like many of my peers, dreamt of fame and fortune, yet, at the same time, I was grateful for any crumbs that came my way. Being older in years, but still very naïve, I was under no illusion that life as an actor was a bed of roses: that I would spend more time doing other odd jobs than in work. One day, I bumped into Jeremy Young, who asked me how it was going. I told him that I was going to give it six months and if the work didn't come in I would try something else. How insecure and unstable a breed we actors are! I had been out of work as an actor for a few months or was it just weeks? What chance did I have when there were far better actors than me that had never worked in the profession? It wasn't long after seeing Jeremy in the street that the work picked up. So when my fifteen minutes of fame eventually came, I had to pinch myself. I couldn't really believe it. I still saw myself as a jobbing actor, and as for being a sex symbol, well I have always thought of myself as a tall, skinny, ugly bloke. So I couldn't take it at all seriously. Fortunately the hysteria in the papers and the stories about my past never really allowed me to wallow in my newly found fame. Maybe all those sensational headlines were a blessing in disguise!

My fortunes now began to change. I had been asked to go and meet the director of a new play at the Bridge Lane Theatre in Battersea. The play was about a prisoner, and written by an ex-prisoner. I read for the director and author, but didn't mention my prison past. Strangely, I didn't get the job because I didn't look like a bloke who could be a prisoner. Nevertheless, I had done well enough to be recommended for a single-act play set in a television newsroom. The play was directed by Laurens Postma, a hip American-sounding Dutchman with brilliantly quirky ideas, who was basically a film-maker at heart.

While I was rehearsing the play, I had bumped into two totally different people from my past. One morning I was having breakfast in a local café when I felt I was being watched. I turned round and saw a guy whom I recognized from the army at the next table staring at me. After a few moments he apologized for staring and asked if he knew me from somewhere. When I said who I was he had a completely different reaction from the bloke on the train. He was very nice and friendly, and was genuinely pleased to know that I was doing all right. He had, he told me, got over the dose of syphilis he had caught from a girl all those years ago in Osnabrück.

After a performance one evening, the director took the cast out to this Italian restaurant near the theatre. Over dinner I looked up and, staring at me open-mouthed, was my old platoon commander, Chris Carter. He just got up from his table and said, 'It bloody well is, isn't it?' and he was like a puppy with three tails. He was working in security, whatever that meant. He gave me his card and told me to ring him, and we would meet up for a drink. I did and we met in some pub in the heart of Belgravia.

Back at Piero's, Lady Di was now a frequent visitor to the shop, and Anna Harvey, who at the time was editor of *Vogue*, would pick stuff for her to wear. When this fantastic herringbone coat with a velvet collar was spotted on her, Piero was at last rewarded financially. As people swarmed to get the coat from him, it made up for all the years of non-payment from her. It was Piero who had supplied Lady Di with those funny-collared blouses she was famous for wearing.

We would also have to take a selection of clothes to her at Kensington Palace to try on. Sadly, by the time the rejected clothing came back it was always too late to put them on sale as the season's latest, so they always ended up in the sale. Piero was completely laidback about the whole thing, and just shrugged his shoulders as if it didn't matter.

I only ever saw him lose his temper once. Greta Scacchi had been brought into the shop by a BBC designer when she was about to film *Dr Fischer of Geneva and the Bomb*. The designer had been in previously to fit Angela Douglas out for a quiz show, and had seen an absolutely fantastic blouse. Although not suitable for Angela Douglas, who was Kenneth More's widow, she had decided it would be perfect for Greta. Unfortunately Greta ran around the shop in it with only her knickers on, eating a huge pear. Suddenly Piero appeared from his office downstairs and screamed at her to get out of his shop. He threw her clothes at her, and after she had taken the blouse off he threw her out on to the street. When the costume designer tried to explain who Greta was, Piero shrugged his shoulders and went back downstairs.

One day I was looking after the shop with two young female assistants while Piero was off in Italy, as he was increasingly prone to be. As I stood by the front door, looking up and down the Fulham Road, I suddenly saw two men, slightly the worst for wear, walking in our direction. One of them was John Bindon, who had wreaked havoc on the location of 'Jake's End' in Southampton. I could see they were popping in and out of each shop as they made their way up the road. Calmly, I went back into the shop and told the girls to switch off the lights and go downstairs. I then locked the doors, sat just out of view in the cubbyhole between the two parts of the shop and waited for them to pass. As they reached our door they stopped and tried to open it. Once they realized we were closed they started to bang on the door. Eventually they moved on, but I didn't open the door for another half-hour. When I eventually told them to come up from downstairs, the girls looked at me as if I was mad. I had to tell them that a few drunks were heading for the shop and I felt it was better to lock up rather than have them come in. If only they had known . . .

Apart from the celebrities who came into the shop – some of whom were downright obnoxious – we also had some regular customers who were strange. One woman, who was titled, only came into the shop to try clothes on – never buying anything – when it was her time of the month. She would stand in the changing room, wearing nothing but a huge sanitary towel, making sure everyone could see her. Why Piero tolerated this I will never know. I remember once a lady came in and ordered so many clothes that she decided to leave them in the shop, saying she would come and collect them with her husband later. She paid by credit card and left. After a few weeks, we decided to telephone her, and spoke to her husband. He calmly said that he was so sorry to put us to this inconvenience, and that his wife every now and then went on a spending spree; this she would do in half a dozen shops, and would then, conveniently, forget what it was she had bought. It was only when the credit card bills arrived that he would know what she had bought, and he would then arrange to have whatever it was delivered. Piero told us that if she ever came in again we were not to serve her.

While at Piero's I had done two sitcoms for ATV and Central, which were filmed at Elstree. The first, 'Hello I Thought You Had Gone', was a pilot episode for a series starring Peter Jones, of 'Rag Trade' fame. The director was Shaun O'Riordan, who had been a regular as the son in 'The Larkins', a very successful television series starring David Kossoff and Peggy Mount. He seemed to like me and was very pleased with my performance. But when the series was commissioned, my part was turned into a female role. I then did an episode of a Donald Churchill and Joe McGrath series called 'Good Night and God Bless', which also starred Donald Churchill, and Judy Lowe. From the moment the series was conceived, the programme was doomed to be trouble. Joe McGrath was a director in his own right and had worked with some of the comedy greats, both on film and on television. Donald Churchill had been around for years and was a well-regarded comedy actor and successful playwright. Central Television, although aware of both Joe's and Donald's credentials, wanted Alan Dossor to direct it, as he was one of the new breed of television directors who had a good track record in regional theatre. Sadly, the mix of talent didn't work, and Alan Dossor became increasingly frustrated with interference from both Joe and Donald. This culminated in a stand-up row in a field near Borehamwood, where a tea urn was thrown and Alan disappeared. Luckily, I had finished filming my scenes; the only reason I was in the field was that I was waiting for a car to take me home. The only other thing the series was noticeable for was the television debut of Lesley Ash.

I was also cast in a film called *Morons from Outer Space*, which starred Mel Smith and Griff Rhys Jones. It was filmed on a new section of the M25, and the scene I was in, playing a traffic policeman, dealt with the aftermath of a space rocket landing on the M1. I drove out to the location, and as I followed the signs, I saw a couple of men walking towards me. I stopped the car.

'Where can I park?' I asked.

'Are you action vehicles?' came the rather theatrical voice.

'No, I'm in the film.'

'An artiste,' he said. He looked at me and said, 'Who's casting this?'

When I told him he said, 'Oh really . . . and whatever happened to . . .'

I was then treated to a long list of the poshest actors. I parked the car in the designated area, where make-up and costume and the Winnebagos were located. I was shown to my Winnebago, and waited for my call. Mel and Griff popped in and then disappeared off to filming. I had arrived at four o'clock in the afternoon and was still waiting to be used. Every so often the second assistant director would pop in and say, 'We will be with you soon.' Midnight arrived and I still hadn't been used, and believe me there's nothing more glamorous than being stuck in a Winnebago on your own, in the middle of a field off the M25.

Suddenly, the door opened and the second assistant stuck her head round and said that we were breaking for supper and after that we would be on my scene. As soon as I had eaten I should pop into make-up, and then I would be taken to the set. I had spent so much time on my own waiting that I was beginning to feel like Rudolph Hess. I collected my food and made my way to what I thought was the dining bus. I was dressed as a motorway traffic policeman, as I entered the bus, the chap I had met as I pulled up in the car earlier was sitting on a table with several other smartly dressed people. He was regaling them with stories of whom he had worked with, and was reeling off a list of names of the great British and American actors. As I made my way up the stairs, he stopped in mid-flow and bellowed, 'Young man, this is for supporting artistes only,' and waved me off. Bloody hell, he was only an extra, whose job it was to get out of his car on the motorway and look at the damage caused by the rocket crash. Feeling rather foolish, and biting my tongue, I stood outside and ate my food. As I was putting my plate and knife and fork in the bowls provided, he appeared from the bus just as the second assistant arrived with Jimmy Mulville, who was playing the sergeant with me in the scene. We were whisked off to make-up and then miked. All I had to do in the scene was pull up on a bridge overlooking the motorway. Jimmy would get out and, after surveying the scene, which stretched out for what would appear to be miles and miles, would get on the radio and report the congestion. I would then get out of the car and walk round behind him and say that great comedy line, 'Shall I put the cones out, Sarg . . .?' Not the greatest debut in the world.

I did, however, reluctantly take my aunt from America to see the film. It was dire, though when it came to my line the place roared. My aunt, obviously very much on my side, beamed. Personally I couldn't wait to get out. As we left the cinema she turned to me and said, 'It was worth it for your line.' Now to get a part in that film I had had three interviews with the director, and each time he had asked me the same questions; and each time I had given him the same answers. So obviously he was either mad or thought that I was three different people.

Matthew Robinson, who had written the play I had done at the New Bridge Theatre, popped into Piero's one day and asked Jane and myself over for Sunday lunch, as there was something he wanted to talk to me about. After lunch he said that he was directing an episode of 'Doctor Who' and would love me to play the lead villain, a mercenary Dalek trooper. I was flattered, and of course said yes. He gave me copies of the script and said my agent would be contacted and a deal would be done.

I read the four scripts, and waited for the call. But instead of my agent calling, it was Matthew, who asked me to pop in and see him. When I arrived again at his house he seemed rather sheepish, although slightly angry. He told me that when he told the executive producer, John Nathan Turner (who in fact was plain Jonathan Turner), he wanted me, Turner replied, 'He's not a star, darling. I must have a star.' Matthew had tried to plead my case, but it fell on deaf ears. But all was not lost: there were two other parts that I could do. Matthew pointed them out to me. One was substantial and appeared in one of the four episodes, while the other was really only a cypher as Davros's assistant, Kiston. (Davros was the leader of the Daleks and was the Doctor's sworn enemy.) The assistant, however, was in three episodes. I of course said I wanted the more substantial part, but Matthew convinced me to be Kiston in that it meant more episodes and more money. It also meant I would be around the studios more. Moreover, beggars can't be choosers.

I was contracted and had a fitting for my costume, and then went into rehearsals. Peter Davidson was the Doctor; Rula Lenska was in it, so too was Rodney Bewes. The part that Matthew wanted me for

originally was to be played by Maurice Colbourne, who had been in
'Howard's Way'. Rula was superb and a great company member.
Rodney Bewes was another matter: he seemed friendly enough, until
he saw a bigger name in the canteen and then he would scurry off to
sit with them. He had to be killed in the show, so he would spend
most of his time lying on pillows in the rehearsals reading the paper.
Rula wanted to introduce me to her boyfriend; he was coming into
the studios, and would meet us in the bar. It was Dennis Waterman.
He probably won't remember the meeting, but I do.

On the producer's run, Rula and I, apart from playing our own
parts, were running around making gunfire and laser gun noises, and
also playing all the parts that would on recording be played by extras.
How Nathan Turner made any sense of it I will never know.
Rodney, once killed off, just lay there reading his paper. When we
eventually filmed his death scene, where he was exterminated, he
appeared to die of pre-menstrual tension, which I must admit was
novel.

After each day's filming we tended to go straight home, but on the
last day, we were all invited to the bar for a drink. The floor manager,
a lovely, colourfully dressed lady called Corinne Hollingsworth, was
getting married the next day. John Nathan was there, and every time
I looked in his direction, I caught him staring at me. Either he fancied
me (which I hoped was not the case), or he had been so impressed
with my acting that he regretted not giving me the part that Matthew
had wanted me for. Sadly, I suspect it was the former rather than the
latter. Corinne and I would cross paths again later, when I was on
'EastEnders'.

While I was rehearsing at the BBC rehearsal rooms in North
Acton, I heard of a drama in pre-production, called 'Knock Back',
about a prisoner who had fallen in love with a social worker. It had
originally been a book, and was written by a chap called Pete Aitken,
with whom I had been in prison. The basis of the story was that the
relationship had stopped the protagonist being released or even
considered for parole; he had been sentenced for shooting a car dealer
with a shotgun. While he was in the Scrubs, he had upset a few
people and had to be whisked out quite quickly. At his next prison

he had met this social worker, and a loving, tender, non-physical relationship had eventually blossomed into true love. While the cynics among you might be wary of believing it, having been in a similar situation, I would be reluctant to say that much of it wasn't true to life.

I found out who the director was and, with the help of Corinne, put a handwritten note in the BBC internal mail system, asking Piers Haggard for a meeting. Well, I didn't hear anything back while I was rehearsing and filming, and as I had only a few days left on 'Doctor Who' I thought I had missed out again. Then I got a call from Vernon Conway, who ran the agency with Bryn, who said he had got me an audition for a thing called 'Knock Back'.

I duly presented myself in Piers's office, where I found him eating his lunch. He said that although the series was based on a book, the script was still being written; only the two leads were in place. Derek O'Connor was to play the convict, and Pauline Collins the social worker. Now Vernon Conway had told me that he had got me the interview, but as I glanced at Piers's desk I could see my handwritten note. Piers asked me if I had a speech I could do for him, as he didn't have a script for me to read from. I pulled out my old chestnut – Tempest's speech from Alan Bennett's *Forty Years On*. He laughed a lot, and although he said he couldn't promise anything, he would do his best to find something for me in it.

From 'Doctor Who' Matthew went off to direct on 'Coronation Street', and later offered me the part of a mate of Geoffrey Hughes's character who would end up having a fling with Bet Lynch. I told Matthew that although I was flattered I didn't want to do a soap. He said he understood, and didn't pursue it any further. Thankfully, I did say no because I got a nice part in 'Knock Back', which was now to be a two-part series. I was to play one of the Great Train Robbers. I got a call from the director, who said how pleased he was that he could use me, but apologized that the scripts were being rewritten every day. He also apologized that he could only find me a part as a prisoner, as he felt that, although I wasn't right for it, he did want to work with me. Strangely, two people who had felt I wasn't right to play a prisoner; both of them knew nothing of my past.

I now got a call from Matthew, who wanted a favour from me. He had been asked by Julia Smith and Tony Holland, the two people who had taught me at drama school about television technique, to help set up and cast a new soap the BBC were doing, set in London. He wanted to put my name forward to play a character that possibly would be only in the first six episodes. Well, having already refused Matthew once, I was hesitant to do it again, as he might think me ungrateful. And so I said yes. Meanwhile, 'Knock Back' had fallen foul of a strike by BBC prop men, and kept getting put back, but I kept getting cheques and new contracts. I met with Julia for an hour and then I was taken in to see Tony Holland and we spent another hour together. They asked me to read the part of Pete, the barrow boy in the market. The series at that time was called 'E8'. I read for them, though at no time did they mention that they remembered me from Webber Douglas; I didn't mention it, either.

I left with the familiar words, 'We'll be in touch' ringing in my ears. No sooner had I arrived home, though, when Matthew rang; he was still in Manchester filming 'Coronation Street'. He congratulated me and said, 'You've got the part of Den.' I told him I had read for Pete. Several days later I received a letter from Julia, which read:

> I thought you might like to be put out of your misery, so I am writing this brief note to say that all being well and other things being equal, I hope you will be joining us on 'East 8' to play the part of Den.

At the bottom of the letter, written in biro, were the words: 'Long live the W.D.!'

The strike affecting 'Knock Back' seemed to go on and on, and every time I would be out of contract another would come through the post. Then Central wanted me for a children's series called 'Dramarama'. The lovely casting director Derek Barnes wanted to cast me as the one adult among a huge cast of kids in a play set on a narrowboat. Obviously I phoned the 'Knock Back' offices and they agreed to my appearing, as the strike was ongoing. So I did the kids' drama, and then I was offered *Brighton Rock* at the Belgrade,

Coventry. Again I had to clear it and again I was told to go ahead. Unbeknown to me, a few of us still remained from the original cast, and we were the only ones who had been contracted.

I did *Brighton Rock*, playing the part of Dallow. In the studio, appearing in a play about the Falklands War, was an absolutely stunning girl. When we were rehearsing *Brighton Rock* during the day and our nights were free, the cast went to see the play. Not only did she look stunning, she was a brilliant actress or certainly was brilliant in that play. When they were looking for a Greek girl for 'EastEnders' I recommended her, but sadly for the soap she was in Hollywood. She ended up playing Commander Deanna Troi in the new series of 'Star Trek'. Her name was Marina Sirtis. Also in *Brighton Rock* was a fantastic actor called Chris Hancock, whom I was able to get into 'EastEnders' as Dot Cotton's husband Charlie.

While doing *Brighton Rock* I received the official confirmation that 'Knock Back' would go into production. The first filming I did was in an old RAF barracks that had subsequently been used for the Vietnamese boat people and, now empty, would be turned into Leyhill Prison. I did the first few days' filming and went back to London, waiting for the next call. All my scenes were to be done in prison settings. I was then called to Glasgow, where we filmed in a women's prison. After a day or so, the message went around that the author was going to be on set. On a particularly overcast morning, he appeared wearing sunglasses. He was introduced to most of the cast before being introduced to me. As he shook my hand I could see the recognition in his eyes behind the stupid sunglasses he was wearing. I am sure he was paranoid that I would recount the last time I saw him: being whisked away by the prison officers, as half of D wing were after him for owing them huge amounts of tobacco for money they had sent into his account. Or maybe it was vice versa, and several people had had their stashes found by the prison officers.

He just nodded to me and left. To my surprise he didn't watch any of the filming. Why come all the way to Scotland to visit the film set of a book you had written, only to say hello to the cast? I read some time later that the lady in the relationship had lost her son in some boating accident. And not long after the series was released she and the author had split up. After filming and having been at home for several weeks it was confirmed that I was indeed to be offered the part of Den in what was to be 'EastEnders'.

18

JUST ANOTHER JOB

Jane's brother had just got married and was on holiday in the States, and we were going to meet up in New York. As we were packing the afternoon before the flight, the phone rang. It was Jim O'Brien, who wanted to know what I was up to. He said that while editing *The Jewel in the Crown*, he'd been talking to the casting director of a series called 'Bulman'. One of their guest actors had broken his leg playing football, and they needed someone in a hurry to replace him.

'Of course,' I said, 'I'd love to.'

'OK. Can you get to Manchester tonight?'

'Of course, no problem.'

I was told that the casting director would call me back, within the hour, to confirm. Although Jane had been looking forward to our break in New York, she has always been immensely supportive and didn't hesitate in telling me I had to go for it. So we rang the railway station to check the train times. I had an hour to get a train to Manchester.

No sooner had we put the phone down, than the casting director was on the line. Could I go directly to the Midland Hotel in Manchester? A room would be booked in my name, and a script would be waiting. So that was that. I kissed Jane goodbye, told her to have a great time in New York, and raced to get to Euston Station.

On arriving at the hotel, the script was at reception, along with a call sheet. I was to be on set at 7.30 a.m. Luckily the schedule confirmed that I had no dialogue for the first few days. It was basically going to be stunt days, and I was down for some stunt driving. I got a message that the others were in the bar so, being a conscientious soul, I went down and met the guys. They were all stunt men. Over a drink, the stunt co-ordinator told me what was scheduled for the next day. The day's filming entailed lots of running around the streets of Manchester, which was doubling for London. The rumour went that some years before Granada had been stopped from filming in London, when they blew up a car in the Strand Underpass and brought the city to a standstill. Whether that story is true is anyone's guess, as I had heard the same one about Michael Winner, as well as many others.

The director was a cigar-chewing Canadian called Bill Brayne. My first job of the day was to drive a Jag round the corner at breakneck speed, narrowly missing a dustcart. The rehearsal went fine and we prepared to shoot it. We got the shot, no problem. Next, the car was fitted with a camera to get my reaction as I was driving. While the camera was being fitted, I was regaled by the stunt co-ordinator, whose name was Peter Brayham, affectionately known as 'Pebbles', as he wore the thickest-lensed glasses I have ever seen. Pebbles told me about all the jobs he had been on, and everyone he had worked with, including Hollywood stars.

As I returned to the car and squeezed in from the other side, I saw that not only did it have a camera rigged to the driving door, but the back seat was now occupied by the sound crew. Crammed in by my knees were a lamp and a mike. The dustcart was positioned in place just ahead of me, so we had to reverse up the road to get a good run at it. While the second assistant set the scene up, I had to hold the clapperboard up to camera, call out the scene and take number, wait ten seconds and then drive. I was ready. The dustcart was ready. The sound crew was ready. Everybody else was ready. The only trouble was, the car was not. It refused to start.

Bill Brayne blew his top, and I felt terrible. As the driver, I thought it was my fault. The stunt co-ordinator tried, the car wouldn't go. The car supplier tried, the car wouldn't go. They tried everything they could before realizing it was only the battery. It was dead. A new one was found and we did the scene. In one take, too.

Later, I was in a different car, which my character had hijacked from a girl in a petrol station. The whole thing was going to climax with the police forcing me to crash as they chased me. Ultimately, I would be shot by them as I tried to escape the burning car. The hijacking scene, and the subsequent pursuit, would be filmed the next day. That day we would film the initial high-speed chase in the Jag, the final crash and shoot-out. After lunch I was introduced to the special effects guy. He was in a wheelchair, had one leg, two fingers on one hand and three on the other, plus he was blind in one eye. I was reliably informed he was the best in the business.

I drove the hijacked car for a while, and was told to stop just short of the wall it was going to crash into. I volunteered to do the crash myself, but that fell upon deaf ears, so the stunt co-ordinator did it. When the episode finally went out though, the stunt man could clearly be seen wearing a crash helmet! While the crash was being filmed, I was rigged with exploding blood bags, which were to be detonated by remote control. A lorry window was also rigged to explode as I ducked and dived as the police opened fire on me.

Eventually, after a few rehearsals for camera and the police team, we started to shoot the scene. I emerged from the car that the stunt man had crashed for me, and made my way towards the lorry next to which I would eventually be shot down. I was carrying a gun and fired at the police. This was great fun! As they fired back, I heard a pop as the window of the lorry behind me splintered. I then felt a small tap in my chest as the first blood bag exploded. I looked down at it as I had been instructed to, and then felt another one. I reacted to that too. Then I felt the most excruciating pain as the third bag exploded and I fell back, as we had rehearsed, and slid down the side of the van. I had a large, blood-soaked sponge attached to the back my head, and we filmed my slow slide down the lorry's side. I didn't need to act out a slow death, here – I was in agony from that third explosion.

After that I was taken back to Granada Studios to get cleaned up. As I walked from the car park to the studios with the assistant director, Julie Goodyear (brassy barmaid Bet Lynch from 'Coronation

213

Street'), was coming out of the reception. She took one look at me and screamed, 'Get him away from me!' As I had never met the woman, I was a bit puzzled by her reaction. But when I got in front of the mirror I realized why she was so shocked. I was covered in stage blood, and looked like something out of a horror movie.

The next day involved escaping from a police car, the hijacking, running around Manchester and the robbery itself. I had awoken with the most searing pain in my chest. It really hurt whenever I moved. I put it down either to being unfit, or just sleeping badly. As we entered the Granada studios a very attractive young Liverpool-sounding woman got into the lift with us. The stunt guys – being stunt guys – moved in and started trying to chat her up. She was applying for a job as a presenter. She obviously got the gig, as she appeared on our screens for years to come. The woman's name? Debbie Greenwood.

The filming went well, although every time I ran I was in dreadful pain with my chest. The following day, I was to be involved in scenes with the main character, Bulman himself – Don Henderson. I didn't know it then, but Don was to have a major impact on my future career. As a man and as an actor he became a mentor and a role model to me – there cannot have been a more generous and selfless individual in the profession. I had one scene with him where he arrested me after I had been captured. Then there was a scene with him in the back of the police van, where I would pull out a hidden gun, hold him hostage until they uncuffed me. We did the scene, and that was that for the day.

A few days later, we were filming the actual robbery, and then the punch-up scene with the stunt man. We rehearsed the punch-up scene until it was ready to be filmed, straight after lunch. As I entered the dining car, Don was sitting there with his wife, the actress Shirley Stelfox. With typical modesty he introduced us and asked me to join them. He told me that he had seen the rushes (unedited scenes) and they looked fantastic. He finished his meal and went off – home, I assumed.

The stunt fight was being filmed by the stunt co-ordinator, a procedure known as second unit filming. The choreography was meticulously worked out, not just for filming but for safety reasons,

Our wedding day.

Says it all . . .

A West End debut.

The cast of *Rick's Bar*.

'Children in Need' with Don Henderson and Geoffrey Hughes: 'The Andrews Sisters'.

With Robert Stephens on '99–1'.

'99–1'.

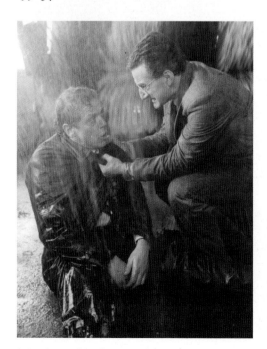

'99–1': another fine mess I'm in.

With Liza Goddard in 'Woof'.

With Geoffrey Bayldon
and Melinda Messinger
in 'Fort Boyard': fun
in France.

Not dirty now . . .

On the set of *Shadow Run* with Michael Caine.

Dad: the best friend anyone
could have.

Panto with Joe Pasquale.

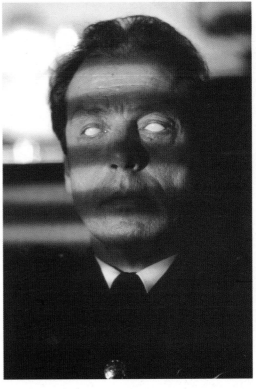

The Uninvited: the eyes have it.

Dirty Den returns . . .

Jane and the boys.

too. I had the next day off, but stayed in Manchester and just chilled; I was still in considerable pain with my chest.

On my final day's filming there was a lot of driving and driver's reaction scenes. Again cameras were rigged, on the car as well as inside it. There was also going to be a camera car in front of us, filming from all angles. Once again the sound man was in the back. We shot it every which way but loose. I had driven around this council estate for hours and eventually the sound man and cameraman asked Bill if we had enough footage. Bill just looked up, twirled his cigar in his mouth and said, 'One more.'

We went again, driving hard. The camera position was resited from some distance away. But I could smell burning . . . and I was getting hotter and hotter.

Suddenly, the sound guy screamed, 'We're on fire!'

As I craned my head back I saw flames.

I drove the car straight to where the crew was assembled, slammed on the brakes, and dragged the sound guy out of the car.

Bill Brayne was furious, and ran over to find out why we had stopped. I turned to him and said, 'Fire!' Suddenly he saw the flames for himself and screamed, 'Fuck!' Fire extinguishers appeared and the flames were put out. The sound guy thanked me. The camera crew checked the gate of the camera to check it was all clear and it was a wrap – we could go.

On returning to the studios, I bumped into Jim O'Brien, who had come down to the make-up room to say hello. After a celebratory drink and a Chinese meal with the stunt guys, I returned to the hotel and made my way to the station. Back in London, my chest had become even more painful. I went to the casualty department at our local hospital, and only then, days after the event, did I find out I had a broken rib. The ultra-powerful charge that should have blown the window out of the lorry, had been used on a blood bag instead. The feeble blood bag explosive had been used on the window! No wonder the special effects guy was in a wheelchair with one eye and only five of his allotted ten fingers! Although I had a broken rib, I did count myself lucky that it wasn't worse. I mean I could have lost a leg, and ended up playing Long John Silver for the rest of my life.

★   ★   ★

Even though I got the part in 'EastEnders', other parts were still being cast. On several occasions I had to go to the 'EastEnders' office, just off Shepherds Bush Green, to meet those being considered for the members of my family. I was told that I shouldn't let any of the auditioning actors know that I had the job, as this might influence how they performed in front of Julia and Tony.

On one occasion I met Letitia Dean, who would play my daughter Sharon in the series, and she seemed a very sensible young girl. Another time I met an actress called Jean Fennel, who also seemed very nice, if a bit tense. Finally I met them both together. After the audition we made our way to the tube station, Letitia hardly saying anything and Jean telling us how she was going to be the new Bet Lynch. Jean, however, was never going to be anything like Bet Lynch. After about fifteen minutes of this monologue, which even carried on to the tube platform, Jean caught her train and Letitia and I just looked at each other and both shook our heads. Letitia asked why Jean was so excited, seeing as how she hadn't got the job yet. I said, 'She may well be the new Bet Lynch, but as far as I'm concerned it's just another job.' How wrong I was.

Meanwhile, back in the real world, Jane sold her house in Chelsea and bought a wreck in Fulham, for its potential. The place had brown walls and black ceilings, so we spent most of our free time painting it from top to bottom in white. How anyone could live in such a dark, depressing environment was beyond me, but we did manage to make it habitable.

I now had to attend an 'EastEnders' cast meeting at Elstree, so I caught the tube and train to Elstree. As I left the house, the sun was shining, but as the train pulled in at Elstree Station, the heavens opened and it started to pour. Even though I tried to shelter under the canopies of a number of shops, I ended up soaked. I made my way to the studios, resembling a drowned cat. After being shown where to go, I arrived at the room where the cast and everyone had assembled. Letitia was there, as was Jean Fennel, Julia Smith and Tony Holland. No one commented on my appearance, although I was conscious that I must have looked ridiculous. After a brief introduction, Julia and Tony started to move through the room. When they came to me they started talking about my character having a dog. After several minutes, I was put on the spot and asked what breed of dog Den should have. We discussed the merits (or otherwise) of Rottweilers, Alsatians and Dobermans; and after a few flippant remarks about a tape machine that barked, or a stuffed dog on wheels, I said in a rather camp way, 'What about a Poodle?' They both laughed, and moved on. Several other people introduced themselves but not for any length of time, so I left and returned home.

Rehearsals weren't due for a couple of weeks and the scripts weren't ready, so it was back to waiting for the phone to ring. My agent, however, thought that until I got 'EastEnders' out of the way, it would be pointless going up for much else. The contract was only for a few episodes – although there was an option to keep me longer if needed – but I hoped that that wouldn't be the case.

Bryn Newton had left the Vernon Conway Agency for Saraband. When he left Vernon he said that he would take only four of his clients with him, but I should wait until he had settled down in his new job. When, after a few weeks, I still hadn't heard from him, I wrote a letter and hand-delivered it to Saraband's office. I then received a call from Bryn, saying that although he hadn't forgotten me, he was trying hard to convince Sara that I was worth taking on. She had agreed the other three, but wasn't sure if I had star potential. (She hadn't even heard of me.) Eventually Bryn won her over and I joined Saraband. With the BBC being new to soaps at that point, it didn't have much experience of ongoing contracts. The BBC simply classed the contract under their special low category, and basically it was take it or leave it. But it was money coming in and yet another job on the CV.

Eventually the first day of rehearsals came and I made my way to BBC Television Centre, where a coach was to take us to Borehamwood. The BBC ran an hourly shuttle service from White City to Borehamwood Studios, which in the early days was a godsend for me. Most of the cast was on the coach, and several of the faces looked familiar. I travelled out sitting next to Bill Treacher, who was to play Arthur Fowler, and he regaled me with stories of all the shows, films and television he had been in. He looked familiar, so I asked him if he was the little man who lived in the freezer in a frozen pea commercial. I then made a joke about how he looked bigger off screen than on, but it went completely over his head, as he continued his conversation about all the commercials he had filmed. And I realized that he had also been in a commercial with Jane.

When we arrived we were given scripts and had a read-through. We were to work on the first script, but not record, as we had a few weeks to rehearse before filming the twelve episodes before the series hit the screen. We rehearsed for a few days, and then we put a few select scenes together for recording. In one particular scene, Den's wife, Angie, drunk and flirtatious (especially with Arthur Fowler), needed to be carried upstairs. It became increasingly difficult, as Matthew always wanted a better take. Nevertheless, it was an important scene in the first show and set up the frailties of Den and Angie, and their relationship with the other characters in the Square. Trouble was, we never seemed to get further than Angie sitting on Arthur's lap.

We came in one morning and were told to go to the wardrobe area to try on the clothes we had selected, as well as pick out various jewellery pieces that we felt our characters would wear. Julia was very pleased with the choices of nearly all the characters until it came to Angie's clothes.

'Jean, that doesn't look quite right,' said Julia.

'But, I feel, my character wouldn't wear that, she'd look much better in this,' replied Jean Fennel, who was wearing a ridiculously gaudy and sluttish Bet Lynch outfit.

After ten minutes of this kind of to-ing and fro-ing, Julia snapped. 'Don't tell me about your character, I fucking invented her.'

Jean burst into tears and rushed out.

Someone was dispatched to see if she was all right, and we got on with choosing the jewellery. Most of the stuff was your archetypal, brash, clunky watches and bracelets, as well as other stuff that spivs and wide boys wore. But there on its own, sticking out like an oasis in a desert, was a very sophisticated silver watch. Thankfully, everyone had ignored it, so I picked it up and asked Julia, mindful of how she had reacted to Jean, 'Could I take this? I think it makes a statement about Den.' She looked at it and looked at me, smiled, and said, 'Yes, it's the sort of watch his mistress would give him.' Mistress? This was news to me; but as it was the watch I wanted, I let it pass.

We were all given a tour of the Square itself, and what a sight it was – absolutely phenomenal. The designer, Keith Harris, had done a fantastic job; it looked so real, but it wasn't until you went inside that you realized it was all fake. The set was slightly smaller than a real square, which explains why the characters look smaller whenever they go out of the Square on location. Previously the area used for Albert Square had been a German building site in 'Auf Wiedersehen Pet'.

After visiting the Square, we were shown the interior sets. The Queen Vic, being my place of work, looked like any pub of a certain age, but as I gazed at the pictures on the wall my heart sank. I couldn't do the job; the photographs were all of old Arsenal players. I looked at Keith, and he saw something in my face that told him I was troubled.

'What's wrong?' he asked.

'Sorry, I can't do the job,' I said.

'But why?'

'Den can't run a Gunners' pub. Look, he might be slightly dodgy, but a Gooner he isn't.'

Keith laughed. 'Leave it with me.'

Within the next twelve hours, all the Arsenal photographs had been replaced with West Ham memorabilia. Now, I could live with that. Years later when I played the Arsenal manager in a Nick Hornby film, I justified it by wearing a West Ham tie. Fickle, us football fans.

Eventually, we had reached the point where Matthew was happy with all the scenes we were to rehearse. We would, in a few days' time, properly record the first episodes of the show. So, at ten o'clock, we assembled in the green room on the fifth floor awaiting our call, and at ten-thirty we went through our paces for Julia and Tony. My exquisite opening line – the first flowery sentiments of Dennis Watts, Esquire, to seduce the breathless public – went as follows:

'Stinks in 'ere.'

Poetry in motion, I think you'll find. We finished our scenes and were told to wait, while Julia, Tony and Matthew went off in a huddle. After ten minutes we were told to go home. On the way home, I kept thinking that I had been crap, and when I arrived and Jane commented on how early I was, I said, 'I think I'm going to be sacked.'

After about an hour, the phone rang and Jane picked up. Her face was tense and her hand shaking as she handed it to me.

'It's Matthew.'

'Are you all right?' Matthew asked.

'Yes,' I stuttered. I wanted to add, 'But *you're* not, are you? Spit it out!'

He spat it out.

'I have some bad news for you.'

My heart sank; so I had been right after all: I was to be sacked after ten minutes of the biggest break I was ever going to get.

'Look, Matthew, I'm really sorry; I've let you down. I've let everyone down . . .'

'Leslie, shush! It's got nothing to do with you. It's Jean . . .'

He then told me they were looking for a replacement for Jean, and they hoped to have her in place when we started shooting. If not, it would be no problem, as they would just shift the schedule around. He would see me the following Monday at Elstree. Obviously, I was elated that it wasn't me who'd been sacked. But I did feel sad that Jean had gone, since apart from her intensity and obvious excitement about being a major player in a new soap, she was a very nice girl, and I couldn't see much wrong in what she was doing. Julia, however, thought she was wrong, and Julia was *the* boss.

Several female members of the cast went to Julia and asked for the part, and when they were told they were too old or too young to play opposite me, they came up with actors' names who could play me to accommodate themselves in the role of Angie. Julia pooh-poohed the idea and set about finding a replacement Angie. A day later, I was sitting in the canteen, when Julia appeared with a younger woman. She introduced her as Anita Dobson, who would play my wife. After a brief chat she disappeared with Julia. The following morning, when we arrived to rehearse, Anita was there and we did the scene that had caused Jean so much trouble. We sailed through it. Anita was phenomenal, and earned a round of applause at the end of it. We had a technical run in the afternoon with cameras and lighting in recording order, and then a run of the two shows in story order, with the writers and Julia and Tony in attendance. When we had finished, Matthew disappeared with Julia and Tony and the writers for a note session. We all went home.

The following morning we were given our notes by Matthew. We rehearsed those scenes that had to be reblocked, and then shot several other scenes, before going home and relaxing before being called at eight o'clock the next morning for camera rehearsals prior to recording in the afternoon and evening. Studio days were Wednesdays and Thursdays, while Fridays were exterior days. We would also be rehearsing all day Saturday. The morning session from eight until lunch would be camera rehearsals, and then after lunch we would film until four, when we would break for tea, and then camera rehearse the scenes until evening break, when we would have supper and then film until ten o'clock. It was gruelling, and put paid to the lie that actors have it easy.

The days went well. I was sharing a dressing room with Bill, although the Beales and Fowlers had their own. Anna Wing was playing Lou Beale, the matriarch of the Square; Wendy Richard was the daughter, Pauline, who was married to Arthur; Susan Tully was their daughter Michelle and David Scarboro was Mark, their son. Peter Dean, who I had thought was magnificent in a television series a few years earlier called 'Law and Order', with Derek Martin and Ken Campbell, was to play Lou Beale's son Pete, Den's best mate; he ran the market fruit and veg stall. His character was married to Kath, played by Gillian Taylforth, and they had a son called Ian, played by Adam Woodyatt. The wonderful Gretchen Franklyn, who was related to Clive Dunne, was to play Ethel, Lou Beale's best mate. Letitia Dean was playing my daughter, Sharon. We had Sue and Ali who ran the café, played by Nedj Salih and Sandy Ratcliffe. Shreela Ghosh, whom I had met in India on *The Jewel in the Crown*, was playing the Indian shopkeeper, and Ross Davidson and Shirley Cheriton were playing Debs and Andy, the love-struck couple in the Square. A black actor called Oscar James was Tony Carpenter, the builder, and Paul Medford was his son. Oscar had done some terrific stuff at the Royal Court, but as the series went on it became evident that he was struggling with the quick learning process that filming a twice-weekly soap required. Paul was a tremendously talented kid who, it was obvious, had a great future. John Altman was the Square's wayward tearaway, Nick Cotton.

We had to have photographs taken outside the Queen Vic, and Terry O'Neil came to do a photo-shoot, in which we all had to be in costume, for a weekend supplement. But when the article came out it mentioned only the Beales and Fowlers, plus a short piece about Shirley Cheriton, but as they all had a track record, this was understandable.

Eventually, I decided, after talking to Matthew, that it was perhaps best if I mentioned my past. Matthew took it completely on board, although he said he would never have guessed. He felt, after reflecting on it, that I should tell Julia, so I made an appointment and told her. She was very kind and just told me not to worry about it.

Unknown to me, the heads at the BBC, Michael Grade, Bill Cotton and Jonathan Powell, had seen the first few episodes and had instructed Julia to push the publicans to the fore. This must have made both Julia and Tony laugh, as a few years ago they had approached the same people with a project about an alcoholic, flirtatious, pub landlady, married to a Jack-the-lad womanizing husband. It was to be called 'Pearl and Swine', and was to be set in a pub in Osterley. The BBC rejected it on the grounds that the public wouldn't take to a couple like that . . .

Apart from the cast, crew, producers and directors, another major contributory factor in getting the show right was the supporting artistes, those people you see in the background of every television drama. After my experience on *Morons from Outer Space*, I soon realized that not all were to be tarred with the same brush. In the main, they were absolutely fantastic, and of course an essential part of any show, but as with anything else, you had the few that let you and themselves down. Some could be even more competitive than the actors. Nothing demonstrated this more than when we filmed the exterior shots in Albert Square, especially in the market place. Peter Dean, as Pete Beale, ran the fruit and veg stall, but the other stalls had to be manned, and to see some of the supporting artistes (who must have realized that this was an opportunity to get a regular slot every week) fiercely compete for roles as stall holders was something out of a situation comedy. And some have made a nice few bob out of it. Then you had the other few who, although in the scene, made sure they were never seen, so as to either just take the money and run, or to make sure they were called back. But in the main, they were a good bunch, and some have become great mates.

After filming a few episodes with Matthew, we had a new director, floor manager and assistant directors, and it became more apparent with each episode that some of the supporting artistes were playing a different character each week. One, for example, was a gas man working in the road, in the following episode a Salvation Army *War Cry* seller, and then a policeman. So I approached the powers that be, and suggested that we should have a book that was a general reference to who was what, thereby saving a huge amount of embarrassment. This they agreed to, and with my help managed in those early days to co-ordinate the background characters into some sort of order so this wouldn't happen again.

After a few weeks of filming, my agent phoned to say that the BBC had picked up my option; I was to be there for a full twelve months. Funny thing was, my overwhelming emotion was sheer relief. Julia and Tony had had – out of necessity – to edge forward an episode to see what would work on screen, and what worked only on paper. Some very talented actors were let go, and it wasn't down to their ability: it was simply what seemed like a brilliant idea or storyline was just not going to have the legs to sustain an ongoing life in a weekly, prime-time soap. So, while my delight at being retained was palpable, it only came to me as a delayed reaction.

Everyone was nice and we all got on great, although it was becoming more and more apparent that Bill Treacher was becoming frustrated with David Scarboro, who was playing his son, Mark. Bill, being of the old school, and David, being a sort of James Dean-type method actor, and a little bit undisciplined, although extremely good on screen, had several clashes. Bill would offer advice and David, being young, obviously took umbrage at this, and continued to do things his way, which made Bill more and more furious, so much so that Julia called them both in, and warned David about his behaviour.

It was also apparent that Shirley Cheriton and Ross were becoming very close, although this could be put down to their learning lines together. Several other members of the cast were always commenting on it, and whenever they disappeared together, to learn lines, the rumour mill started to grind.

Eventually it was launch day, and a press showing was arranged at Television Centre. We were all paraded to the press wearing blue sweatshirts with our characters' names on them in white. Peter Dean did the introductions in his chirpy Cockney sparrow way, plus a sprinkling of Cockney rhyming slang, and we were all then left in the room with the press. Obviously they hadn't seen the first episode yet, so we mingled and answered questions. They surrounded Shirley Cheriton en masse and a few chatted to Wendy, and after a while we were taken back to Elstree to do our filming or rehearsals.

That night we had a private showing of the first episode in the main rehearsal room. I was sitting next to a man about my age, who looked important, but I hadn't seen him on the show. It looked good, but I cringed every time I appeared, as I hated seeing myself on screen.

The episode finished and the man shook my hand and said, 'Fantastic. Well done. What do you think of it?'

'It's all right, but I hate that music.'

He laughed. 'By the way, I'm Simon May, the composer.'

Well, talk about putting your foot in it! Even all these years later I still feel pretty stupid about it, although I still hate the music . . .

The show was to be aired the next night on BBC1 at the prime-time slot of seven o'clock. February 19, 1985 – the date should be etched on my heart for all the grief and glory that followed. We were all told we had to watch it in the BBC club, where food and drink were laid on. I still hated seeing myself on screen and couldn't wait to get away. Matthew had arranged that Jane and his girlfriend would meet up with us both at a restaurant not far from where we lived, and so as soon as the programme ended we hightailed it out of Elstree and met up with the girls. Jane thought it was great, as did Sara. After the meal we made our separate ways home, and it was back to learning lines and an early night, as I was expected in the studio the next day. The answerphone was swamped with congratulation messages and the phone didn't stop ringing all night from friends and family. Of all the well-wishers to phone, the man who was proudest was my Dad. Never a man of words, he tried to explain his delight but he didn't have to. I could hear it in his voice – he was choked with pride.

So 'EastEnders' was a success, it seemed. And like anything else, once the first one was out of the way, you could relax a bit. All that was left now was the critics' reaction. As I went to sleep I am sure I had a smile on my face, yet at the same time I was wondering what the critics would say, would they like it, but most important of all, would the audience like it? Because one thing is certain: no one ever put a blue plaque up to a critic. And the audience are the only people in my business that count. They pay my wages.

19

AN OVERNIGHT SUCCESS

When I woke up the next day, I flew in and out of the shower, grabbed a quick cup of coffee and armed with the day's script, headed for Elstree. When I say woke up, that was not strictly true: I hadn't really slept much, as I had gone over all the scenes in my head from the first show and had analysed (and hated) them. I kept thinking I could have done them better, and I was still analysing them as I arrived at the studios, when this exotically dressed apparition, wrapped up to the eyes and wearing dark glasses and a hat, sailed past me. It was Shirley Cheriton, looking like something out of a French movie. When I commented that I hadn't recognized her, she replied that she didn't want to be recognized. When I entered make-up, for their cursory thirty-second look at me, everyone was all reading various reviews of the show. The viewing figures were good and the hierarchy at the BBC was pleased. I, it seemed, was someone who looked as if he knew what he was doing and in a poll conducted by one tabloid newspaper in the East End of London I had got the viewers' vote.

I went on set, and when Peter Dean turned up I asked him what he had done the previous night. He said he had gone to his brother's club, and that an old mate of mine had sent his regards. When I asked

226

who, he said Frank O'Connell. Oh shit . . . Frank O'Connell had been in Wormwood Scrubs with me. He was also the chap I had had my only fight with inside, and had come out of it looking a fool.

'Oh, really?' I said.

'Yeah. He said he knew you well,' Peter replied.

Thankfully, it was time to rehearse. We dropped the subject, and I hoped that that would be the end of it. I bumped into Julia and Tony, who both congratulated me and said they had some great storylines in store for me. Once I had finished recording I made my way home. I wouldn't be called until late the following day.

The next day the papers were still full of the show: there were several articles by members of the cast. When I arrived at the studio the first person I bumped into was Adam Woodyatt, who asked me if I had seen Susan Tulley or Letitia Dean. When I said, 'No, why?' he told me they were very upset. Typically, I thought I must have said something to upset them, and told him I would apologize. Adam said, 'It wasn't you. Peter said something about your past.' I was furious and went to see both Tish and Susan. They asked me if it was true, and I told them I was sorry they had found out this way, but it wasn't something I was proud of and really didn't want to shout it from the rooftops. They just said, 'Oh, Les.' I also said I would understand if they didn't want to talk to me, to which they both told me to shut up, of course they would talk to me. I then went back to Adam and said, 'Where's Peter?' He said he would go and find him. He returned saying he had told Peter I was looking for him, and when Peter asked why, Adam had told him the reason. Which might have been the wrong thing to do.

Within fifteen minutes there was a flurry of activity, and people started to run about the place. Peter, it seemed, had collapsed with a suspected heart attack in full view of the staff in reception. An ambulance was called and he was rushed to hospital. I felt terrible; had Adam's message to him from me been the cause? I left a message on his answerphone, saying I hoped he was going to be OK.

Well, the next morning who should stroll in as bright as a button, but Peter? He told me his 'heart attack' was only indigestion, and he apologized profusely about his behaviour of the day before. He didn't know what had come over him, but he wasn't himself. I told him not to talk about me and my business or he and I would really fall out. I also asked him why he had told only the youngsters on the show, and he mumbled that he didn't know. Things were never the same between us after that. Fortunately it didn't seem to affect any other members of the Fowlers and Beales. Nevertheless, it soon became very evident that there was a huge rift in the camp, with little cliques beginning to spring up.

I was then approached by the series' publicity woman, Cheryl, who said that the *Sun* newspaper wanted to talk to the nation's number-one pub landlord. 'Oh, for God's sake,' I said, 'I'm an actor, not a publican, and anyway I don't want to do any interviews; I'm too busy.' I had made a vow to myself very early in my career, after reading a horrible article about an actor I had admired, in which he was systematically ripped to pieces by a newspaper. If I were ever successful I would try not to do interviews. Cheryl looked worried and said she wasn't sure how she was going to put them off, but maybe we could do it another time.

I had made my way to the canteen, and was just sitting down to eat my food, when I heard my name being called. I looked up and was told I had a phone call. Thinking it was Cheryl, I answered it, but it was a female reporter from the *Sun*, who wanted to talk to me about my time in prison. I told her to go away, and hung up. I then rang Jane and told her the press had found out. She told me not to worry about it.

I went off to see Cheryl, who had also been contacted. Suddenly the place was alive; the studios were surrounded by waiting press, and some had even tried to bribe their way in to take pictures. Julia asked if I wanted to go home early and I said no, I'd finish my scenes. She said she was going to have to issue a statement. I offered my resignation but she said no, she would phone Michael Grade. He also said I wasn't to resign; we would ride it out together.

At the end of the day I was smuggled out of the studios and driven home by Matthew Robinson. There were no press in evidence, so Matthew dropped me off at the corner and I walked towards the house. Suddenly this chap appeared, wearing what looked like a green Gestapo-style leather coat. He asked me if I had any statement to make. I said no, and that a statement had been issued by the BBC. When I got home, Jane was in tears. Apparently the press had been screaming through the letterbox, 'What's it like to be married to a killer?' 'Why pick on her?' I thought. I was the criminal; her only crime was to fall in love with me. Suddenly, a note appeared through the letterbox from the man in the green coat, saying he had been on to his office and they had no knowledge of any statement issued by me through the BBC. I ignored it and spoke to my agent, who had been briefed by Julia. I had a glass of wine, looked at my lines, and went to bed.

The next morning the newspaper headlines screamed at me wherever I turned. Every front page had the same sort of headline: ' "EastEnders" Star is a Killer'. The front of my house was under siege, as was the studio. Matthew picked me up and drove me to Elstree. Once I arrived I wrote a letter of apology to the cast, stating that if they didn't want to work with me I would understand. I stuck it on the noticeboard. When I returned to the green room, the cast called for that day had assembled. Wendy Richards on seeing me flew across the room and flung her arms around me. I looked at the board, and saw my note had gone. No one shunned me or said anything. I could now get on with filming the show.

Every day brought another stream of headlines, quotes from people who were at school with me, so-called friends and neighbours, and people who had been in the army and prison with me. There was also a lot of rubbish from people who had never met me. There were pictures of me at my courts martial, pictures of my family, and of anyone I had ever passed in the street. The newspapers were screaming for the BBC to sack me. Polls were conducted, but the answer from the viewers and readers was always the same: leave him alone.

We had been under siege non-stop for two days, and Jane found it impossible to leave the house without half a dozen reporters and photographers ambushing her. We had to rely on friends to do our shopping. I, being in the studios, was protected from all this, but as I left home or work I was followed by a convoy of Fleet Street's 'finest'.

Sunday's newspapers brought no respite, and we had to keep the curtains shut – actually, they weren't curtains, but bits of calico and old sheets we had stuck up until we could afford curtains. But we knew the street was full of reporters, and silly money was being offered to neighbours for any information they had. Now I knew how Custer must have felt at the Battle of Little Big Horn.

Matthew Robinson rang and invited us over for lunch, but we told him it was impossible to leave the house. He said he would ring back, and when he did he had a plan: a red Citroën 2CV would appear outside our house, and when we saw it we should rush and get in. Once we had driven round the corner we were transferred to his BMW, while the press ran to get into their cars. As we went one way, to his house for lunch, the press were following the 2CV all the way to the television centre, where it pulled into the staff car park. The headlines next day were of the 'Den Escapes Press in High-speed Chase' variety. Seeing as the journey from Parsons Green to Shepherds Bush was entirely within a built-up area, with dozens of traffic lights and roundabouts, how high speed came into it I will never know, but I guess the headline was far more sensational than 'Den Escapes Press in Five-mile-an-hour Car Crawl'.

The press intrusion at home finally abated because I had not responded to any money offers or made any comment at all. Sadly, though, the headlines didn't stop, and obviously a lot of people were still making money out of me, selling stories, both true and false.

I had now been offered my first public appearance at a shop in Harlow, Essex, and after the necessary clearance, I prepared myself and headed off. As I was sure that no one would turn up, I decided to arrive early. The signing wasn't until 10 a.m., and I arrived just before nine. No one turn up? The queue stretched all around the block, and what was supposed to be a two-hour signing lasted for nine hours. I quickly ran out of photos and was signing anything shoved in front of me.

I had a break from the filming for two weeks, so we decided to go to Australia, but I could only get a twelve-day visa. We arrived in Adelaide, saw all Jane's family, and then drove to Canberra, then on to Sydney, where we saw Keith Michell in a play. He had been directly responsible for Jane and my meeting, as she had popped in to see him while he was appearing in a play in London to ask his advice about her career, and he had told her to try Webber Douglas. We stayed at Surfers' Paradise for two days and then it was back to Adelaide and home to England. After dropping Jane at home, I made my way back to 'EastEnders' and got ready to rehearse and film my exterior scenes.

'EastEnders' was an immediate and runaway success, and Den's volatile relationship with Angie was one of the most popular aspects of the show. It seemed like we were pushing back the boundaries with each new episode. But towards the autumn of 1986, when we'd been up and running for about eighteen months or so, Tony and Julia had the audacious idea of devoting an entire episode to Angie and Den. This had never been attempted before in television history. The whole attraction of soaps is that they're entertaining without being overly demanding and part of the formula is to keep things moving, cutting from character to character, scene to scene. How on earth were Anita and I going to keep the nation watching all by ourselves? Well, we'd reckoned without some of the very best storyliners and writers in the business. When we became privy to what was in store for our characters, we couldn't wait to start shooting. First, Angie was to tell Den she had only six months to live. Smitten with remorse for his loose and philandering ways, Dennis sweeps Angie off to Venice to woo her and win her back. Mistaking Den's guilt-driven ardour for true love, Angie confesses that, actually, she might not strictly have been telling him the truth about her terminal illness. Den is so overjoyed with this reprieve that he gives Angie a Christmas present to savour: he serves her with divorce papers. It was all absolute genius, and we were licking our lips at the roles, the storylines and the impact this would all have on our viewers. It was only a soap, but we were aware of the part it played in its fans' everyday lives. 'EastEnders' was absolutely huge, and throughout that period it felt as though we were at the very epicentre of all that mattered in the world.

So much so, that it transpired that the cast were to make a Christmas record of Cockney songs, in conjunction with a chap called Eric Hall, and a record producer, Tony Parnell. Because I had been away and hadn't been there for any discussions, I ended up singing 'Henry the Eighth'. I must say, having heard it, it is possibly the worst song on a dire album. I don't profess to be a singer, but I know I can sing better than the final result suggests.

Eric Hall had a number of footballers on his books and when he found out I was a die-hard West Ham supporter (although I hadn't been for a while), he asked me to go to a match with him. I was chuffed to be asked. I went with him and Ross, and at half time I was asked to draw out the lucky programme number on the pitch. As I stepped on to that hallowed turf and made my way to the centre circle, all the matches I had seen and the players who had been my heroes came flooding into my head. I could hear the roar of the crowd, cheering each and every player and all the goals they had scored. Suddenly I was being nudged by Brian Blower, the commercial manager, who said, 'Listen to them.' The crowd was singing 'There's only one Den Watts'. Later, after the Den-being-father-of-the-baby episode, it would turn into 'There's only one Dirty Den'.

Players came up after the game to say hello. I was in seventh heaven. Brian Blower had said, 'If you want to come again, just give me a call.' He gave me his card. I booked a ticket for the next match and went straight to the game from rehearsals, and took my place in among the West Ham fans. This was not a good idea, as the first half was almost entirely taken up by programmes being thrust in my face for me to sign. At half time I was approached by a smartly dressed steward who told me Brian wanted me; and he was a bit upset. 'Brian?' I thought, 'who's Brian?' but as I was escorted around the stands, I realized who he meant. As Brian approached, he called out, 'Why didn't you call me?' I told him I didn't like to, but he plonked me in the directors' box and after the game told me that I was never to buy a ticket again. Sadly, because of work commitments, I couldn't perform the opening ceremony of a new building at the club some time later, so Michael Cashman performed the ceremony. (Michael was the show's first gay character, Colin. Predictably, the tabloids had a field day with this, slashing banner headlines such as 'East Benders'. Very droll.) Ironically, I had been the one who introduced Michael to West Ham in the first place. He's a brilliant actor, and although doing well in his new career as a Euro MP, Michael is a great loss to the acting fraternity.

Around this time the pressures upon me, which seem so trivial now, had begun to take their toll. I had trouble sleeping, and so got the doctor to give me some sleeping tablets on a rollover prescription. One day, after a period of a huge amount of press intrusion, I was so depressed when I arrived home that I just rolled up on the floor and cried. A combination of overwork, press hounding and lack of sleep had reduced me to this. I couldn't go on. I went to the bathroom, grabbed a bottle of sleeping pills and swallowed the lot. When Jane found me on the floor, she phoned an ambulance and tried to make me throw up. I remember I had a deep sinking feeling, as if I was being engulfed. Then everything went blank. That was all I remembered. By all accounts, I had waved the paramedics away when they arrived. I realized the next day how stupid I had been; however tough things were, they could only get better.

'EastEnders' and Den and Angie went from strength to strength. Michael Grade then had the brilliant idea of moving the programme's time slot from seven o'clock to 7.30, following a dinner party, at which some friends said it was on too early for them to see. When it was moved to its new slot, the viewing figures shot up. I was now being offered masses of personal appearances. At one time I could have done one a night, but I realized that if it hadn't been for 'EastEnders' I wouldn't be doing any at all. So I made sure they never affected my work on the show. Others weren't quite so sensible about it, and fell foul of Julia Smith over it.

I was also being offered lots of awards: tie wearer of the year, jewellery wearer of the year, rear of the year, even glasses wearer of the year, despite the fact I didn't wear glasses. I always said no, as I was working when the awards ceremonies were being held. When my agent informed the various societies that I wouldn't be there to collect their award, and asked could a friend attend on my behalf, the same answer always came back: they would give the award to someone else. I still continued to fill the front pages, though, and only on a few occasions during my time on the show was the front page devoted to someone else. One of these was Fergie and Prince Andrew's engagement. I wrote them a note, saying 'Congratulations on the engagement', and also thanking them for taking me off the front page. They sent a lovely note back, thanking me for my best wishes, and saying also they were glad they could help. When I met Fergie years later, at a pantomime performance, she reminded me of it.

I did win a Sony Award, though, for the man who had made the most impact on television that year, and after the ceremony I travelled back on the tube to home carrying my crystal bowl in its box on my knee. How glamorous is that!

I was also being offered lots of television interviews at this time, but wary that I would be asked questions about my past, I declined. When I turned Michael Aspel down, the show's publicity people replied that they would fly my favourite actress in from America to be on the show, so I relented and said, 'OK, I would love to be on the show with Marilyn Monroe . . .' Funnily enough, I never heard from them again.

I now seemed to be working non-stop. I was always the first one in to work and usually one of the last to leave. The stories about me got bigger and more sensational. At one point I was convinced if I broke wind I would be accused of causing an earthquake. I had decided to sue the papers over certain of these stories, but not about my past, however falsely it was portrayed. This was because if I had said this was false, and that was true, then the whole thing would rear its ugly head again, only this time it would appear as if I had authorized its republication. Since I had never talked about it until now, and was, and still am, deeply ashamed about it, I felt it was something between me and my maker, and not for public consumption. I sued only when I felt it was right. If stories lied concerning my work ethic or my home life, or when something was completely false and had appeared just for sensationalism, I sued. Suing newspapers is a double-edged sword, and very expensive. Also, because newspapers are childish, they will keep running stories that aren't the subject of the court case. Money was thus being poured down a bottomless pit; it disappeared as fast as I was earning it, and the papers, although they knew they were in the wrong, kept it going for as long as they could, hoping that my money would run out.

Members of the cast who had been released from the series were selling stories about 'EastEnders', most of them untrue. But as they had committed themselves to flash cars and a lifestyle they thought would go on for ever, bankrolled by the series, they were left in financial turmoil, ready to be thrown a lifeline by the press. They knew 'EastEnders' sold newspapers, and no one wanted to hear how lovely and how nice everyone was, and how it was a joy to go to work, so for huge sums of money they were ready to slag everyone off, usually Anita, Wendy, Julia and me.

One day I was a racist, the next homophobic. I remember one article written by the self-proclaimed 'Queen of Fleet Street', Jean Rook, which devoted a whole column to how I would sit, lonely in the corner of the canteen, ignored by everyone. As several cast members had been sitting with me at the time she claimed to have observed this, she had obviously not bothered to clean those ridiculous Dame Edna Everage glasses she wore.

At home, we needed two phones, one for business (always on answerphone), and our hot line, for which only friends, agents and family had the number. One night I arrived home and checked my messages. There was one from a journalist, asking if I had a comment about the headlines in the following day's papers. I obviously didn't reply. By now I had told the BBC press office that it would save a lot of time and effort if they didn't bother to ring me about anything in the papers, as I had no intention of replying to any of the stories.

The next morning I drove into work, and stopped at a petrol station to fill up. As I went to pay, the headline screamed out at me: 'Dirty Den is Racist'. I found out later that Sally Sagoe, who had come into the series to play Tony Carpenter's wife, had sold a story about her time in 'EastEnders', which said I had described her as a 'man in a frock'. I admit this, but in the following way. Oscar, who played Tony, was a good actor, but couldn't cope with the pressures of learning lines on such a quick turnover, and as the Carpenters were the only black family in the Square, the BBC decided to bring help in for him in the shape of a wife. Sally was very glamorous, but she did have some terrible dialogue. She was in the dressing room next to mine, and she came in once to ask my advice. I looked at her script and I could see where the name Tony was whitened out and her character's name typed in. I offered her the advice that unless she wanted to be a man in a frock she should change it ever so slightly. This harmless remark was then turned on its head. Instead of helping to keep Oscar in the show, she speeded up his departure and, of course, hers. As for the racist remark, I had appeared in a scene in the pub as Dick Turpin, and a writer trying to get authentic Cockney had put in the phrase 'big, sooty horse', which, unbeknown to him, had racist connotations. When this was pointed out to the producers, we reshot the scene, substituting 'black' for 'sooty'. But the line including 'sooty' was put out in the transmitted programme. As I left the petrol station and was about to get into my car, a blue van appeared and half a dozen black guys got out, each one carrying a newspaper under his arm. As the first one saw me, he shouted out, 'Hello, Den,' and they all shook my hand, asked for an autograph and thrust the newspapers at me to sign. I did so, signing them with the names they gave me; the last guy just laughed and said, 'Put "To Sooty" man.'

Because the character and I were the same to a lot of people, it became harder for the public to figure out which was Leslie Grantham and which was Den. In fact, some people even called me Des and others Len. I remember being at a dinner party one night, and this woman was there who worked in film. After about an hour of name-dropping about films she had worked on and the directors and stars she had worked with, she decided to go round the table, asking people what they did, either smiling or looking sad at the answers they gave. It was a common experience for me then; people would just come up and tell me they never watched 'EastEnders', and then proceed to tell me every storyline. Thinking that she was one of these, and not wanting to hog the evening, when she got to me I replied that I was a publican. I knew straight away by her reaction that she knew who I was, and was being clever. Shortly afterwards, she left.

A few years later, while filming a series called 'The Paradise Club', several of our crew had worked on a film with Kiefer Sutherland about an American serviceman who had killed his girlfriend while being stationed in the UK during the Second World War. And everyone had been invited from our show to attend the film's end-of-shoot party by the co-ordinator of the film, except for me. When our co-ordinator asked why I hadn't been included, he was told I had been extremely rude to someone on the film some time ago. Well, of course, it was the woman at the dinner party, so our entire crew didn't go. Which annoyed her even more.

Once, travelling back from work with Matthew, he looked quite worried, so I asked him what was wrong. He said that he had got his new set of scripts and he had to find a Mum for Nick Cotton; he was trying to think of someone who could play the part. The previous night I had seen a rerun of 'The Sweeney', in which there had been an older actress who I thought was brilliant. I mentioned her to Matthew and he asked me if I knew her name. I said I didn't but I'd have a look in the *Radio Times*. When I arrived home, I looked up the programme and the name June Brown stood out. I phoned Matthew. Ten minutes later, he called me back to say she was with my agent and was it a plot? Just coincidence, I said. I then phoned Bryn and warned him that he might get a call, as I had suggested June Brown for a part. Anyway, the rest is history: June has gone on to be one of the nation's favourite cigarette-smoking characters. She is also, I might add, a superb actress, although a bit eccentric. June will not mind my saying this, as she knows it herself.

'EastEnders' continued to fill the front pages, and no one was safe, although certain stories were obviously planted by members of the cast. What was great about the early days was that the spirit and camaraderie were good, and the cast was adamant that they wouldn't talk to the papers, as they couldn't be trusted. Information, however, was still getting to the papers about storylines and people's private lives on set. Everyone had their own ideas as to who the moles were. Trouble was, no matter how much money people were earning, they always wanted more. And of course every now and again a cast member who had left, been killed off or sacked sold a story, so it was like a non-stop roller coaster; you never knew what was going to be written about you. Much later, as the cast split into several different camps, resentment began to creep in.

One day, I was called into Julia's office, and told that she had a problem. Straight away I thought I had done something wrong, but no, I had been given a best actor award by the Variety Club. However, she felt that this would create even more upset in the camp, and that I should decline it. She would explain my reasons to the Variety Club. I suggested that maybe it might be better if they made an award to the whole cast. Julia looked at me as if I was mad, but she said she would put it to them. Luckily they agreed, but insisted that I pick it up on behalf of the cast. So everyone was happy.

By this time, Ross Davidson and Shirley Cheriton's affair had become public, although they couldn't understand how . . . Anita had also become involved with Tom Watt, which was a very unlikely combination, but they seemed very happy together, although Anita later would try to influence his involvement in scenes.

David Scarboro had been released from the show. He was a very talented boy, but he was undisciplined. He still had the same mates and was doing whatever he wanted to in his private life – and why not? Sadly, the pressure of press intrusion took its toll and after a serious drinking binge, he threw himself off Beachy Head.

In the series, he and Michelle were sharing a bedroom, and around that time, Michelle was supposed to fall pregnant. I have always believed that the father would have turned out to be her brother, as Julia and Tony were so groundbreaking in their storylining. Where they went, others followed. Obviously, to change the storylines would require a Herculean effort. But Julia and Tony came up with a Who-Dun-It that soon gripped the nation. Every male cast member was in the frame. Every newspaper was having guesses. The *Telegraph* came up with names for us; I think either Ali or Andy was prefixed with 'Amorous', or maybe it was 'Randy Ross', 'Naughty Nedj', and I got the name 'Dirty Den'. Scripts weren't, as was reported, written with numerous different endings. Tony and Julia called me up to the office, and I was told I was to be the father of the baby. 'Great,' I thought, we would be filming off site. Julia said, 'I would tell you to not tell anyone, but I don't think that's needed in your case.'

I was sitting in the tea bar a few days later, when Susan sat down next to me. She looked at me and said, 'Thank God it's you,' meaning that I was the father of the baby. I said, 'Well, Sue, I'm glad I'm not the father of Lou Beale's baby.' We both laughed. I told her I was looking forward to the scenes by the canal, and that I hadn't mentioned it to anyone. Meanwhile, we were given the scripts, and because the scene was to be filmed out of sequence, it would not appear in any scripts. There was a time difference between the filming of the 'father' script and the filming of the next script in sequence, so it could be kept under wraps. The episode leading up to the revelation entailed all of us suspects receiving a phone call, and heading off to a mysterious destination, a very clever move by Julia and Tony.

The day before the filming, Julia was furious: she had been informed by the outside broadcast department that she couldn't use the normal film crew but had to use a outside crew. Now we had some of the most fantastic film crews working on our show, although it was shot on video, or tape. However, by using an outside unit, it would have to be shot on film, making it look different. And obviously our crews would love the chance to get out of the studio. Julia was so incensed that she went to Michael Grade and told him if she wasn't allowed to use her own crew she would resign. Anyway a compromise would be worked out: she would use her crew for this shoot, but obviously the Venice trip would be crewed by a film unit. Julia kept her job, our crew was happy, the film unit was happy, and the rest is history.

Julia had phoned me at home to tell me they had a problem, but told me to be on standby; I was not in the studios that week. Eventually she phoned to say that it had been sorted. A call sheet was faxed through, giving the location. I made my way there and we rehearsed and filmed the scenes. Julia was directing, and she had worked out precisely everything she wanted. Even Roly behaved himself! The only thing we could not control was the weather, although, as Julia was only too keen to point out, the outside film crew would not have coped with the pace. Suddenly, after lunch, the skies clouded over, and it was an afternoon of stop–start. Then a patch of blue appeared in the clouds above, and we went for the last scene of the day. It all started well but, halfway through, it began to pelt down. When you film scenes in the rain, you have to employ specialist water units to bring in a rain machine, as normal rain doesn't look like rain on screen. But if you are filming a sunny scene, rain shows. As I felt the first drops fall, we were by the bridge over the canal, and at the end of a speech I gently led Susan Tully under the bridge. Julia was amazing: she cut and reset the camera position, and we filmed the rest of the scene under the bridge. Julia and the crew were ecstatic, and we wrapped. Once again we were sworn, on pain of death, to keep the filming quiet. Which of course we did.

When these episodes went out they were a great success. Once broadcast, the name Dirty Den stuck, and my profile was raised even higher. The wink I had snuck in to an episode, as in the script it had said 'Den acknowledges Michelle silently', was something that became synonymous with the character.

Personal appearances became an even more regular occurrence, and now women of all shapes and sizes were throwing clothes at me and stripping off. At one such gig, I was escorted by my agent Bryn, who until that point had tended to treat my tales of near-riot scenes with an element of cynicism. At the switching-on ceremony of some Christmas lights, though, he got it first hand. The crowd surged forward and knocked my agent to the ground; more familiar with a genteel mêlée for pre-theatre canapés than a stampede for Dirty Den's autograph, the poor man was in real fear for his life. After that he would only accompany me to what he considered 'safe' events. In some seaside resort, the venue was huge and the disc jockey was Ann Nightingale. All the fans wanted to do was touch my hand. She reported on her radio show and in her newspaper column, it was as if I was Jesus Christ, which was quite funny really as I felt I had had more bad publicity than Adolf Hitler.

At this time, Jane and I decided to do some building work. Given that she was the one blessed with good taste, it fell to Jane to oversee the refurbishment. She was also pregnant with Spike.

'EastEnders' had finally got their act together and had put out letters asking us to submit holiday dates, so they could plan storylines and filming. On the form it quite clearly stated that unless we heard differently, these dates would be firm. I heard nothing, and the dates I had tied up had been when Jane was due to give birth.

At one personal appearance in the Midlands, Don Henderson, whom I'd met on 'Bulman', turned up to say hello. I was pleased to see him, as I had endured about an hour of having my crotch grabbed as I walked around a crowded pub. I say walked, but it was more like inched, as you couldn't really walk for the crowds. Don whisked me into a back room, and told me that on the day the papers had revealed my past, he had happened to be in the publicity department, when a newspaper had called to see if they had any photos of me with a gun in the show. Don had told the publicity officer to say no. Don and I became great friends from that day on until he sadly passed away.

My life was now very hectic: appearances in the show were full on, and Jane was having difficulty with the pregnancy. She had lost several babies before, but all in the early stages. She was continually confined to her bed, but I of course was keeping the pregnancy quiet. No one at 'EastEnders' knew, and only a few close friends were aware of it. As I left each morning, I made sure she had enough food for the day, and installed a television in her bedroom so she wouldn't be bored.

At work, rather than using the green room phone, I would use the phone at the main desk as I was leaving the studios to see if she needed anything picked up on the way home. Only Wendy had a phone in her dressing room, and rightly so, as she was a star. I was still sharing with Bill Treacher. As I was halfway through one such phone call, I was suddenly aware of a hand reaching across and pressing down the cradle of the phone. As I whirled around I saw it was a security man.

'What was that for?' I asked.

'I've been told by the studio manager that cast members aren't allowed to use the phones,' he replied.

Well, I saw red.

'In that case, when I can use the phone, I'll be come back.'

I handed him my scripts and dressing room key and made my way to my car. By the time I had reached the front gate, the studio manager was there and, visibly shaking, assured me that I would have a phone in my dressing room by Thursday.

'Look, if I get a phone, then everyone should have one. Thanks but no thanks,' I said.

'Not by Thursday,' he said, 'but by Monday.'

Having been assured that I could use the reception phone, I took my script and my dressing room key back and went home.

The next day I was informed that I could move dressing rooms. When I asked why, I was told that it was unfair for me to share a room, and that some more had been released. I was offered two, one in the main block with the others or one slightly larger, with a shower and loo on the next corridor. I decided that I would take the one with a shower and loo. I found out later that it was Tom Jones and Engelbert Humperdinck's dressing room, when the studios were used by ATV for their spectaculars. Breaking the news to Bill, I said that as he had a heavy workload coming up, it might be better if he had privacy, and Bill agreed. The rest of the cast had phones installed in their dressing rooms a few days later.

Letitia and Susan were still using public transport, and I was picking up Gretchen Franklyn every day. Also, if we finished early, I would drive Letitia, Gillian Taylforth and Susan Tully home after rehearsals, and sometimes Wendy too. With the storylines in the show, it was becoming even more difficult for the younger female members to use public transport, as they were easily recognized and were suffering a lot of verbal abuse from blokes who thought that they were like their characters. In conversation with them I realized how stressed they were and so I approached the new production associate, Corinne Hollingsworth, who was the first assistant on the 'Doctor Who' I did. She completely understood Letitia's and Susan's predicament, and made transport available for them.

The time was getting nearer for the birth, and we had moved into a friend's flat in Fulham, above his photographic studio. I eagerly awaited the end of the recording day.

Although I had finished for the day and was about to go home to await the birth of our first child, there was still a lot filming to do, and as I left the studios and waited for the barrier to be lifted the security men on the gate said, 'Have a nice time in Venice.' Puzzled, I replied that I wasn't going away.

I thought no more of it until I got home, but no sooner had I got through the door than the phone rang and it was Cheryl from publicity. She told me about the press conference that had been arranged at Heathrow the following morning, prior to filming in Venice. I told her she must have made a mistake; I wasn't going to Venice. I put the phone down. And then all hell broke loose.

Julia had been informed that I had refused to go, and rather than talk to me had found out where my agent was (he was in fact in Brighton watching a client in a play at the Theatre Royal), driven down there and explained that although they knew I had booked my holiday, someone had messed up and not informed me. The truth of the matter was, as admitted later, that no one wanted to tell me they had boobed, hoping someone else would do their dirty work. So nobody did. At four in the morning, Julia was on her hands and knees in my front room, begging me to go. I had by then explained why I couldn't, that my wife was about to give birth, but after she promised that I would be flown home at the first sign of the baby, I reluctantly agreed.

After hurriedly packing I waited for the car that was taking me to the airport, where I had decided to circumvent the press by going straight through passport control to the lounge. I popped into the toilet on the way, but unfortunately because the airport had a deal with the press to allow photographers behind the passport control, they spotted me and followed me into the loo. As I made my way to the lounge, the photographers knocked down an eighty-year-old woman, and I stopped and picked her up. Funnily (but predictably) enough, the headlines the next day blazed out that I had knocked over a frail OAP.

On arrival we were greeted by what appeared to be the whole of Fleet Street, and we were followed day and night. Julia was again directing, and the storyline was part of that ongoing epic about Angie having only six months to live. Den discovers a previously sealed-in soft side and whisks Angie off to Venice for a second honeymoon.

243

Unbeknown to him – and it could only happen in soap land – Jan, Den's mistress, was also there with an Italian gigolo. We had met the Italian actor who was to play Jan's lover the night before we were to film these scenes, and he was an extremely handsome man. Well, as soon as Anita and Jane How saw him, they were like flies around a honey pot. Buttons became undone, so as to expose a bit more cleavage, and myself, Julia and Tony might as well not have been there. Sadly, all the flirting came to nothing, as he had no interest in them whatsoever. Still, it was fun to watch two fellow professionals making such thorough fools of themselves.

We couldn't escape the press, so I completely blew their minds by joining them at their restaurant for a drink. All knew by now that Jane was expecting, so they all tried to outbid each other to fly me back if and when she went into labour. I was happy enough to have a drink with them, but I told them I was not going to answer any questions. Which, surprisingly enough, they agreed to. Now that was a first . . .

The filming went well, and we finished off on the Orient Express. I rounded off a successful shoot with the bizarre experience of a shoot of an altogether different kind – popping clay pigeons from the back of the cross-channel ferry! My one experience of this sport had been at a wonderful, old country house hotel in Cheshire the previous Christmas, where we were spending the holiday with Jane and her parents. Invited out to have a crack at shooting with some fellow guests, I must admit I was dubious as to the pleasures of shooting pottery discs out of the sky. But it seemed rude not to have a go, and out I went. On closer inspection, my shooting partners – who seemed oddly familiar – turned out to be Roland and Curt from Tears for Fears. 'Everybody Wants to Shoot a Bird', it seems!

On arrival back in London, I was met by Jane and her younger brother Michael. By now Jane was heavily pregnant, and about to give birth, but luckily she had the good sense to wait till I was home. The next day was a normal studio day, and on the way to work I dropped my car in for its service, and had made arrangements to pick it up the next morning, on the way into work. When I arrived home that evening, Jane was cleaning the flat. Straight away I guessed –

don't ask me how, but I knew – she was about to give birth, so I phoned the hospital and booked her in, grabbed a bag and dashed to the hospital. Within an hour, two cameras were handed in, along with a wad of cash: the press had tried to bribe two nurses to take pictures of us. Within three hours, a photographer was also found hiding in a cupboard. Someone at the Portand Hospital was obviously earning a packet, tipping off the press about which celebrities were having babies. Luckily the medical staff were more discreet.

Eventually Jane gave birth and I watched. She was obviously in great pain but had declined any drugs; she never took any sort of drug, not even aspirin. Our son Spike was born. I went home and slept for a few hours and then went to work. After picking up my car on the way, I was crossing the road, waiting on the central reservation, when suddenly a white van smashed into me side on and totally wiped out my car. I was left struggling to get out. On hearing the crash, the guys in the garage ran out and dragged me out of car. The driver of the van was less fortunate: he had broken his neck. They called an ambulance, and then drove me to the studios. Here I was, having just seen the birth of a son, and I had nearly been killed.

When I arrived at the studio, I just did my work and, after finishing rehearsals, went back to the hospital to see Jane. I didn't tell her about the crash. We then had to name our son. I wanted to call him Spike straight away, but after a sort of mild disagreement we agreed on Michael Leslie, which were my names reversed, and he was christened accordingly, although he has only ever answered to the name of Spike. And it suits him. Years later, when looking though a book of babies' names, I found out it means 'the leading one, the bright star'.

Obviously the press were still sniffing around, but I had decided to tell no one. I wanted Jane to get over the birth and settle into a healthy pattern with the new baby. Eventually, she came home, and I hoped we would be allowed to get on with the business of bringing up our son. Suddenly, there was a flurry of activity outside our home, and the doorbell was rung continually. So eventually I went downstairs, flung open the door and was confronted by a gaggle of reporters who all wanted a quote.

'I'll give you a quote. Leave us alone; we're trying to settle a three-day-old baby.'

'We care, Mr Grantham,' they said.

'If you cared that much, you wouldn't ring the fucking doorbell all night. Now fuck off,' I replied in a less than ambassadorial manner.

Funnily enough, the doorbell didn't ring again that night, and the story the next day proclaimed that I was over the moon about the birth of our son. I must have been on such great form that I transmitted my real feelings subliminally, through the medium of 'fuck off and leave us alone!'

Obviously my being at work left my wife very vulnerable, and while I was at the studio she was continually under siege, so much so that Spike had to be given a dummy to calm him.

My relationship with my sister and mother, meanwhile, was becoming more and more strained. My sister couldn't wait to appear in the papers, seduced by the money and the chance to be photographed in glamorous clothes. Over the years she has managed to make a healthy living from the press.

Obviously my relationship (or non-relationship) with my mother and sister caused some grief with my father, but he was totally on my side, and some time later would disown both my mother and sister for continuously selling stories.

Shortly after the birth of Spike, I was approached by Danny Boyle, the head of drama at BBC Northern Ireland. He wanted me for a drama loosely based on the Littlejohn brothers, who had worked for military intelligence, had gone renegade and ended up working for the IRA. Julia said no, but Danny was very ambitious and gatecrashed a party where Michael Grade was and talked to him about it. Michael then told Julia to arrange it. So, after a lot of rearrangements, I flew to Belfast to shoot the Irish parts of the film. I was booked into the Europa Hotel, but as this was the most bombed hotel in Northern Ireland, it was decided to put me up at the Wellington Park. When I arrived there, it looked like something from a war movie. It was surrounded by barbed wire and security gates. The trouble was that, after a day's filming, to get to your room you had to go through the bar area, which was packed with hundreds of young people on a night out, so after running the gauntlet of the patrons you spent half the night trying to ignore knocks on the door. Filming was also a continuous peep show: wherever we filmed, thousands turned up, no matter what time of day it was. I had a permanent RUC escort and had to wear a flak jacket when not filming. After the Belfast filming it was off to Amsterdam to film there.

When I returned to London, it was strange to find the tube closed and a queue going on for ever around the terminal with people waiting for taxis. Although there had been a slight delay in Amsterdam for wind, I was oblivious to the fact that a huge storm had ravaged half of the UK. As we made our way to Fulham, the result of the storm became apparent. I began to wonder if Jane and Spike were safe as I saw trees lying on their sides, cars crushed by falling trees, and so on. What should have taken forty-five minutes on a good day took nearly two hours, but when I arrived back at the house, which we had now moved back into as the building work was finished, I found Jane and Spike were still fast asleep. They had slept through the whole storm.

Although I had been away filming in Belfast and Amsterdam for a fortnight, as soon as I entered the studios it was as if I had only had a day off. It was back to the usual grind. Two days later, I was informed that I would have to shoot some of the Amsterdam scenes again, as the sound equipment had not turned up in Belfast from Holland. This obviously was going to cause Julia a problem, but Danny Boyle was adamant that he could work around my scheduling, and so as soon as I had a break in filming I went off and reshot the stuff. It also became obvious that the equipment had been lost on purpose. Apparently, Danny had upset someone and the sound tapes mysteriously had disappeared.

When I had shared a dressing room with Bill Treacher, he was adamant that he would never do any interviews with the tabloids. 'Good for him,' I thought, and he was true to his word until one Sunday newspaper decided that he deserved an award for his breakdown scenes. Then, a huge spread appeared, showing Bill at home with his wife. As I arrived for rehearsals on the Monday, someone said, 'Have you seen Bill?' and when I said I hadn't, they said, 'He has gone all glam.' Bill, although never scruffy, always wore ordinary clothes to rehearsal or to the studio. I was shown the article. Funny people, actors: they hate being in the papers but love to buy them to gloat, laugh or snigger at what is written about others. There was no doubt about it: Bill's house was extremely smart, and quite rightly he was proud of it, but I did feel he had sold his soul. As we rehearsed, Bill arrived, and he looked like Noël Coward, wearing a bright pink Pringle sweater, a checked shirt and a cravat. He had the air of someone who was up his own arse, and when he came through the door to rehearse his scene, he complained that the furniture was in the wrong place, and did a huge diva number.

As soon as I had finished my rehearsals I shot down to wardrobe to see if they had any cravats. They had a few, but not enough for what I wanted. When they asked what my plan was, I told them. They couldn't promise me anything, but they said they would see what they could do.

After the technical run, one of the wardrobe department came up to me with a box of cravats. I put one on everyone, including Roly and the bust of Queen Victoria that had pride of place on the bar of the Vic. I even gave Julia and Tony and the writers one to wear, telling them to just go along with it. When Bill walked through the Queen Vic's doors, and delivered his line, he stopped dead in his tracks. After taking in the fact that everyone was wearing a cravat, he just fell about laughing. Bill had a great sense of humour, and took it well. He never wore a cravat on set again, or a pink sweater for that matter either.

Julia also had a great sense of humour, although sometimes it took a while to sink in. The papers were always having a go at her, calling her the hatchet woman, saying she was sharpening her knives to slash the cast numbers. I nicknamed her Rosa Klebb, after the wizened old Russian in the Bond film who had knife blades hidden in her toecaps. When we had bets on horses in the show, we even had the winners' or losers' names begin with Rosa. And I was always calling her Rosa, so Julia took this to be a compliment. But after one episode's producer's run, when Den had won a substantial amount on a horse called Rosa's Revenge, she was at the note session with the writers and director, and she said quite innocently, 'Leslie's named that horse after me. How sweet.'

Obviously, the writers and director and Tony Holland all knew the truth, and they took great delight in telling her what the name really meant. At rehearsals the next day, the director started to give us Julia's notes, and when he got to me he said, 'Julia wants you.' So I trotted down to the second floor to see her. She looked at me and said, 'Ah, Mr Bond . . .' in a strange guttural voice. I looked at her, and she said, 'I'll give you Rosa Klebb,' and laughed. And as I left she said, 'Only you could get away with it.' Julia and I got on fine. Once she had approached me about the discipline of the cast in the studio on recording days. Directors, it seemed, were reluctant to tell actors off, and she wondered if I could have a word. I said yes, but I doubted if it would do any good. Eventually, I suggested that she come on set and bollock me, therefore proving a point. This she did, and as I left the studio to go to my dressing room, I bumped into her. She was visibly shaking, and was so upset at shouting at me that she had to apologize. When I pointed out to her that I had suggested it, she smiled and hugged me. God knows what the rest of the cast had made of her screaming at me, but it certainly improved discipline.

About this time, Julia decided that she needed a bit of recognition for her contribution to the show, understandably, as she had created, with Tony Holland, a phenomenal piece of television history. She appeared on chat shows, and had magazine and newspaper articles written about her and Tony. These were positive rather than the usual 'Hatchet Woman of Albert Square', and quite rightly so. She also picked up a BAFTA award for her outstanding contribution to television. Julia was basking in this glory, when it all suddenly went wrong. She and Tony had gone on holiday, and she was snapped topless on her hotel balcony. At this point, she decided that she had had enough of being a celebrity, and went back to being the reclusive hatchet woman that we all knew and loved.

Suddenly my life was turned upside down as well. Out of the blue I received a phone call from my mother.

'How could you ignore your younger brother, in his hour of need?' she screamed.

'What? What are you on about?' I said.

I had seen Philip several times in the last six months or so, and I knew he was buying a flat not far from me.

'Is he in some sort of financial trouble or having trouble moving in?' I asked. 'I'll give him a hand.'

'It's got nothing to do with the flat,' she said, 'he's in hospital with some sort of cancer. For once in your life, be a proper person and visit him.'

Philip was gay, and the more I saw him the camper and more outrageous he seemed to become.

When I arrived at the hospital, and asked where the ward was, I was told to wait and a doctor would come and see me. When I asked him about my brother, I was told he had discharged himself and gone home to his flat. I left, and only as I was travelling home did it cross my mind, that it wasn't cancer at all. When I arrived at the flat and saw Philip, I knew straight away. He had AIDS; he looked frail and pitiful. Chatting with him as he struggled to show me around his new flat, it was obvious he had nothing to eat in the house. I told him I would be back in a while, and driving home, which was five minutes away, I realized that he had no warm coat and it was freezing cold. I rushed into the house, grabbed my credit cards and an overcoat that I had worn only once. I then rushed off to the local supermarket and stocked up with food for him. Arriving back at his flat, I proceeded to cook him some food, told him some cock-and-bull story about the coat, and told him to phone me if ever he needed anything or was sick. He assured me he would, although he had friends who would be popping in. He also said he was sorry. (Sorry for what?) I told him not to be silly, and just to relax.

I continued to keep in touch and it was obvious that he was on a downhill slope. Eventually he was admitted to hospital and, as ever, the press found out and burst into the ward he was on, and snapped away. I received a call from him shortly before he eventually left this world and he asked that I not attend his funeral, as he didn't want it to turn into a media circus. Reluctantly, I agreed. He also said he was sending something over for Spike. What a guy: he was on his last legs and wanted to send something to his nephew. When it turned up it was a beautiful plastic book in the shape of a duck that babies played with in the bath.

My sister, of course, couldn't wait to inform the world of how I had snubbed Philip.

My only regret about Philip dying was the fact that when a journalist arrived at my door to ask if Philip had AIDS, I had denied it, as Philip had requested. I felt that this was wrong, because AIDS isn't something to be ashamed of. In this world we live in, though, it's better to keep quiet, and by giving him a few more moments' peace and quiet, I felt it would make his final days more bearable. Philip's ashes were scattered in Putney Cemetery and sometimes I wander in and walk around, hoping if he is watching, he might feel better. At times I wish it had been me, as Philip was a nicer person than I will ever be. He was one of life's lovely guys and had such a tragic death. Such a loss. My mother would never acknowledge the truth, and always quoted the fact that he died of pneumonia.

Everyone wanted to visit the set of 'EastEnders'. Frank McAvennie, the West Ham forward, came to see me to have his picture taken with me in the Queen Vic. Princess Di arrived and remembered me from Piero de Monzi. We also had our picture taken together. Douglas Fairbanks arrived; he had had an office in the studios during the war and it had since been called Fairbanks House. Terry Wogan, too, broadcast from the set.

After the Princess Diana visit, I was continually requested by her courtiers to pop over and see her. It wasn't just myself who formed the impression we were the Princess's favourite new toy. It certainly felt that way when she'd visited the set, toured the studios and met the cast. After politely rebuffing the Palace on two or three occasions, the calls ceased. She'd found a new toy.

Stories continued to appear in the papers, even the most personal stuff that only our family and friends were privy to. We began to get paranoid about everyone, and both Jane and I became reclusive. But our phones would ring at odd times and even when we picked them up, they would continue to ring. BT came every day to fix them – always the same bloke, always the problem remained. We ended up having to employ an engineer, who found and removed a bug.

Although a car was provided if we needed one after recording, I tended to drive in to work. If it was a nice day, I would walk to the BBC studios at White City and pick up the shuttle to Elstree. One such time, as I boarded the shuttle, a few people gave me a bit of grief, and as they were normally people with whom I had a laugh and a joke, I didn't quite know how to take it. It was the same reaction when I arrived at Elstree, so, completely flummoxed, I thought I had best go to the press office, in case something was in the paper about me. Suddenly Julia appeared and asked if I was all right, and when I said no, and described to her the reaction at Television Centre and on arrival at Elstree, she told me that there had been a death threat directed at me and security had been tightened. A lot of stuff had also been recovered from people's cars that had gone missing from the studios. Well, no one had told me, and I had walked for four miles in broad daylight, possibly at the mercy of this lunatic gunman.

Not long after this, I had to put my car in for a service and, because I had a personal appearance booked was about to order a hire one. On asking the prop buyer if she had a contact, she said, 'Borrow that white one.' This car was on loan from Rover, so she cleared it with the company and at the end of the day I drove it home. I had just locked the car door, when I was thrown in the air and landed spread-eagled on the bonnet, with a gun at my head. Suddenly a monotone voice shouted, 'It's OK, it's him.' The assailants were police, and although dressed in civvies, they had the task of guarding my house. They told me that the BBC had received a phone call; someone was threatening to kill my son. And after being furnished with details of my car, which of course had been put in for a service (Julia wasn't to know), the police had guarded the house. When I confronted Julia about it and asked why I hadn't been told, she said, 'We didn't want to worry you.'

By now the rift in the camp was getting wider and wider. Actors are a strange breed and tend to take notice of what's written about them.

If the critics say they are brilliant they believe they are Olivier. If the critics say they are crap, although upset, they obviously think the critics have no taste. Also, because 'EastEnders' was such a success, the show's cast tended to believe they were wonderful, however peripheral their involvement.

Nick Berry had joined the series some time before. He was a great guy, and we got on well. One day, I arrived at the rehearsal rooms on a Saturday morning to block a scene. When I arrived I saw that no other members of the cast were there, and when I asked why I was told that Wendy had had permission to open a supermarket. Bill only had this one scene, and as he was saying his lines at the bar, there was no need for him to come in. Various other people also had only one or two lines, so it wasn't worth calling them in for this one scene. 'Bloody hell,' I thought, 'I've only come in for a walk behind the bar.' I had no dialogue, no business other than appearing from the hall and crossing behind the bar to leave the pub.

The following day I went to see Geoff McQueen, the creator of 'The Bill', who wanted to meet me and talk about the possibility of going to the BBC with a new series. Obviously the subject of 'EastEnders' came up, and I made the comment that it would good if he could write for the show. He rolled his eyes, but before he could reply the phone rang. While he was away, his wife told me he couldn't write for 'EastEnders', as he had a problem with someone in the cast, who he had worked with on another show.

All soap operas have characters that are fondly remembered. In 'Coronation Street' it was Elsie Tanner, played by the wonderful Pat Phoenix. I never met Pat, although she was with my agent, but I was proud to be asked to take part in a memorial concert for her after she died. I was asked to turn up and say a few words and do a raffle draw. As I was doing this, who should walk on stage from the wings but Don Henderson. Everyone was wearing evening suits and huge frocks, but Don was wearing a denim suit. We did the draw together, and he said, 'I'd love to work with you.' And of course we did. He also became Spike's godfather.

The next day, in the green room waiting for the cast to arrive, it was apparent that a lot of people were late. I felt for the runner who, on her first day, was continuously watching the minutes and hours tick away, and when others, in later scenes, arrived they were taken in and rehearsed their scenes out of order. Eventually, the latecomers arrived. Nedj was first, but when told he was late, he screamed at the runner, 'You're lucky I'm here at all.' Peter then arrived and gave everyone, not his usual excuses (that he was out with Janine, a page-three girl, or had been working on the script with Mike Leigh), but proclaimed that he had been to 'The Bill' office, as they wanted him for a major regular character. I turned to Nick Berry and said, 'Have you got a cigarette, Nick?' As he handed me one he said, 'I thought you didn't smoke.' I had packed up for two years, but I said, 'I do now.'

With my fag in hand, I went down to the second floor, and told Julia I wanted to leave. I don't think it really sank in, but after a while she believed me, and although visibly upset, agreed. A few days later, Anita made the same request. Julia thought it was to get more money from the BBC, since I was leaving. Later, I was approached by Julia and told that, after discussions with the writers, it had been deemed I was the one they least wanted to leave, and would I stay for a few weeks? Michael Grade had left the BBC and had been installed at Channel 4. I rang him, and asked his advice as well as that of Jim O'Brien. They were of the same opinion: it wouldn't do me any harm to stay for a few weeks. Others, including my agent, thought I was making it up. When the deal was made, I was to be there for about six weeks, but in that time I was to do a year's worth of episodes. Bill Lyons was to write 'Den's Story', and scenes were to be dropped into episodes over the next year.

Most of this was to be filmed on the run and in Dartmoor Prison. Julia, and other members of the production team, visited Dartmoor to see if we could film there. Julia was unaware of the prison policy that ex-cons were not allowed back in a prison as visitors. When the prison Governor asked who would be in the cast, Julia said, 'I can't tell you; it's top secret.' The Governor must have guessed the truth, and after telling Julia of the rules regarding ex-cons, said that he would agree for me to film there. And we did film it, but part of the deal was that the prisoners were allowed to come and watch the filming. Eventually we finished, although I did still have a clause in my contract for one more day's filming, to fill in any holes.

As I drove back to London to fly off the next day on holiday, I felt both sadness and relief that I was ending my time in 'EastEnders'. I had made a number of friends, from crew and cast, and also a few enemies who would continue to dog me even when I left. Nevertheless, I wondered what was left in store for me.

20

IN DEMAND

As I drove from Dartmoor to London, all I could think of was flying
out to Italy for a well-earned holiday with Jane, who was heavily
pregnant with our second child. When I had first arrived in
Dartmoor Prison, the scripts were still being written, so every day
was a schedule from hell for Julia. For the actors it was a long day,
and for me it was a long night. I was given the next day's script,
sometimes as late as 10 p.m., to learn for the next day. Julia had cast
a whole new bunch to play various prisoners and prison officers, as
well as two regular characters who made the crossover, John Altman
(Nick Cotton) and my friend Michael O'Hagan, who played a
ducker and diver mate of Den's. (Michael was married to my dear
friend Pamela Salem, who had visited me all those years in prison.) I
had also managed to get Jeremy Young the part of 'Officer Stone', as
a thank-you for all his help in getting me into drama school.

On the first day of filming we managed thirteen minutes of screen
time, but on the last day we managed thirty-seven minutes. Julia has
to take the credit for pulling the show through; I don't believe
anyone else could have managed it. No wonder she decided to step
down as executive producer, though she remained as series producer.
I really did love the woman; she was a friend and a confidante who

taught me all I know about television. And when I attended her funeral in 1997, a part of me seemed to die too.

My car phone suddenly rang – I had had one fitted when Jane was pregnant, so I didn't have to rely on the phones at the studio – it was my agent. He wanted to know when I was flying out, and whether I could go and meet a director at the Lancaster Hotel in London. It seemed that Scottish Television wanted me for a major drama series about a boxing promoter. After a brief chat, the director gave me a script to read on holiday.

On our return from Italy, I found, among my mail, a contract for 'Winners and Losers'. Thank God I had liked the script: my agent had done the deal for a series while I was away. But as I trusted him I didn't care. Don Henderson then phoned, asking to meet up and introduce me to Murray Smith, creator of 'Bulman'. He had a rough idea for a brand-new series he wanted to pitch to Don and me. On first hearing his idea – Don was to play a world-weary priest and I was his wayward younger brother, Danny – it sounded a little far-fetched. But Murray was such a wonderful writer, we had every confidence he could make it work. And boy, could he! Within a week Murray had sold the idea to Zenith, run by Charles Denton and Margaret Matthieson, and within a fortnight they had sold it to the BBC. 'Winners and Losers' would be filmed in Glasgow.

Around this time I was asked if I could find half a day to support the Save the Rose Theatre campaign, which was really starting to gather momentum. The remains of the Rose – a theatre dating back to Shakespeare's day – had been unearthed as builders excavated the foundations for a new office block. Many of the heavyweights of British theatre – Olivier, Gielgud et al. – had been lending their support to the campaign to preserve the theatre as a living museum. The great Shakespearean actors all recorded sonnets or passages from their favourite plays which seemed to carry clever, highly relevant messages about the need to safeguard our culture. When my time came, I couldn't think of anything remotely clever or apt so I said: 'If I start quoting Shakespeare at you the bulldozers'll be in like a shot!'

It must have gone down well because the following week I was invited to appear in Tom Stoppard's *Fifteen Minute Hamlet* alongside

Vanessa Redgrave, Ian Charleson, John Alderton, Timothy Dalton and Janet McTeer. Sitting in the audience were Dustin Hoffman and his wife, cunningly averting the public's attention by wearing white sunglasses! The queue for autographs snaked right around the building site and out into the street.

And it was while doing my bit for the Rose that I met the actor Chris Villiers, who introduced me to the people with whom Jane, the kids and I would spend most of our summer Sundays from that point on. Chris was, and is, a gem of a man and a wonderful human being who I'm proud to count among my very closest friends. After a chance remark about playing cricket down at the old Boots sports and social club in Eltham, Chris invited me down to see his loose assembly of actors, writers, directors and even toy salesmen (often all three rolled into one) in action. The were called the Wandsworth Cowboys and the very mention of their name breathes cold fear down the necks of amateur cricketers.

We pitched up there, and were made to feel as though we'd been a part of the family for ever. I bowled a few overs, stopped the game for prolonged cigarette breaks and generally had the time of my life. Jane loved it, too – a haven of normality and tranquillity, and on our doorstep, too. Over the years I've played along such cricketing cowboys as Hugh Laurie, Sam Mendes, Ed Hall, Sam West, Alex Hanson, Tim Wallers, Richard Trinder, Nick Asbery, Richard Avery, Willo Johnson, Gregor Trutor, Sean Dromgoole, and the Bowmans; and the pleasure of this simple pastime has kept me sane during some genuinely trying times. I'd like to think it's a two-way street, too; I've certainly kept the tobacconists and osteopaths and chemists of Wandsworth in business with my creaking joints, dodgy back, spinner's wrist and sledger's elbow over the years. From the day we first trooped down there the Cowboys became true friends, and twenty years down the line we're still all thick as thieves. Thank you, Cowboys, past and present, wherever you may be.

I was now on a roll, and doing quality television. But I still had to fit in a day to film my death scene in 'EastEnders', where I was shot in front of a bunch of daffodils. What a complete travesty it was. The floor manager misunderstood his instructions and forgot all about the flowers, until it came to shoot the scene. Moreover, the supporting actor, who was slated to play the gunman, became so carried away with his role as the man who shot Dirty Den that, although told to keep quiet, he had sold his story to a national newspaper. Needless to say, he had to be replaced at the last minute.

When the first assistant director, who happened to be the boyfriend of John Nathan Turner, sauntered up to me and said, 'John always knew you were going to be a star,' I was unimpressed. I thought, 'Oh yes, so much of a star that he didn't give me the star guest lead role.' Television producers: always wise after the event; it's a wonder that anything gets made.

My demise was to be filmed in a large water tank in Ealing Studios. Keith Harris, the series designer, had re-created a canal, complete with old bikes, milk crates and supermarket trolleys under the water. The man was a genius, and without him, Albert Square would have been a pile of shit.

I had been to Glasgow once before, when I had filmed 'Knock Back', but my only memories of it were being out with Derek O'Connor. We had watched a drunk stagger out of a door, weave his way in and out of traffic, hit a lamppost and then weave his way back in and out of traffic, and fall back in the doorway he had emerged from. Now, if you had done that in an audition, the director would have said you were over the top.

Glasgow, at the time we were filming 'Winners and Losers', was European City of Culture and a huge amount of building work was under way. When I arrived the Glaswegians went potty. I was not allowed to pay a taxi fare or the bill in a café or restaurant. And at one time we were filming outside the best hotel in Glasgow, when the police advised us to get off the streets, as Celtic and Rangers had just finished a match. Suddenly two coaches full of rival fans appeared. When they saw me, the coaches stopped and the supporters poured out. They were screaming my name, and calling me the big man. So much for trouble.

In playing a boxing promoter, I had a lot of scenes by the ringside and quite a few in the bedroom. The unlucky lady who had to do sex scenes with me was a tall, beautiful actress called Denise

Stephenson. After one particularly steamy scene, her agent took her out for dinner and asked her what the sex scenes were like. Denise, being the honest person she is, replied, 'I don't know; he kept his underpants on.' The headlines the next day were all variations on the same theme: 'Dirty Den Keeps His Pants on in Bed'. Luckily I remembered to take my socks off. The press had presumably been told this fascinating information by Denise's agent. She was also the agent who had pocketed Linda Davidson's money, and had ripped off Caroline Quentin for large amounts of money. Be careful whom you trust, especially in my business. It's a shame I didn't heed my own advice.

With Jane due to give birth, the press started snooping around again. One journalist even turned up at the airport, as I was flying home to see Jane, armed with a huge bunch of flowers and a bottle of champagne. He kept saying 'Congratulations'. I just looked at him blankly and said, 'For what?' Now, that threw him.

'Winners and Losers', apart from a few iffy reviews, was a critical success. But when I read the script for 'The Paradise Club' I just couldn't put it down. It was superb, and I was really excited. Jane wanted to go to Australia for Christmas, and I was due to film right up to the beginning of the middle week of December, so she took the boys out there early.

At the time, I was seeing Dad regularly, but because of my difficult relationship with my mother, I would meet him near his house, or he would come up for the day to see us. He was heavily involved in local politics and took his work very seriously. He was constantly being asked to be mayor, but he felt that with my mother's erratic behaviour, he wouldn't be able to do the job properly. And he had had a pretty rough time with the press. I remember when Philip was dying the press were on his doorstep. One morning, as he opened the door and saw who it was, he tried to slam it shut, but they tried to force their way in. Dad went mad, rushed at them and flung his false hand at them. They wheeled round and ran out of the house. His neighbours later told me it was one of the funniest sights they had seen: this old-age pensioner, dressed in a vest and a pair of trousers, chasing these two big lummoxes to their car. My mother, on the other hand, was sometimes seen climbing out of the kitchen window to join the reporters in their car to dish some dirt.

My sister had now moved down to be near my parents, after her marriage had broken down and she had to leave the police house she lived in. My brother John was also suffering a marital breakdown. Sadly, his wife joined the press bandwagon, and sold stories about John, Dad and me. (Bloody hell, we only needed the milkman to do the same, and then everyone with whom we had ever come into contact would have been accounted for.) Like my father, John tended to put up with a lot just for an easy life, so he bowed to pressure and allowed my sister to move into his flat to look after him. Even though I didn't want to have anything to do with my sister, I could see that it wasn't too bad an arrangement for John, who was working nights at the local Johnson's factory. Whereas my mother wouldn't do a stroke of work in the house, my sister was fanatical about cleaning to an almost obsessive degree. To give Angela her due, she is extremely house proud and a good cook. At least John would be looked after.

By now the press intrusion was becoming ridiculous. I had to shoot 'The Paradise Club' at a huge nightclub in Brixton. As I got into the car, the unit driver said, 'Do you want a paper to read?' I said no, but couldn't help but notice the headline: 'Dirty Den Disowns Niece and Her Black Baby'. My heart sank. What was it this time? Obviously I had to read it. Apparently, my sister Angela's daughter, Claire, was living happily with a black guy and had had a baby. All this was news to me. Dad and I never spoke about Angela, so I rarely knew what she was up to. However, it seemed that someone had decided to sell another story. The story claimed I was a racist and all sorts of other crap. Good timing, Sis. Here I was about to film in Brixton, which is possibly one of the most densely populated black areas in London. With some trepidation I got out of the car, and immediately I was surrounded by hundreds of people, all wanting photos and autographs. No one mentioned the article.

A week later another story appeared in the papers, claiming that I had refused to allow my mother to see my children. This was true, as she had sided with my sister over the stories she sold. I decided to cut my mother out of my life. It was only out of my love for Dad that I allowed the relationship to continue as long as it did. Obviously, I was furious at this new revelation. I rang my mother and told her she only had herself to blame. Fatal mistake! This gave her the excuse for another story. When Dad arrived home later that day, he found my mother deep in conversation with a photographer and a reporter. After throwing them out of the house, Dad confronted my mother, who then proceeded to climb out of a window and finished her conversation with the press in their car. This was the last straw. Their relationship deteriorated even more, and although he still relied on her, he now immersed himself in his council work. As she had not had a job since before she married. Unfortunately, when she arrived at work the day after the article appeared, the owner of the shop opened up the paper, pointed to a picture of my sister, and asked if that was her. When my sister said yes, she was asked to leave the shop.

Filming of 'The Paradise Club' finished, and a second series was commissioned. At the press launch, I left the viewing room as soon as the lights went down and returned when I saw the lights go up. The BBC loved it and judging by the reaction in the room, the press loved it too. Unfortunately, a newspaper the next day slammed it on the basis that there was a scene of extreme violence in which I had blown a man's head off. No such scene existed. After a few heated discussions between Zenith and the editor of the newspaper in question, who was adamant that the reporter stood by her story, he was sent a copy of the episode. When he watched it the reporter swore blind that Zenith had deleted the scene, and only when Zenith threatened legal action did the paper relent.

Around this time I was invited to lunch by Mark Shivas, who asked me what I thought was wrong with 'EastEnders' as it had started to slip in the ratings. I told him that where 'EastEnders' went, other soaps had followed, and had beefed up their shows. I told him that the show had become safe; it needed fresh blood, fresh writers and a cast cull. He told me that the show had tried to replace me but it still wasn't working, and would I consider going back. I said no, as I had other commitments. He also then asked if I would go back as producer, to which I replied that I was flattered, but that the cast might have a problem with that. He told me to think about it; he also mentioned how expensive 'The Paradise Club' had been to make. I said that maybe it could be made by Zenith, but use BBC staff. He laughed and told me it was a great idea, but it would never happen. A year later, the BBC did its first co-production, using outside companies and inside staff. After the second series of 'The Paradise Club' had been successfully transmitted, Jonathan Powell, the new head of drama, cancelled the new series (although scripts had been written) and replaced it by that great show, 'Trainer'.

With the commercial channels up for tender, Carlton was bidding to replace Thames as the London-based provider. Carlton had asked Zenith to help with their bid and, if successful, would reshow the first two series and then do several new series. When Carlton started to negotiate, though, it hit a stumbling block. The BBC, although it had paid to show each series twice, refused to show the repeat of the show, thereby stopping a new series being made. The BBC was also talking about other shows for me, and even had Julia working on one of them. But behind it all was the basic premise that everyone wanted me to go back to 'EastEnders'.

I had suggested, at a meeting with Mark Shivas, that Corinne Hollingsworth, who had been a production associate on 'EastEnders' when I was there, should be made producer. She was. I still declined to go back. Apart from game shows and various appearances on 'Children in Need' or 'Noel's House Party', I never did any drama for the BBC. I did, however, film a spoof version of 'The Paradise Club' in an episode of 'The Detectives' with Jasper Carrot and Robert Powell for Celador.

I was going on holiday again to Australia, but just before flying out I was asked to meet the director of *Rick's Bar* in Paul Elliott's office in the Aldwych. After chatting with Gilmore and being given a script, I said, 'Well, in theory, I'm interested, but I'll have to get back to you as soon as I've read it.' On the way home I phoned my agent, and said that I had felt they wanted me. After being in Australia for a couple of days I received a fax from my agent to say the deal was done. Confused, I phoned him.

'What do you mean done? I've only just started to read the script.'

'Things have changed. It's going earlier, and they said you said you wanted to do it. I didn't want to lose it and so I said yes,' he said.

It was a done deal. I was in *Rick's Bar*, which was the play that *Casablanca* was based on, and apart from a few name changes and the ending it was exactly the same as the film. All the hype that was put out at the time, about the script being written every day and no one knowing what each day's script was about until they had got it, was absolute rubbish.

The show would open in Bromley before being transferred to the West End. Rehearsals were in Pimlico and on the first day we gathered: Edward de Souza, Richard Durden, David Weston, Ken Bones and lots of others. As I looked round the room, I saw that the girl playing Else was Shelley Thompson. Shelley had been at RADA when I was at Webber Douglas, and she had been a house mate of Jane in Chelsea.

When we opened, you couldn't get a ticket for love nor money. The author came over, and although now an old man, he was really chuffed and entertained us all. We then transferred to the Whitehall Theatre, which possibly, on reflection, was the wrong venue, but business was good, and the majority of the reviews were favourable. Jack Tinker, John Peter and a few other heavyweight critics loved it, and even Shirley Cheriton, who had been employed by a tabloid, loved it. At the after-show party, held at some nightclub in Piccadilly, where camels and people in fezes were walking around, Linda La Plante came up and introduced herself. She raved about my performance, but said that at the end of the play, when Else is leaving Rick to catch the plane, 'Darling, she left you like she was going shopping at Sainsbury's.'

In Fulham I was living next to Lance Percival who, after reading Jack Tinker's review, popped a bottle of champagne around with a lovely note saying, 'With that review you can now retire.' I met Jack Tinker some time later in Edinburgh as he was doing the rounds at the festival. He spotted me and flew across the road, papers strewn behind him, and said, 'I have to tell you, your West End debut was the most accomplished I have ever seen.' Over the top, Mr Tinker, but thank you. Albert Finney had been offered the part of Rick first, and what a fantastic choice he would have been, but he had turned it down, saying it was unplayable. Paul Elliott sent him the Jack Tinker review and simply wrote: 'It isn't.'

Jane's family flew in for the first night. My father-in-law was a huge *Casablanca* fan, although he didn't (as far as I recall) spout lines from the film. He loved it, but like me, thought maybe there were a few changes needed in the staging of it, as it was a bit hackneyed in places. I would have used some things from the film: at the beginning of *Casablanca* there is that sequence showing the newsreel of the day, building up the scene-setting with a map of Germany's invasion of North Africa. Other things like that were needed.

The next day, as the curtain went up, all I could see was row upon row of people dressed like Humphrey Bogart, in white dinner jackets. It was unreal. At the curtain call, the Humphrey Bogart lookalikes stood up and chanted, 'Better than Bogie', which, however flattering, was, I think, a huge exaggeration.

I was doing the show for hardly any money at all. Paul Elliott had said it was very expensive with such a large cast, and it couldn't run in the West End unless he cut costs. Like a mug, I believed him.

One day, during the run, we were approached by Paul Elliott, who said that business was bad. Strange – we seemed to be full or nearly full every night. He told us that unless everyone took a pay cut, the show would have to close. Every agreed – well everyone except one – even the stage door and bar staff and theatre crew said they were willing, but eventually the show closed anyway.

My West End failure, although a bitter disappointment to me, didn't really register on the Richter scale, and work of various sorts came in. I did a film for Channel 4 directed by Laurens Postma, who had directed the play through which I had met Matthew Robinson. It was called *Gummed Labels*, a strange piece about a talking minah bird. I was playing a psychoanalyst involved with finding a runaway Asian girl. I had also been offered pantomime in Nottingham, with Little and Large, playing Robin Hood in *Babes in the Wood*.

The first days of rehearsal were like something out of a sitcom. Sid and Eddie were fantastic, but the script was not written for names.

We started the read-through; the Dame, Ken Wilson, who although he was seventy and as deaf as a post, said that he would start the panto off with his usual routine. Sid and Eddie then said they would do their bit here, and on and on it went. I just tore pages out and threw them away, and eventually, at the end of the read-through, all I had to do was swing in on a rope, sing a song with Maid Marion, fire an arrow into a bullseye target, escape from a magician's box, and have a fight with the Sheriff of Nottingham. We did three shows a day and Sid and Eddie complained bitterly that they were never off stage. Which reminded me of the old adage from my army days – never volunteer.

During the build-up to the panto, the director had phoned me to ask if I could sing. I told him no, and thought that was the end of it. A few days later I received a copy of a George Benson song through the post, from 'Freddy the Frog', a cartoon film. A short while later, he rang again and asked if I could dance. I said no, but lo and behold a dance routine arrived. Then finally he phoned to say that I was the only one in the show that wasn't to be funny. I was to play it like Errol Flynn, in fact I *was* Errol Flynn. I told him that I wasn't adding six inches to my cock for anyone. Schofield ignored that remark, and put the phone down.

On the opening night, as we were about to go on stage, the director was standing by the door to the backstage area. As we trooped past him, he said drunkenly at the top of his voice, 'You're all shit!' 'Thanks, but I know that already.' During the show I had to fire an arrow at a target on the other side of the stage and, being in full view of the audience, I *did* have to hit the bullseye. After thirty-odd shows and a success rate of about 75 per cent, one night the arrow hit the bull and went straight through. Luckily no one was standing in the way or crossing the wings, as it embedded itself in a wall off stage.

I vowed I would never do the panto again. However, Sid and Eddie had been asked to reprise *Babes in the Wood* in Wimbledon, and as I was only living around the corner, so to speak, they wanted to do it again. I said I would consider it. I had been asked to do a comedy sketch on the 'Children's Royal Variety Show' in front of

Princess Margaret, and while there met a young guy called Jon Conway, who offered me a panto, playing Hook in *Pan*. Luckily it got me out of doing *Babes in the Wood*. At the end of the Royal Variety performance we were all introduced to Princess Margaret, who just wandered down the line shaking hands and smiling. When she got to me, she said, 'I love your voice.' Well, what I was to make of that?

A few years later we were performing at the Royal Lyceum, Crewe, where Princess Margaret was patron. I was playing Count Dracula. The theatre had just undergone a major refurbishment and the Princess was there for its official reopening. It turned out that she couldn't stay for the main performance, so we put on a little show of excerpts and highlights for her. When we lined up for her to thank us, Princess Margaret smiled and complained that my Dracula hadn't done any neck-biting scenes. With that, she disappeared off with some local councillor.

I had for a few years been doing a wine column for the *Sunday Mirror* magazine and various wine slots on 'This Morning' and other magazine programmes. In the beginning, the articles had been written by Hilary Kingsley, whose husband Peter worked on the *Mirror*. But Jane and I felt that the way the articles were going, although informative about wine, were a little bit too geared to 'EastEnders', and other soap operas. And as I had been out of the show for some years now, I found it a bit strange. If I wanted to be taken seriously, the style would have to change. I mentioned this to Hilary who appeared to take umbrage. Eventually I asked my editor, Katherine Hadleigh, if I could try writing one myself. She agreed. Jane and I began to write all my columns.

With each column I was being flown out to various vineyards around the world. This had started when I had raved about a Romanian wine that would be perfect for Christmas. Within twenty-four hours it had sold out. After a while Katherine left the magazine, but I continued to write my monthly column. The trips became more frequent, usually to European vineyards, although I also had a great trip to Sonoma in California. I did an article on cognac, and stayed with the Hennessy family at their estate. After the column came out, they wrote to me saying it was one of the best columns about cognac they had read. Praise indeed.

Eventually the column stopped, because a new editor, an Australian, wanted me to do an exposé of the corruption in the wine industry rather than the 'best buys' column I was writing. It really wasn't my thing. Lots of people used to come up to me and say, 'We tried that wine you recommended and it was fantastic.' Whenever I am in a supermarket lots of people still ask my advice. I am not a wine expert, but I just wanted to blow away the snobbery of it all.

The column only came about in the first place because when I was in 'EastEnders' the press always wanted a quote on what I was doing for Christmas. I was supplied with a Christmas menu and was asked to say what wines I would choose. Referring to Hugh Johnson's pocket wine book, I selected some. This went out under 'Dirty Den's Christmas Choice'. Several years later, it was repeated, and after being asked to take part in a wine challenge I was offered a column. I only know what I like, and that is the approach I still take.

Once on the 'Food and Drink' show I fell foul of Jilly Goulden by using the words 'balls' about wine. I had selected a Californian wine, and said, 'This wine is just like a woman: long legs, tastes nice, good body, and has balls,' meaning it was very fruity. Oz Clarke agreed. We wrapped and the director, Peter Bazalgette, thanked me. As I was changing to go home, I was told there was a problem and my bit would need to be shot again. It emerged that I had upset Jilly by using the word 'balls'. No one else could see the problem, but this time I said, 'This wine is just like a woman should be: long legs, great body, smells delicious, tastes wonderful and doesn't talk back.' As for Jilly complaining about the word 'balls' being used so innocuously, I thought it was a bit rich. Hadn't she started her career writing articles for *Nineteen* and *Jackie*? It seemed rather odd to me. Alas, when the programme went out, my comments about the wine, which used standard expressions, upset some people and a whole programme on Channel 4 called 'Bite Back' was dedicated to this male chauvinistic pig, me.

Being on mainstream television opens up a lot of opportunities. Doors that remained stoically closed in your face miraculously open.

Invitations to openings of swanky new restaurants and galleries proliferate, while you get asked to premières of films and celebrity screenings of new TV blockbusters. Much of it is work, and behind the smiles for the cameras everybody is getting something out of it. But every now and then, celebrity brings with it some genuinely enriching experiences. One of the most pleasurable activities for me has been the opportunity to play in so many charity cricket matches with so many splendid people. There have been numerous wonderful times with the Cowboys, as well as several memorable fundraisers for Jonners.

The Bunburys was sprinkled with England internationals like Robin Smith, Jack Russell, Allan Lamb and the irrepressible Phil Tufnell, and we took on county teams like Worcester and Surrey at postcard-perfect settings such as Blenheim. One time we played an XI selected by the then Prime Minister's wife, Norma Major. The match was played in rural Cambridgeshire, and was unforgettable, not merely for the cricket! I parked up under a tree to keep the sun off the car and, as I got out, was approached by three burly bodyguards, hands twitching underneath their blazers. Crikey, I thought – it's usually just a ticket for careless parking and here am I about to get wasted by the Prime Minister's bodyguards. As they got closer, the nearest delved inside his jacket and pulled out . . . an autograph book. I took a couple of wickets and was caught by Allan Lamb. But the most bizarre incident of the day was yet to come. Promenading around the boundary rope as is my wont, having a quiet cigarette, I was approached from behind by the PM himself who, on catching me, proceeded to pat me on the bottom and depart without so much as a 'Hello, handsome'! I was most distressed by this – could I really resemble Norma from behind? Or perhaps, with my dusky mane, he'd taken me for Edwina Currie . . .

While I'm always glad to try and help with requests for charity fundraisers – since having Danny we've tended to concentrate our efforts on raising money for the Down's Educational Trust in Portsmouth. Jane has devoted every living day to trying make life easier for other parents of Down's children since the birth of our wonderful boy. Through my profile as an actor and her own, she has lobbied hard for Down's storylines and cast in popular television drama, so it's brilliant news that 'EastEnders' is bringing this challenging subject to life via Billy and Honey's newborn baby Janet. The phenomenon of 'EastEnders' alone will bring about more helpful understanding of this everyday condition than decades spent campaigning and leafleting. Good on the producers and storyliners – now let's see how far they decide to take the story. Kids like Danny – and baby Janet – can and do integrate perfectly well into society. It seems a sad fact, though, that money is not made available to support education, training and inclusion. Down's syndrome is still something of a taboo subject, and as long as that persists, its support system will always be under-funded. But as long as there are people like my brilliant wife out there changing people's perceptions, kids like Danny will have the opportunity of competing on a level playing field.

Another satisfying outlet was always pantomime. Some actors view it as unworthy of them, but I shall always love and revere the wonderful world of pantomime. One panto was to be staged in Reading. The cast was Michaela Strachan as Pan, Una Stubbs as Mrs Darling and the Mermaid, Bernie Clifton as Smee, and as it said on the poster a wonderful supporting cast. Business was tremendous and I was booked for Richmond the following year, although Bernie Clifton sadly was not to be with us, which was a real shame, as he was a joy. He would do the most outrageous things. When we were in the Theatre Bar, he would quietly fill up people's pockets with the salt and pepper pots, their handbags with the cutlery, and when his agent came to see the show and left his coat and briefcase in Bernie's dressing room for safe keeping the coat would appear on stage being worn by the crocodile carrying his briefcase. At the time Bernie's wife wasn't well and I think he wanted to be near her the next year. Michaela was superb as Pan, and although only really known for her animal show presenting is a great actress. Una Stubbs has to be one of the most wonderfully lovely people on the planet, again a superb actress and a brilliant comedienne. She was a joy to work with and the show was totally different to the one in Nottingham the previous year. Jon Conway and Nick Thomas were also fantastic and I have had a great relationship with them for many years since. I have also been teamed with that brilliant, funny man Joe Pasquale for more years than I care to remember. I was also doing lots of book readings on tape so work was pretty much ongoing.

I was trying to get projects off the ground, one about an oilrig for Channel 4, which Peter Ansorge had liked; he had commissioned a young writer to come up with some drafts, and I, being the originator, got some money. We wanted Michael Elphick to play the baddie, but he declined because he felt that his public only saw him as a good guy. And eventually, because it would have been expensive, it never got made. I had become involved with Channel 4 because Zenith had got the rights to the Duffy books, which were about a bisexual private eye. Channel 4 was very interested, but sadly the literary agent and the author felt that they shouldn't be a television series but a film. Michael Grade had suggested they were like 'Minder' with thrills, but if we got the rights to the character, it was a worthwhile prospect. He had sent me to see his head of drama, Peter Ansorge, but sadly nothing happened. Carlton, with Zenith, had by now decided that as 'The Paradise Club' was not going to happen they had commissioned Terry Johnson to write a series for me. It was to be called '99–1', which meant 99 per cent boredom and 1 per cent danger in police terms, although with my character, Mick Raynor, it would be the other way round: 99 per cent danger and 1 per cent boredom.

21

THE FUTURE'S BRIGHT

Filming '99–1' was a hoot. The series had a wonderful cast: Robert Stephens, Danny Webb, Adie Allen, Gwyneth Strong and Niall Buggy. Filming, however, was completely manic, but fortunately we had a brilliant young director called Charles MacDougall who would go on to direct 'Desperate Housewives'.

Mind you, it was a wonder I survived the first day's filming at King's Cross Station. I had to drive my character's car down the concourse and on to the station platform and park inches away from a train, which contained the man who had brutally slain my partner. After the usual sound and make-up checks and background action, I set off. As I raced down the ramp and swung the car in the direction of the train, I applied the brakes and lo and behold they didn't work. The distance between the car and the train was shortening, and the car was not slowing down. I suddenly grabbed the handbrake and the car ground to a halt inches from the train, although facing the wrong direction. I could see the panic in the producer's eyes as I got out of the car. He asked the car suppliers why the brakes hadn't worked, and they said they were going to check them the next day. I turned to them and asked if, by any chance, their boss was in a wheelchair, had one leg, was blind in one eye and had half of his fingers missing.

We then carried on with the scene. Luckily the camera operator had had the presence of mind to keep the camera rolling as the car with no brakes roared towards the train.

The first series was a huge hit. When I went to have a meeting with Michael Wearing, head of drama at BBC2, after the first episode went out, the first thing he said was, 'Well, you've seen off "Between the Lines",' which was the channel's flagship show. Robert Stephens, however, was not a well man. I was told that he had had a bad blood transfusion in Italy, having been given the wrong blood, so he was constantly tired. He was also playing King Lear in Stratford while he was filming. We were in the Playhouse Theatre, filming a meeting between his character and mine, and he was struggling to say his lines, not because he couldn't remember them, but because he was extremely ill. Eventually we did the scene, and he apologized about his stumbling over the lines. He also said how good he thought I was. To which I replied, 'You should see my King Lear, Robert.' Sadly, because of his health we couldn't use him in the second series, but Frances Tomelty made a superb replacement.

We also had Terry Johnson direct, another consummate professional. Actually, we were blessed with great directors on that series, one in particular who loved his toys: cranes, water machines, and extraordinary stunts. When the series finished he heard that my agent, Michael Whitehall, was filming a series called 'Noah's Ark', and would I recommend him. I did, and he got the job, after a lot of groundwork on my part. Never trust anyone in this business, though. In spite of everything I'd done for him, he didn't give me a part in the series, and the chap he went with was so bad that they had to overdub him – cheaper than reshooting all his scenes. The viewing figures for '99–1' were good, but sadly Carlton didn't re-commission it.

I was now working on more ideas for television series, and had come up with an idea called 'Who are You?' about an alien invasion of Earth. I had taken my idea to Charles Denton, who was head of drama at the BBC, and he had given both myself and Archie Tait of Zenith a fifteen-minute meeting. After the usual formalities, I punted it to him and he commissioned a script with a view to it becoming a ten-part series. A script was written, but by now Charles had moved on, to be replaced by Nick Elliott, former head of drama at LWT. Because Charles was seeing out his remaining time, we were sent to see Chris Parr, head of BBC1 drama. As I chatted to Chris, there was something about him I couldn't quite put my finger on, and it wasn't until I was travelling on the tube home that it came to me: he was like the white rabbit in *Alice in Wonderland*. He would keep disappearing, although he was still in the room.

After a few weeks, Chris made an appointment to see me again, and told me he wasn't going ahead with the series. I made an appointment to see Nick Elliott. The day before our meeting, his secretary phoned and asked, was my meeting with Nick pleasure or business. I told her it was about a series idea, and she then advised me, since Nick had just resigned from the BBC, that maybe it would be better if I waited a few days until he was in place in his new job – as the head of ITV Drama! So Archie Tait and I punted the show to him as an ITV series. I had decided that I didn't want to be the lead as well as creator and co-producer, so I opted for a smaller role. We got the green light and casting began. Eventually we settled on Douglas Hodge and Leah Williams as our leads.

By now, Jane was pregnant with our third child, Danny. She said from the start that this pregnancy felt different from the others and, though she didn't say so at the time, she had a powerful instinct that the baby had Down's syndrome. The scan proved her instincts were, as always, spot on. You could clearly see his dear little face with his slanting eyes and chubby neck. Perhaps Jane wanted to make sure I was fully aware what we were looking at, and she spelt it out to me.

'We're going to have a little boy with Down's syndrome.'

It took me a while to reply, but I smiled at her and said, 'That's all right. He'll be our child and we'll love the baby we're given.'

Although it was a few weeks before the baby was due, Jane's waters broke early one morning, and after arranging for a neighbour to have Spike and Jake and to get them to school, I took Jane to the Portland Hospital. Shortly after arriving, Danny was born, and even though I was prepared for him, I was still hugely emotional as the little man was placed in my arms. After seeing Jane was all right, I went home, promising to pop back later. When I got home, I just broke down and cried. I couldn't drive this image out of my mind – Down's syndrome kids when I was young, dressed in heavy woollen suits and jumpers and ties, with nuns looking after them, on the hottest day of the year. It seemed unbearably cruel and I made up my mind that only the very best would suffice for my Danny.

I picked the boys up from school, and took them to see their mum and new brother. On the way, I told them all about Danny's condition, but that this wouldn't stop him being a brilliant brother to them, nor for them to be brilliant brothers to Danny. In your heart of hearts though, you'd settle for them to merely accept him. I may well be biased here, but my sons are the tightest, most supportive and loving unit you could imagine. It's common for people today to say that so-and-so was 'there' for them when something traumatic happened. These lads are there for each other constantly, every single day. They have an inner strength, a value system and an unbreakable loyalty to one another that makes me humble. Whatever crap gets flung at me, I have the consolation that each of my sons is a hero to me.

The first night home, we had to put Danny's feet in cold water to get him to feed, and those first few days took it out of Jane. But even at that stage, he had such a strong personality. All these years later, we wouldn't swap him for anything. A few friends and family obviously knew, but it is surprising how you find out who your real friends are when you have a child with a disability. It is amazing how people we thought were friends would cross the road to avoid us, and some we didn't even know, other than by a passing nod, would become firm friends because of Danny.

'Who are You?' was now in production, retitled 'The Uninvited'. I was driving home from a shoot one day, when I got a phone call from Jane, saying the press were at the door and had screamed through the letterbox, 'Tell us about your Mongol child.' I was only a few streets away, so I raced to the house, and as I pulled up a tall man approached me.

'I am sorry to hear about your disabled child,' he said.

(Funny how they are always politically correct to a man, but completely nasty and evil to a woman on her own.)

'Don't you mean my Mongol?' I said.

'Look . . . look . . . I'm . . . really very sorry. Do . . . do you have any comment you'd like to make?' he said, and went very red.

'Why do you keep saying you're sorry?'

'I'm sorry . . . I mean . . .'

'Look. Here's my comment . . . It could be worse.'

'Worse . . . How worse?'

'He could be French,' I replied.

We filmed 'The Uninvited' in Norfolk and apart from a few scares it went well. I say a few scares; one was major. Douglas Hodge, who could aqua dive, was filming in a tank in London, and according to the production team, we had a top underwater cameraman. By two o'clock, after nearly six hours, he had not shot a single foot of film. In fact he had not even entered the water. Of course, it transpired he was not an underwater cameraman at all; in fact he was not even a cameraman. Later on, an actor was to throw a huge paddy, because he had been promised he could leave after his last shot, which would have been – if all had gone well – at ten that night, since we were doing a night shoot. But by eleven we hadn't quite finished, and he was getting really angry. I had left to get back to London, when I had a phone call saying that he was demanding a car. When I said, 'OK, but didn't he drive himself to the location?' I was told he was too tired to drive, and that he wanted his car driven to his house as well. I, of course, said no. His car could be left at the hotel and a car could take him home and bring him back, end of story. Well, he got his own way, and when I heard about it I was furious, and told him in no uncertain terms that he was taking the piss. The only reason he was in the thing anyway was because I didn't want to do the lead, as well as everything else.

After 'The Uninvited', I created another series with Zenith called 'Bomber', and left it with Archie to come up with a list of names of writers. While I waited for this, I had to work, so I did a few little films and a series called 'Fort Boyard'. My agent, Michael, was adamant when approached about the series that I wouldn't do it, but I then got a call from Joe Pasquale, who had said that his mate was directing and producing it and would I meet with him. I did, and also saw the executive and head of entertainment at Thames, Richard Holloway, who had been the floor manager on the sitcom I had done for Central, 'Goodnight and God Bless'. They showed me a tape of the show, which was a huge hit all over Europe. It had a certain familiarity about it; it was like 'Crystal Maze'. The presenters of the show were very nice, kindly people to the contestants, and I said I didn't think that was me, and they agreed, saying that they wanted me to be horrible to the contestants. I signed up and we did the show. The French hated the fact that we changed the format, although I am told at the next television festival it was the English version they showed and several new countries lined up to take part in it.

The fort in question was a real Napoleonic one in the Bay of Biscay, about ten kilometres out from La Rochelle. To get there we had to be transported by boat, and then winched up in a witch's basket into the fort. If the weather was bad – and this happened only twice – we were flown in and taken off by helicopter. We worked three days on and three days off. The series lasted for several years, and by the end we had won even the French over. At each end of series, the crew would throw the new boy on the crew overboard, usually the director or a young trainee, and as we finished what was to be the last series, I was the one to go in the sea as we headed for the boat's docking place. The crew told me I was the first foreigner to be awarded the honour.

My father had been busy doing the local elections and helping his friend become Mayor, and after the latest mayoral race I had gone down to take him and his mate out to lunch. His friend had won, so it was a nice celebratory lunch in one of Dad's favourite watering holes. After lunch I drove Dad back to his house. My mother was in a nursing home by now, so Dad had the place to himself. I told him I thought he looked a little tired and suggested he have a nap. I then left him and drove home.

The next day I received a call from the girl who used to come in and tidy up for him, and do a bit of ironing. She had arrived at the usual time and found him nearly starkers, pouring boiling water on his cornflakes. He had also emptied a bag of sugar on the floor. I told her I would leave straight away. I then rang his friends, who all had keys, and told them what the girl had said. When I arrived at the house, it was probably the hottest day of the year, and the front door was open and his friends were sitting there, but there was no sign of Dad; they hadn't seen him. I drove around looking for him; I even phoned the nursing home my mother was in to see if he had paid her a visit. After driving around, I gave up, and went to the house to wait for him. Eventually, he turned up. He was dressed to the nines; he had on his best suit, hat, scarf and overcoat. He looked surprised to see us.

'Where have you been?' I asked.

'Out,' he said.

'Out where?'

'In the garden.'

'I looked in the garden and didn't see you.'

'I was in the loo.'

'The loo in the garden?'

'Yes. The loo in the garden.'

'But we haven't had an outside loo since 1947.'

His friends left, promising to keep an eye on him. I helped him get out of his heavy, hot clothes and decided I would stay with him, thinking it was probably a combination of the heat and tiredness due to the hard work he had put into the mayoral elections. I phoned Jane and told her what I proposed to do, and sat and chatted to Dad. He had a visitor, a sister at the nursing home that housed my mother. She had seen my Dad at the Mayor's election and thought he looked tired, so she was popping in to see him. I treated us all to fish and chips and after she left I put him to bed.

My father was a stickler for timekeeping and never got up later than 6.30 every morning. So I was up bright and early, ready for him to come down the stairs so I could make his breakfast. At eight, he still hadn't appeared, so I popped upstairs and looked in on him. He was fast asleep, so it *had* been tiredness, I thought. Eventually at about 8.30, I heard a crash, I raced upstairs and saw him lying on the floor, trying to put his trousers on. I asked him if he was OK and he replied he was, so I told him breakfast would be ready as soon as he came downstairs. After a while, I heard a *schhhhh, schhhhhhhh, schhhhh* sound like someone dragging something across the floor. I raced upstairs. Dad was in a bad way. I put him back to bed and sent for the doctor. He tried to eat, but said he wasn't hungry. I phoned his friends and told them what had happened.

When the doctor arrived, he said Dad had had a stroke, and needed rest. Jane suggested that he come to stay with us, but in discussion with his friends they thought that wouldn't be a good idea, as he had no friends in London; all his friends were down where he lived. I phoned around to try and get some nursing for him, and eventually it was decided to put him in a nursing home. I made enquiries and the majority of the homes in the area were full, although there was a space in the same home as my mother. He didn't want to go there, so I phoned social services who, when I said his name, rushed around and came up with a little one, not far away. But they did warn me that, if I was looking for somewhere in pristine condition, I would be disappointed The place was in need of a lick of paint, but the care, by all accounts, was superb.

After speaking to the owners, I decided that Dad should move in. The ambulance came for him, and I had bought him new pyjamas and a dressing gown, and filled up a bag with toiletries and a few things he needed until it was time for him to be up and about. To see this man sitting looking so frail and pathetic in the back of the ambulance was desperately sad, because up until a few days before, he had been running around like a sixteen-year-old.

I went to see him every day at first. He had given me power of attorney and called a solicitor in to execute his will, adding a proviso that if he should die – although at this point in time it didn't seem a probability – he didn't want my sister or my mother at his funeral. I popped into the house and realized that his clothes weren't suitable, so I bought him some new ones from Marks & Spencer so that he would look good when I took him for walks. Sadly, that wasn't to be. He began to regress, and after a while it was obvious he was not with it, and although he recognized his friends and family, he became very tired and would soon fall asleep. He was now being spoonfed.

It was tragic to see this, and I prayed that he wouldn't be this way for too long.

We had booked a holiday in Australia, but the day before we were due to go, the home phoned to say they felt he was on his way out, so we cancelled it. One morning I received a phone call, and I was a bit sleepy, but I made out the words 'nursing home . . . who's going to pay for the funeral . . . ?'

'Why?' I said. 'Has my Dad died?'

'No,' said the voice on the other end, 'it's your mother.'

'I guess I had, then,' I replied.

Apparently the home had rung my sister and she had told them to ring me, which I guess was understandable, as I had put stuff through her door saying that Dad was too ill to carry on dealing with my mother's pension and that she had best deal with it. She had returned the envelope to me at the nursing home my father was in, saying, 'No.' She couldn't be bothered.

My Dad's will had left her a large sum, in case she sold a story saying I had pocketed it all. I phoned her sister in America and her brother's family and told them. I then went down to the nursing home and on the way arranged for the funeral, at the same time sorting one out for my Dad, just in case. After donating my mother's television to the nursing home, I drove to the home Dad was in, and told him the news. He just lay there, not moving. I said, 'Don't expect too many Christmas cards this year, your wife's dead.' Not very subtle, I know.

Two days later I was booked to do a night shoot and, as luck would have it, instead of finishing at four in the morning we wrapped at nine. As I arrived home, I saw Jane put the phone down; the nursing home had phoned to say Dad was on his way out. We drove down and, sure enough, he was going fast, but he was fighting it. I looked in his eyes and suddenly saw the faces of people I knew like my brothers and my aunts and uncles and his mother, also a lot of faces I didn't know. I stared at them and I realized that they were his friends and family. I told him to get in the boat, as the ferryman was waiting to take him to see his mates and family. I spouted name after name, and suddenly a tear appeared at the corner of his eye and rolled down his cheek; he grabbed my hand and squeezed and then seemed to fade away. As I bent to kiss his head and say goodbye, he sat up; I then smelt burning and he was gone. With a last wave we left.

As we were leaving, the undertaker arrived and said, 'Grantham? I have a woman of that name in the funeral parlour.'

'Yes. That's Dad's wife,' I replied.

'Shall I put them next to each other?'

'No, just in case she kicks him during the night.'

I drove in silence all the way home, and when we arrived at the house I went into the back garden and lit a cigarette. I looked up at the sky and saw what appeared to be a bright light travelling; suddenly it stopped, got bigger and then disappeared, and I knew he had reached his destination. I finished my cigarette and went back in the house. Dad was gone . . . my only real friend had gone away.

22

A BLACK DAY

Having just phoned my aunt in the States to tell her about her sister (my mother) dying, I dreaded to have to tell her about my father. She was preparing a Thanksgiving dinner, and she was more upset about my father's death than about her own sister. She said she would try and fly over for the funeral. My mother's brother's family was the same: they seemed more upset about Dad's death than my mother's. I told them that there was no need to come to either funeral, as they were being held on separate days. They reluctantly agreed.

The day of my father's funeral arrived. It was truly memorable: a lone piper played 'Danny Boy', and his old mate from the regiment wore his uniform and led the funeral procession, followed by other members of the regiment. My aunt from the States had arrived. She had been at her sister's funeral, where only a few people had turned up, and then stayed the night locally and came to Dad's funeral.

After the service, the funeral cortège drove through the army section of Aldershot, where the flags were flown at half-mast, and then past Boots the chemist, where the staff stood outside and again the flag was at half-mast, past the council offices, where it was declared a half-day and the flags again were at half-mast. Finally on to the crematorium, where they played 'My Way', corny I know, but as Dad had been born in the same year and on the same day as Frank Sinatra, it was only fitting; he was a great fan of Sinatra's, and the highlight of his life was when he had seen him at the Albert Hall. Dad had lived six months longer than Sinatra, hadn't made as many records, but I am sure the people who came in contact with him loved him as much as Sinatra's fans loved Sinatra.

The service was just coming to an end, and as the coffin started the last phase of its journey, my sister arrived, threw a rose on the coffin, handed the vicar a bottle of whisky and left. Talk about timing! Everyone was appalled, but I am sure Dad would have laughed out loud and said, 'Silly cow!' The fact was that Dad, in his will, had stated that my mother and sister were not to attend his funeral. Obviously my sister disregarded his wishes.

After the ceremony at the crematorium, we had a do at the British Legion. We all left and went our separate ways, knowing that he had been seen off in style. Here was a man that had given so much, and was loved, greatly. He never moaned, he just got on with life, and I am sure in death he has reorganized it up there so it works as slickly as a Boots warehouse.

I don't think I have ever come to terms with my father's death; how could someone so kind and generous not be here?

Life carries on, though, and I have had to put my grief to one side, get on and support myself and my family. I have always felt that a certain something was missing; I know everyone who knew him felt the same.

Work continued to come in. 'Fort Boyard' was a success for Channel 5 and panto was a yearly event. I had been offered a film with Michael Caine and enjoyed the experience immensely – we got on like a house on fire. The film was called *Shadow Run*, and it was by the same man who had written the first television play I had been in, 'Jake's End'.

I was offered a tour in a play called *Theft*, with Roy Hudd. Roy has a reputation for being great fun. But when we were in Bournemouth, doing six weeks on the pier, he spotted that the front two rows were full of either Japanese or Chinese and so decided to do a whole kung fu routine, which only he found funny and which completely confused the rest of the audience and cast, as it had nothing to do with the play.

I had become very friendly with an actor called Peter Alexander. I had a room at the Royal Bath Hotel, who sponsored the summer season at the pier and gave a room over to the 'name' in the play. One Saturday, between shows, Peter and I decided we would have a cream tea at another hotel further up the hill, and while there we were joined by a woman who made a great thing about 'Oh sorry, I thought I knew you.' After a few minutes' polite chat, during which she enquired if we were staying at the hotel, we left, although we did pay for her baked potato. That was the end of our conversation with the woman, or so I thought.

We returned to the pier and after a spot of sunbathing, we did the evening show. Afterwards I drove to London. The show in Bournemouth was to last six weeks, and when I returned to the hotel after my weekend in London, my room phone was full of messages. When I played them, they were hang-ups. We did the show on the Monday night and after a meal I returned to my hotel, and was just dropping off when the phone rang. It was the woman from the cream tea afternoon; she had phoned to say how nice it had been to meet actors who seemed like nice people, and to thank us for paying for her food. I didn't even know her name. Another satisfied customer, I thought. As I settled down to fall asleep, I assumed this would be the last time I would hear from her and that there was no way that she would see the play. How wrong I was and what a nightmare was about to begin.

23

BOMBED OUT

Merrily proceeding through life doing various guest appearances in shows such as 'The Bill', 'Wycliffe' and 'Heartbeat', I was also still trying to get series ideas off the ground, and one day I received a phone call from my agent telling me that he had had a very strange call from Archie Tait at Zenith, asking if one of their actresses was available to do a series called 'Bomber'. This, of course, was originally my idea. I called Archie – I hadn't heard from him for a while – and asked what was going on. Apparently the series had been given the green light, and was going into production. I asked why I hadn't been told, why hadn't anyone been in touch, why hadn't I seen any scripts, met the writer and so on and so on. Archie made some excuses – the usual stuff. They had employed some writer who didn't like writing for a named actor. My reply to this was that he wouldn't have had the gig at all if it hadn't been for me . . . also, he had made it all posh, as 'that's how it was' in the bomb disposal squad. Well, I am sorry, but I'm sure no policeman walks around San Francisco saying, 'Hey punk, make my day,' but they turned that into several successful films. I was told that there might be a part in it for me if the director thought it was OK. Unfortunately, the director didn't.

I think maybe I must have missed something here. I came up with an idea for a television series, Zenith was paid to develop the scripts, and a writer was paid to write it. In addition, Zenith stood to make a huge percentage of the budget to keep paying the wages of people who sat in their offices. I hand it to them on a plate and get nothing. I thought, 'I'm getting fucked here,' so I spoke to my agent, who in turn tore a strip off Zenith, and refused to let them make it unless they paid me. So a deal was done, and the series made, with me getting a credit for my 'original idea'.

Obviously, I didn't learn my lesson, as I had been dealing with the BBC about several ideas, one called 'Dead Files' about a police team investigating old unsolved crimes, and one called 'Spent Force' about a team of ex-policemen invalided out of the force who became vigilantes. Both these ideas were with the same man, and we had lots of meetings. Eventually, I got a letter eighteen months later, saying that neither idea had been green lit, but that if I saw something on the screen in the near future similar to or the same as my ideas, they hadn't stolen them.

One night, late, sitting in the garden enjoying a glass of wine, as the weather was really hot and humid, the phone rang, and thinking it must be for one of my boys, I ignored it. On calling back, though, the phone was answered by Jon Conway, one of the owners of the company I did panto for. Gareth Hunt had collapsed on the press night of a play on Bournemouth pier and Jon wanted to know how quickly I could learn the part of Sidney in Ayckbourne's *Absurd Person Singular*. I asked him when he wanted me on, and he said right away. I had a copy of the play in the loft and sat up learning the part all night. I travelled down to Bournemouth the next morning, sleeping on the train. On arrival I was booked into the same hotel as before, and after a quick bite to eat I arrived at the theatre and waited to rehearse. Sadly, one of the actresses decided she would turn up late, and was more worried about whether her photo, which was life-size, would be taken down and replaced with mine. I just said, 'Stick mine over Gareth's; that'll be OK.' She didn't speak to me for the next few days, so I decided I would put the fear of Christ up her. She had moaned non-stop about the understudy, so on the Friday night I said at the top of my voice to the understudy, 'You're on tomorrow, I have had enough.' Well, suddenly, both of them were all over me like a hot rash. I felt like saying, 'Go take a running jump.' Anyway the word had got back to the producers and the director, who all knew that because I had taken over it was a sell-out season, and they were lucky the play was still running.

Actors are a funny lot, especially when they are up their own arses. How different it was when I was asked to take over from Adam Faith. Adam had died while on tour with a play called *Love and Marriage*, and I had been asked to take his part. I had learned the lines and travelled to Brighton for a few days to rehearse in the day, while the understudy was doing the part at night. Lizzy Izzen and Stephen Boxer were very good. We opened in Guildford, and on the opening night, I had to show a golf club that had been twisted by my wife in the play. As I swung this club, the head flew off and hit a woman in the front row in the mouth. I stopped the play and asked if she was all right, she said she was, and just kept saying, 'What a day I've had.' After checking she was OK, we started the play again. We sent her flowers and champagne; the poor woman had been on chemotherapy, and her treat on the day she was released from hospital was to come and see me in the play.

I had also been doing a film, *Charlie*, in South Africa, about the Richardsons, a south London gangster family who were contemporaries of the Krays. Various other bits and bobs also came up, while I was doing *Love and Marriage*: I was asked if I would like to meet the executive producer of 'EastEnders', a meeting was set up and we had a good lengthy discussion about whether I would be willing to return to the show, to tie in with its twentieth anniversary. After getting some assurances about the storylines, I agreed to think about it. The executive producer, although slightly nervous – maybe because she didn't want to be seen with me because it might get leaked to the press – was a lovely lady, who obviously cared about the show. Her name was Louise Berridge. After a few days of thinking about it and working out my availability (I was in pantomime), we decided to agree to do it. After a lot of negotiations, a deal was struck and we had a meeting in a Chinese restaurant in north London near the studios. As I arrived with my agent, we were informed by Louise that the press had found out about the meeting, and a compromise had been struck to give a photo to a paper of us meeting. Obviously, the press office had leaked it. Maybe alarm bells should have been ringing then, but it was too late: the deal was done. I was told the storyliner would be in touch to discuss storylines with me, but apart from a phone call from his holiday home in Spain to say hi, I never spoke to or saw the man again, unless it was across a crowded room, where he was holding forth surrounded by sycophantic actors.

As the news was now leaked to the press that I was returning, I had to run the gauntlet of many press interviews. A meeting was set up to have lunch with the producer of the first episodes to be shot on my return, with Letitia Dean who played my daughter Sharon, and with Nigel Harman, who was playing the son I had never known. This was at a restaurant near the studios. I arrived, and the first person I saw was John Bardon, now a major character in the series. I had worked with him when he had done an episode of 'The Paradise Club', so I went over to say hi. He kept on about how bad the food was in the canteen in the studios; that was why he was eating in the restaurant. Nice to see you, too, John.

The producer, named Colin Wrattan, was a very nice bloke, and Letitia hadn't changed one bit since I had last seen her many years before. Nigel was, and still is a great guy. We seemed to get on like a house on fire, and this was to be continued when we eventually ended up on set together. I was subsequently to meet the director at my agent's house a few weeks later, and like Louise, Colin, Letitia and Nigel, was really up for the first time I was to reappear. It would be like old times, working with Letitia again . . . sadly no Roly, as he had gone to that great big kennel in the sky.

Obviously the scripts were a secret, but I would be furnished with them as soon as they were written. A lady named Sara Phelps would be handling that department. When they arrived, they were good, in fact they were bloody good. I looked forward to my first day back in Albert Square.

24

'HELLO, PRINCESS'

I arrived early at the studios, and had a costume meeting. Louise had decided I was to be in monochrome, black and white, which was fine by me. Although I think I would have preferred to have dressed up a bit more, as if I really *had* just returned from Spain after nearly fifteen years. The series had a spin-off show called 'EastEnders Revealed', and it was something I had done a few times, but today it was to follow me around as I made my way around the various parts of the studios.

One of the first people who came up to say welcome was Laila Morse, who plays Mo Slater. She was and is a great mate; there were times when she was the only normal one in the place, and that is saying something. I saw Wendy, who obviously had had a lot to contend with over the years healthwise, but was still the mainstay of the show. Pam St Clements, although she was on holiday, sent a message; and June Brown, who just made me laugh all the time with her eccentricity. Adam Woodyatt hadn't changed: he was still the same young kid now, as he had been all those years ago. Several members of the crew, who had been there the first time around, and whom I had met several times during my years out of the show, made an effort to say hi, welcome back, as did a lot of the extras, such as Jane Slaughter, Joan Harsant, Leroy and many others.

I had met Scarlet Johnson at a soap awards ceremony a few weeks before, but she wasn't due to arrive until we did our scene later. My first scene was to be in Angie's Den, my only scene of the day. All I had to do was walk out from behind a plant in the studio and utter the immortal line: 'Hello, Princess.' I had been there since ten in the morning and at 9.30 at night I finally did the scene.

'Hello, Princess,' I said.

'Cut!'

I received a round of applause . . . God knows what would have happened if I had stepped out and recited Hamlet's soliloquy.

After a quick drink in the bar, I returned home and learned the fifty pages for the next day's filming. Although focusing on the Watts family, it was basically a two-hander with Sharon and myself. The first scene we did was nearly thirty-two pages long, but we managed to get through it. Eventually, we finished the first four episodes and my return was complete. A lot has been made of my relationship with Phil Mitchell, and, although he seemed wary at first, Phil was great to work with. The whole of the second floor at Elstree had tuned into the studio and waited with baited breath, apprehensive about what might happen. Nothing did . . . .

The schedule was hectic: each night I had reams and reams to learn. I would arrive at home late, learn thirty to forty pages and then set off early next the morning to get to the studios, where I was either first in, or Laila beat me to it. If I wasn't filming, I would be followed by 'EastEnders Revealed' or doing lots of photo shoots for every magazine going.

I was to be in the show for a few months, and then, in the storyline I was to go back to Spain, when in reality I was to be in Belfast, doing a panto. During those first few months it was obvious that few were taking the show seriously; they didn't know their lines and the job seemed an inconvenience to their social lives. It was pretty galling to a lot of people who had anything up to twenty-five pages of dialogue to find that, although they were word-perfect, others in the scene had only a few lines and they hadn't learned them. The show was overrunning each day, and at the end it was the same people who were bailing everyone else out, by getting through the script quickly to finish on time.

The time came to leave the Square and depart for Belfast. Jane had taken the boys off to Australia for Christmas to see her family. I arrived in Belfast and started to rehearse. The Dame was played by John Linehan, a well-known Belfast comic and a great person. The Fairy was a wonderful Scottish actress and singer, Ali McKinnon. I was playing Dirty Rat, which anywhere else would have been King Rat, but as King Rat was the name of some IRA terrorist, that had to go. But Dirty Rat (Dirty Den – Dirty Rat, geddit?) was a natural change. Apart from one performance when some desparate smoker lit up in the loo and the whole building had to be evacuated – I stood outside the theatre throughout signing autographs and having my picture taken – the pantomime season was a great success.

Sadly, this wasn't to be the case off stage.

Jane arrived back from Australia, while I had flown back the day before from Belfast to stock up the house with food, had met them at the airport and, after a cup of coffee and a snack, I caught a flight back to Belfast. (Jane brought Danny over later to see the show.) As soon as I finished in Belfast, Jane, Danny and I headed off to South Africa for a ten-day break before returning to Albert Square to restart filming. Everything was peaceful and hunky-dory. We returned to England ready for the next lot of filming relaxed and refreshed – the calm before the storm.

25

SEX, LIES AND THE INTERNET

Ever made a mistake – *known* it was a mistake, even as you were doing it, yet you carry on regardless? It's a bit like the wet paint syndrome – you know how it's going to end up, yet you have a sucker's instinct that *you* are going to be the *one* who gets away with it. I'm sure I'm not alone in experiencing this, yet I'm equally sure that creative types – and actors in particular – are more vulnerable than most to the need to just *see* if the paint is still wet.

We spend our lives playing other people. The very best training in the world will not make an actor out of you if you don't already have that complexity in you – the duality (or plurality) to be several different people, all at once. I make this observation not to absolve myself of yet another gruesome chapter in my life (as always, I hold my hand up to my mistakes – then kick myself hard, where it hurts). No, I'm saying this because I am genuinely interested in the factors that motivate us to do the things we do. And looking at this episode in particular – the chain of events that led to my being suspended from 'EastEnders' – it really does feel like I'm watching somebody else in a film, wilfully getting closer and closer to the wet paint. The top and bottom of it is that I got caught in an Internet sting. I can't help wondering why I was there in the first place, though.

I was never even that interested in pornography. Even in prison, the only centrefolds I had on my cell walls were Messrs Moore, Peters and Hurst. But my belated discovery of the Internet was, I confess, a revelation to me. Before I get to the heart of what actually happened, let me just divert to make a couple of observations. Fame (or celebrity, as it's more often called, now) is a weird entity. It is very hard to stay absolutely grounded and sane when so many people – hundreds, thousands of them in every town and city – act so oddly around those they consider famous. (Years ago, a lad I knew was first to spot a warehouse inferno and call the emergency services. He was interviewed for ten seconds on the news and, for the next few days, was mobbed with autograph demands. Today he'd have an agent and three series of 'Celebrity Love Island' behind him.)

How many celebrity magazines are there, or magazines that focus on the lifestyles of the rich and famous? There are dozens. People are very, very interested in the famous, some to the point of obsession. And while the vast majority of fans are incredibly patient, loyal and lovely, standing for hours in the rain just to wish you well, there are plenty of others who don't, or can't behave naturally. There's something about the whole celebrity sideshow that makes them behave oddly and treat you as a deity. Over a period of years, I think that affects your own sense of normality.

My second observation develops out of the first: people assume you're living a glamorous life. It's the first thing they say to you – that must be *so* glamorous. Now, I'm not knocking it – it is, and always has been, an actor's life for me – but that perception of red carpets, premières and champagne at sunset on a Hawaiian beach is the icing rather than the cake itself. What actors actually *do*, day after day, week in, week out, is wait. We live in a waiting room. We learn our lines and, for the most part, we sit in a dressing room or somewhere else on set and wait to deliver these nuggets. When I first started out, different actors would kill the time in different ways: they'd do the crossword; they'd answer fan mail. Why, some would even converse with each other! But you can imagine my delight when I stumbled upon this newfangled contraption called the Internet. You could get a one-page summary of a Harold Pinter play;

you could get a potted CV of the commissioning editor you were due to see at Channel 4. And there was, of course, the wet paint element to it, as well. You could tap in these three letters, and a world of boundless, scary, fascinating, hilarious possibilities would open up. Just three letters. S E X.

Just writing this, I realize all over again how crazy my behaviour was. I was married to a beautiful, talented woman whom I loved, hugely; we had three great kids, whom I adored and respected. I'd become known through a series that emphasized family, and I had a brilliant one of my own that I cherished. And I was successful at the only thing I'd ever really wanted to do – acting. I was, in every sense, living a charmed life. So why, then? Why delve further and deeper into that sordid world? Because it was there, I think. And it was so very, very easy. Far *too* easy, as it turned out.

I would spend hours looking at various sites, all of them absolutely free, and at first I couldn't believe my own eyes. I'd absorb it all, not participating myself but watching the conversations as they appeared on the screen. Before I knew it, this was the first thing I would do when I got to my changing room. Switch on my laptop. Log on. Tune in. Watch. I was hooked.

In between filming, I was emailing people, looking at the web and having friendly and sometimes sexy conversations with complete strangers. I was mystified when some of them said they had been speaking to me earlier that day. Earlier? I hadn't been on. Other discrepancies arose, until I realized that someone was hacking into my computer. It got worse. While I was in Spain shooting a front cover for the *TV Times*, one of the tabloids ran an interview with a woman, who another actor and I had made room for at our table in a crowded hotel tearoom. She was now saying she had been my lover for two years, which was untrue, and I had been bombarding her with phone calls. Although I had had several phone conversations with her, some completely inappropriate, the first I heard about it was when a reporter on the *Observer* asked me for a comment. I got straight onto my agent and this quickly became a matter for the police. We discovered that someone had been claiming to be me, calling my phone provider and bank for copies of my telephone records and bank statements.

But there was worse to come and, this time, it was myself who played the role of the Fool. A few weeks earlier I had an email from a woman who worked at Yorkshire Television. She said she was a fan and was pleased to see me back in the show. She asked could I send her a signed photo, which I did. So far, so good. Absolutely nothing to raise suspicion. A few days later she emailed me again to say she had received the photo, and thanks. We exchanged a few more emails, mainly making fun of the tedious side of television studio work. At this stage I checked her out on the Internet. It all looked kosher – she was a weather presenter who had also done one or two other items for Yorkshire Television. We began to chat on Messenger, where she introduced me to her mate 'Amanda', a dancer from Sheffield. I sent her a photo, too. Around this time, I should have smelt a rat. What a fool . . .

Amanda started sending photos of herself, and asked if I had a web-cam. I said I didn't, although the laptop did contain an in-built camera. Her pester power was admirable. She played me and played me, targeting the vanity all actors try to hide. I should have seen the light but I was blinded by the flattery of a vivacious, flirtatious twenty-three-year-old dancer, a girl who wanted to have fun. Suddenly, those endless hours in the dressing room between scenes were not so dull. Suddenly, I had company – and I liked it. I wouldn't have minded if those breaks between takes went on all day. I had Amanda – my virtual, online, dial-up pal. Little by little she cranked up the intimacy. Crazier and crazier, I complied. Questions about 'EastEnders'. Questions about individual cast members. Oh, the agony of having to recall all this all over again because now, of course, it's so obvious the entire operation had been a sting, a scam. But she got me, and got me good. If I have any recriminations, they're mainly aimed at Grantham, L.

Suddenly the screen went blank, and Amanda had gone – if she had ever existed at all. The next thing I knew it was all over the papers. It was my birthday and we were heading out to have lunch, when a reporter turned up at my front door and thrust the newspaper containing the story through it.

From that moment on we were under siege.

I have no excuses. I had let everyone down – my wife, my children, and of course the show itself. Life didn't seem worth living. Once again I had done a terrible, gross and stupid thing. Having worked so hard to earn myself a national profile, I had loaded up the rifles and had handed them out to all those shadowy figures, to take a potshot at the fool on the hill. I brought it on myself. These were people I didn't even know – some who I had had conversations with, some I had only ever had a drink with, and some who I'd bitten off too much with on the Internet. But they had one thing in common – they were now all making money out of me. And just as things couldn't get any worse, who should spring up in print but my own dear sister. She was calling herself a publisher now – but the only things she ever published were stories about me.

26

FACE THE MUSIC

As the reality of what was happening sank in, I became as depressed as I had ever been in my life. I also became detached, and couldn't bear to look at myself in the mirror. I tried to lie my way out of the situation, especially with Jane, instead of facing up to it like a man. Things got so bad that one night I tried to kill myself.

I got hold of a Stanley knife from my toolbox and, having tied an elastic band tightly around my arm, started to hack at my arms, trying to get at the veins underneath the skin. In my pathetic stupor I didn't even feel a thing. I only managed to make minor lacerations. I even tried to slash my throat, but couldn't go through with it. I gave up and went to bed.

Sleep, however, was the last thing on my mind; I just lay on our bed, numb from depression. After a few hours, I got out of bed and made my way into the garden. On the grass, I found one of the children's skipping ropes, which I tied to a branch of a tree. I took the end of the rope, made a neat noose, and tried to hang myself – but even in my darkest hour, farce was to dog my efforts. As I jumped the branch broke. Undeterred, I located a heavy pipe overhang and attached the rope to it and prepared myself to jump. I murmured a quick apology to all of those I'd hurt so badly and, convinced that long-term I was doing them all a favour, I closed my eyes and jumped. Nothing happened. Well – when I say nothing happened, plenty did, but nothing that ended my wretched life. I'd reckoned without the new consistency of your common or garden skipping rope (nylon with a rubber casing) which meant that, placed under pressure, it simply stretched. Looking back now, I can just about – *just* about – say that I'd like to see a CCTV video of that botched attempt. What must I have looked like, the tragic, fallen hero, noose around his neck and ready to end it all, when I close my eyes and perform a perfect little jump . . . straight down on to the front lawn! I opened my eyes and, finding myself in Wimbledon rather than Heaven or Hell, accepted that, even as a potential suicide, I was crap. That, or someone was looking out for me.

But I still felt deadly low and beyond motivation or medication in the morning. I couldn't move. Jane, although still raw from this latest humiliation at my hands, did what Jane always does. She got directly to the heart of the matter and assessed that it was love, support and sympathy I needed rather than the cold shoulder. She propped me up in bed, told me I wasn't going into work, and phoned my agent, who came round straight away. She penned a short statement for the press and bought me a crucial twenty-four hours of comparative peace of mind.

After a lengthy discussion with the producer, and realizing the trouble it would cause the production if my absence was too prolonged, I went into work, followed by London's paparazzi corps. When I arrived at Elstree, I went straight to my dressing room, changed and went out on set. Fortunately, given my state of mind, only two people made negative comments; the others just laughed. Nevertheless, I am sure they all wanted to say something. It took me a while to get around to see everyone, as we were filming the infamous fairground collapse at the time.

After a brief meeting with the bosses I was told I would be fined – the fine being donated to charity – and no other punishment would be forthcoming. The papers were full of the story, and of course I was followed everywhere, as were Jane and the children. I had managed to get through the day, but I still had to make it through the night. I got home to a frosty reception from the boys, who were adamant they weren't going back to school the next day. This is the side of my misdemeanours that always hurts most. It only takes a moment to make a mistake, but the result of one second's thoughtlessness can last a lifetime. It's hard enough for my boys to live with my job and take all the ribbing on the chin, even the stuff that's well-meant. Most of the jibes they have to face up to are pretty vindictive though, and my Internet folly was only going to fan the flames. Whatever rubbish they read in the papers, they knew they were going to face ten times worse in the playground – and it was all down to me. Their father, for God's sake, the man whose given role it is to protect and provide for them. Once again, I had let everyone down, badly.

I still had a lot of lines to learn and a lot of work to do, but I was in denial. (It's the state I naturally enter when I just can't cope.) As I sat in the kitchen, learning my lines at two in the morning, I snapped: I couldn't go on, not in this way. I grabbed a backpack, which I loaded with bricks and a pair of dumbbells and set off for Wimbledon Common. It was pitch black when I arrived, and I made my way through the darkness to the lake. After smoking my last cigarette, I entered cold water, the heavy pack strapped to my back, and waded in until my feet no longer touched the bottom. The weight of the backpack dragged me under, but I simply couldn't make myself sink. I just floated there, alone in the night. No matter how hard I tried I couldn't drown myself, so I tried to stay in the water and die of hyperthermia. After two hours I realized it was hopeless – and pretty damned uncomfortable – and made my way home, soaking wet and freezing cold. By this time, Jane had woken up and was driving around looking for me. Fortunately, it was pouring with rain, which conveniently hid the fact I had been in the lake. When Jane returned and saw me in the kitchen, she asked where I had been and I said, 'For a walk.' Which, I guess, was true.

The next morning we went to see a solicitor, but because I was in denial and couldn't admit my behaviour fully, it was a waste of time. If I had sued and pursued the entrapment line, it would still have left me wide open to other things. I also didn't want to get in to a Gillian

Taylforth situation, and have to lose the case on other aspects of my behaviour. Since then, I have sought counselling and therapy to try and get to the heart of my seemingly self-destructive nature. Without wanting to disparage the (somewhat pricey) insight of the professionals, it's my wife who seems to have hit the nail on the head. Her take on it is that actors are born of a necessary duality – they are, in the purest sense, two-faced, and have to be in order to play out a role effectively. My own duality is extreme, however, and if I can't master it for my own benefit, I am trying my very best to win through for the sake of my boys, and my ever-faithful wife.

While I was safely ensconced in the studios of the BBC, Jane and the boys were being hounded by the press. It was a very distressing time for the whole family, none more so than Danny, who having Down's syndrome, was the most vulnerable of us all. I could see Jane was suffering too, trying to run the house, get the boys off to school and just hold everyone together.

Although we had an unlisted number, the phone would ring day and night with people either trying to get a quote or just making derogatory remarks. If they couldn't get a reaction from me, they hoped that, by putting the family under pressure, it would solicit some kind of response from me – anything at all would do, so long as Dirty Den said it.

For my part, all I had to do was run the gauntlet of photographers outside the house in the morning and try to elude the pursuing press pack. Once inside the studios, I was fairly well protected, although the good folk of Elstree did make money by renting out rooms in houses overlooking the set. As I left the studios, the routine was the same: followed home, to be met by the baying press pack. They were offering money to our neighbours to get into their gardens and try to take photographs from there. GMTV sent a female reporter and cameraman, and after repeated doorbell ringing, were told in unambiguous terms that I wouldn't make a comment. Then they hit on the bright idea of just ringing the doorbell, and when we answered the intercom, they wouldn't reply. However, they would crouch down out of sight, hoping we would open the door and they could surprise us and film us.

But not all of those ringing our doorbell were quite so juvenile. Because Danny is like any other normal child, he feels that he should answer the door. When he did, he was repeatedly questioned by one particular journalist. I'd use the term 'journalist' with caution here, as I seriously doubt whether a true journalist would interview a ten-year-old with Down's syndrome. There are rules to the game: harassing a kid like Danny is not part of it. Danny has a lot going on, with speech and occupational therapy, just to keep up with his peers. To set him up and abuse his innocence like that takes gutter journalism to a new low.

My family was being hounded and their lives made a misery, so I moved into a flat in Borehamwood to try and deflect the pressure away from them. It backfired, and only handed the press a whole new angle: 'Dirty Den's Missus Kicks Him Out'. Untrue, but another good story. 'Dirty Den in a Dingy Flat'. Several of the other residents in the block were offered money for pictures of their flats, but by now were so dismayed at the description of their homes as 'dingy' that they all refused.

I tried to keep as low a profile as possible, but was continually followed. When I popped over to see my cousin in the Elephant and Castle, the press leapt to their usual assumptions. When they asked about her relationship with me, she told them to enquire at Somerset House. If she hadn't, the poor girl would have no doubt been all over the papers as my latest affair. She has been an absolute gem to me all my life and still is to this day, as are other members of my family, especially my cousin in Manchester. Several friends also called round to offer support to Jane and the boys, and while many of my producers and directors at 'EastEnders' were wonderfully supportive, quite a few people decided not to get in touch. Although understandable, it still saddens me that people from the profession should choose to believe everything they read. Just one more of life's lessons all in all.

The paparazzi now seemed to know my every move, and at work a lot of people came under suspicion. Months later, I was to be told by one paparazzo who the mole was. This person had had access to all my addresses and phone numbers, as well as the schedule; he also knew exactly what time people would be picked up from home. I was doing a tour of *Beyond Reasonable Doubt* and living in the flat but regardless, this paparazzo had an uncanny knack of turning up wherever I happened to be. Whatever time I left for work he'd be there but, even more uncannily, he seemed to know exactly when I'd be leaving, and from which gate. One time, though, I got lucky. He followed me into this car park, and as I parked he came out of nowhere and parked beside me.

'Just leave me alone,' I told him as I shut the door.

He flinched, thinking I was going to deck him. When he realized I wasn't, he said, 'Oh, come on, please, just give us a quick picture of you.'

I laughed. 'After all this?'

'All right,' he squirmed. 'I'll do you a deal. You pose for me and I'll tell you who the mole is inside Elstree.'

'So it's someone inside the studio, is it?' I said. 'Keep talking.'

'One picture, and I'll tell you.'

I did. And he told me. The mole no longer works for the BBC. My paparazzo snitch also gave me a number to ring if I was harassed by other snaparazzi; but as I thought this was a ploy to find out where I was, I threw the piece of paper away.

The work schedule didn't lighten: it was week after week of storylines. One day I was told that I had to see Mal Young. He told me he was loath to do it, knowing full well it was a set-up, but certain members of the cast had demanded I be punished. I was suspended from the show, though this would only come into force once my current storylines had played out.

I never found out for sure who complained, but I have a fair idea: probably the same actress who sent pictures of her large breasts to male members of the cast. So much for the one-off punishment. I finished the rest of my work and prepared to take a break. Before I left the majority of the cast and crew took the trouble to tell me to hang on in there. They were pleased I was still here. Just.

27

BEGINNING OF THE END

The enforced break was, in some ways, a blessing in disguise. While theme parks aren't my own particular cup of tea, we had a great family holiday at Disneyworld in Florida, and I was able to just kick back and reflect upon the mad roller coaster journey of my life – from Camber Sands to Blizzard Beach via Wormwood Scrubs and Albert Square. I had much to reproach myself for, but so much more to appreciate. The simple fact of being able to bring the family on holidays like this, and others, was one of the luxuries we could now afford.

Wherever we went, Jane and I had an ongoing joke about the local water supply as a result of our first posh holiday in the Caribbean. We both had good careers as soon as we left drama college and, while it was myself who became a household name through 'EastEnders', Jane won roles alongside Glenda Jackson, Alan Bates, Roy Dotrice and Bill Nighy to name but a few. After Spike was born she was offered a lead role in the new Dennis Potter production and was also asked to be the Face of Estée Lauder. Realizing she could never hand our little newborn over to a nanny or a nursery, she turned both down. By then, Dirty Den was a living legend, so we felt confident in the decisions we were making: so much so that, as soon as baby

Spike was old enough to travel, we headed off on holiday to Barbados, somewhere we'd always longed to visit.

We stayed in a beautiful old colonial-style hotel with private chalets in its manicured grounds. Jane wanted to give Spike his bath, and turned on the taps. The water gushed out an odd, cloudy constituency. We called reception but they didn't seem to take our misgivings seriously. Rather than cause a scene less than an hour after arriving there, I volunteered to go out in the hire car and pick up some bottled spring water from a roadside store we'd passed on the way. They had only two bottles in stock, and seemed to think it mighty odd that I should want, or need, any more than that. I asked where the next shop might be and was pointed in the vague direction north. Over the next hour and an half I called in at six roadside shops and picked up thirty-odd litres of spring water. I hauled them back to the chalet, too. Only the very best for our Spike! Satisfied that his delicate, newborn constitution would not be troubled by iffy tap water, I settled back at long last, feet up on the veranda. As I flicked through the local guide and magazine, picking up tips on local beauty spots, the best beaches and restaurants and so on, my eyes fastened on an article about Barbados spring water. At first I felt a mite foolish, but then I had to laugh out loud as I digested the news that Barbados's local water supply is renowned for being among the purest in the world. At its finest, it is so mineral-rich that it takes on a slightly cloudy hue. Happy days! Whenever we go anywhere now I lean across to Jane and say: 'Wonder if the water's OK to drink?'

After seeing out my suspension in Florida, I returned to 'EastEnders'. The scripts were not great, however, and were still late in coming. Again, it was back to the first-in last-out syndrome, so the hours were long. Nothing really had changed in my absence; the same core group were working their butts off and were always word-perfect, while the usual suspects were still so busy partying and having a good time that they forgot why they where there. It amazed me how, after just a few episodes on screen, newcomers to Albert Square would become increasingly grand and demanding. As one of the original cast from the very first show I was always going to be protective towards 'EastEnders', but I'm not one of these who just harps on about how great everything was in the good old days. It's as simple as this. I loved the show. I love it now. I've seen at first hand the blood, sweat and inspiration that everyone pours into that miraculous production – from Julia and Tony who created the thing, to the continuity kids who spot that a pint sometimes gets bigger, the longer Adam Woodyatt sups it! So to see some of the newer breed swanning around the Square without due care and respect was, I'll admit, a bit galling at times. My view is that progress is great, but not for the sake of it. Some of the new faces on 'EastEnders', behind the scenes as well as on camera, would benefit from doing their 'Knowledge' before they started throwing their weight around. Lecture ends.

Louise Berridge was trying to turn around this perception that the show was losing its edge, but was often stymied by certain actors failing to produce the goods, and writers whose scripts were either late, flimsy or both. Eventually, I saw the change in Louise; she began to look ill. I think the pressure was not merely getting to her, but starting to overwhelm her. I asked her outright how much of this downturn was a fall out from my so-called revelations, but she assured me all that was firmly in the past. One day, I was standing out in the car park just going over my lines, and she seemed really on top of everything, happy, in good health and bright-eyed. We had a long chat, and she seemed on top of the world. I didn't guess she had just resigned, but the relief must have felt like sweet liberation to this good and talented woman. Everyone, cast and crew, attended her leaving party and a lot were in tears by the end of the evening.

Our new executive producer was to be Kathleen Hutchison from 'Holby City', which was filmed at Elstree in the studios next to 'EastEnders'. Kathleen had her own views on where 'EastEnders' was going wrong, and how to fix it. She thought that the show would benefit from the verisimilitude of being shot on single camera, rather than multi-camera. This is how a lot of front-line documentary and news footage is gathered – often with jerky, live-as-it-happens camera angles. It was a bold move, and one which worked best with the bustling exteriors of the market. My view of production was always pretty simplistic: make the best use of what's there in front of you. As we had several cameras and many excellent operators, it didn't make sense not to use them. But that's why I'm an actor, while others are directors and producers.

One afternoon I was told that Kathleen wanted to see me, so I waited outside her office for nearly two hours. Eventually, I gave up and left, and went back on set. She flew down to see me, and apologized for keeping me waiting. She wanted to talk about storylines. I told her I wasn't interested in my storylines, but she was adamant that I was to hear it; my character was going to become darker, and even more evil than he normally was. And at that exact moment it just hit me. Things were changing. It was inevitable they would change and I was only going to end up bitter and angry if I stayed around complaining. I knew it was time to go. Kathleen viewed Den as some gangland big hitter, little realizing that the Dennis Wattses of this world are always big fish in their own little pond. I'd grown up with Dens since I was a little boy, duckers and divers, chancers and charmers rather than hardened criminals. The middle-class executives who populate the corridors of power in TV drama are all obsessed, at arms' length, with working-class lowlife. Yet, when confronted with the real thing, they prefer their own, dumbed-down version of it. So Den Watts, the love of my life, was going to make his move up the criminal ladder and it just didn't ring true to me. But if my attempts at bringing Den's new role to life didn't quite have the tone or the menace Kathleen was hoping for, it wasn't for the want of trying. Maybe I just didn't have the heart to destroy Den like that when it all came down to it, but I still gave it my best shot. Among all the things I love in the world, 'EastEnders' is one of my most cherished treasures. I'm proud as Punch to have been, not just a part of the show but one of its all-time icons. I'm Dirty Den. But as I made my way up to see the execs for my future-planning meeting, I knew in my heart of hearts that I was out. To my mind, 'EastEnders' is at its very best when it speaks to, and for, the everyday people of Britain. It's a microcosm of society, set in a bustling little square in east London – not a hotbed of gangsters and villains. The Dirty Den we know and love might succumb to a cargo of illegal hooch, but he'd be out of his depth ordering hits on local crime lords. I didn't want to play him that way, but it broke my heart when they told me that he, and I, would be going soon, never to return.

On my final day, I was touched to learn that the supporting artistes had been jostling to be there in my last scene. The producer of the episode, Jo Johnson, organized a replica Queen Victoria bust and the entire cast autographed it. Everyone left a message – some I never expected. All my old pals from the show came to wish me all the best. For some, like Wendy, it must have been like watching a whole slice of her life sail away, for ever. It was incredibly emotional. As I left 'EastEnders' for the last time I couldn't stem the tears. A big part of me would always remain in Albert Square.

THE END

As I finish this book, I realize that I have not covered a lot of things, I have tried to be as honest as I can, and I think have dealt fairly with all that has gone before. What the future holds is anyone's guess . . . Can I ever get back to normality? I have carried on my business of working as an actor, and have tried to repair the hurt and damage that I have caused my family by my irresponsible and shocking behaviour. Only time will tell if my wife and family forgive me. When I look at them and see how much they have supported me through thick and thin and through my latest débâcle, I can't help but think how lucky I am to have such a wonderful family. And how I wish it could be so, so different . . . how the time left on this planet should be nothing but happiness for us all. Only time will tell if I can forgive myself, although I have never forgiven myself for what happened in Germany all those years ago.